LOUIS D. BRANDEIS

Louis D. Brandeis

American Prophet

JEFFREY ROSEN

Yale

UNIVERSITY

PRESS

New Haven and London

Yale University Press books may be purchased in quantity for educational,
business, or promotional use. For information, please e-mail sales.press@yale.edu
(U.S. office) or sales@yaleup.co.uk (U.K. office).

Set in Janson Oldstyle type by Integrated Publishing Solutions.
Printed in the United States of America.

Library of Congress Control Number: 2015957835
ISBN 978-0-300-15867-0 (hardcover : alk. paper)

A catalogue record for this book is available from the British Library.

This paper meets the requirements of ANSI/NISO Z39.481–992
(Permanence of Paper).

10 9 8 7 6 5 4 3 2 1

Frontispiece: Louis Brandeis, Library of Congress, Prints and Photographs
Division, from the George Grantham Bain Collection, LC-B2-5213-10

ALSO BY JEFFREY ROSEN

*The Unwanted Gaze: The Destruction
of Privacy in America* (2000)

*The Naked Crowd: Reclaiming Security and Freedom
in an Anxious Age* (2004)

*The Most Democratic Branch: How the Courts
Serve America* (2006)

*The Supreme Court: The Personalities and Rivalries
That Defined America* (2007)

Constitution 3.0: Freedom and Technological Change
(coeditor, with Benjamin Wittes) (2011)

To the memory of my grandmother
Bertha Wolinsky Katzenberg Gittler
June 15, 1903–August 14, 1998

CONTENTS

LOUIS D. BRANDEIS

——————◆◆◆——————

Isaiah and Jefferson

Louis Brandeis was the most important American critic of what he called "the curse of bigness" in government and business since Thomas Jefferson. And in 1934, he was increasingly alarmed about the centralizing tendencies of Franklin D. Roosevelt's New Deal. Concerned that big corporations were driving small farmers off their land, Justice Brandeis summoned Adolf Berle and Rexford Tugwell, the Columbia Law professors who had designed the early New Deal agencies, to his austere Washington apartment on California Street. Pacing around the room, which was decorated with prints of classical ruins, Brandeis denounced "corporate farming" and warned FDR's Brain Trusters that big businesses "were controlling the nation's destinies." He had voted to uphold the New Deal in the year since FDR's inauguration, he told them, but "unless he could see some reversal of the big business trend, he was disposed to hold the government control legislation unconstitutional from now on."[1]

The prophet made good on his threat. On May 14, 1935, Brandeis warned Roosevelt through their mutual acolyte and future Supreme Court justice Felix Frankfurter that the "eleventh hour" of the New Deal was at hand.[2] And two weeks later, on May 27, 1935—known as Black Monday—the court handed down three unanimous opinions striking down elements of the First New Deal on the grounds that they created unchecked, centralized federal power. When Roosevelt first heard of the court's decisions, he was stunned by the justices' unanimity.

> "Well, what about old Isaiah?" he asked of Brandeis.
> "With the majority," his advisor replied.[3]

Isaiah, however, was not finished with his prophecies. He summoned another FDR advisor, Tommy Corcoran, to California Street. (Although the new Supreme Court building had been completed the previous month, Brandeis refused to move into his chambers, viewing the Marble Palace as an extravagant monument to big government.) "This is the end of this business of centralization," Brandeis told Corcoran. "I want you to go back and tell the President that we're not going to let this government centralize everything. It's come to an end. As for your young men, you call them together and tell them to get out of Washington—tell them to go home, back to the states. That is where they must do their work."[4] He told another advisor, Benjamin Cohen, to deliver another prophecy to the president and Felix Frankfurter. "You must see that Felix understands the situation and explains it to the President," Brandeis said. "They must understand that these three decisions change everything. The President has been living in a fool's paradise."[5] Brandeis's prophecies proved to be accurate. After his rebuke at the hands of the court, FDR changed course and, in the Second New Deal, his advisors relied explicitly on Brandeis's teachings about the importance of protecting economic liberty by restoring competition rather than increasing government centralization.

Why did FDR call Brandeis "old Isaiah" or, in the affectionate letters he wrote until the justice's death in 1941, "My dear Isaiah"?[6] He was responding, in part, to Brandeis's appearance: Brandeis's wife and others compared him to Lincoln, with his imposing height, high cheekbones, and bright, gray-blue eyes; but by the age of seventy-eight, which he had achieved on Black Monday, he did indeed resemble an ascetic Old Testament prophet: his impressive shock of black hair had turned an unruly gray, and his taut, intelligent face had been chiseled by a lifetime of intensely disciplined reading and writing on behalf of personal and economic liberty. Isaiah, too, was the prophet through whom God spoke to denounce the people of Zion for having forsaken morality, exhorting them to be his agents in redeeming not only the nation of Israel but also the entire world. Through Isaiah, God promises that he will "apply judgment as a measuring line and retribution as weights"[7] and, for those who satisfy these exacting standards, "also make you a light of nations, that My salvation may reach the ends of the earth."[8] This combination of loyalty to a people defined by justice and righteousness and a universal aspiration to the moral improvement of all free men and women would come to define Brandeis's vision of Zionism and Americanism.

Isaiah's crusades for personal and religious freedom also prefigured Brandeis's own. The prophet foretold the birth of King Cyrus, who, nearly two centuries later, conquered Babylonia and, around 539 BCE, issued a decree permitting the Jewish exiles to return to Israel and to rebuild the Temple as part of his policy of religious tolerance throughout the Persian Empire. Isaiah expressed a fear that the Jewish people would backslide into the moral corruption he had believed caused their exile, emphasizing that ethical behavior was as important as religious ritual. In May 1916, while the Senate was debating Brandeis's

Supreme Court nomination, William A. Blackstone, a fundamentalist Protestant clergyman, presented Brandeis and President Woodrow Wilson with a petition comparing Wilson to King Cyrus and urging him to call an international conference to endorse Brandeis's vision of a Jewish homeland in Palestine. Brandeis, in other words, is a spiritual descendant both of Isaiah and of Jefferson, who owned two copies of Xenophon's book on the education of Cyrus, *Cyropaedia*, one of which he inherited from his intellectual mentor, George Wythe. Jefferson was similarly inspired by the great king when he wrote the Virginia Declaration of Religious Freedom.

FDR was not the only one of Brandeis's acquaintances who detected something of the prophet in his countenance. Brandeis's deep ethical sense, rooted in his burning determination to protect individual liberty and economic opportunity for the "small man"—workers and farmers and producers, who were being menaced by corporations and financiers—led him frequently to denounce injustice in a prophetic mode. Here is a firsthand account of Brandeis's "prophecies" by his law clerk Dean Acheson, who went on to become secretary of state under Harry Truman, another Brandeis admirer, who professed his complete agreement with the justice on the curse of bigness. When a Harvard professor asserted that, in international law, moral principles were no more than relativistic generalizations from the mores of a particular time, Brandeis erupted with fearsome indignation. According to Acheson: "The Justice wrapped the mantle of Isaiah around himself, dropped his voice a full octave, jutted his eyebrows forward in a most menacing way and began to prophesy. Morality was truth; and truth had been revealed to man in an unbroken, continuous, and consistent flow by the great prophets and poets of all time. He quoted Goethe in German and Euripides via Gilbert Murray. On it went—an impressive, almost frightening, glimpse of an elemental force."[9]

Recognizing Brandeis as an American prophet seems more relevant today than ever. Brandeis's consistent opposition to the curse of bigness made him one of the greatest constitutional philosophers of the twentieth century. He is also the Jeffersonian prophet whose prophecies have been most consistently vindicated. The "people's lawyer" who predicted the crash of 1929 was the most ferocious critic of economic and political consolidation in an age of "too big to fail." More than any other Supreme Court justice, he can instruct us in the need for translating the constitutional values of privacy and free speech in an age of technological change. And as the leader of the American Zionist movement, he was the most prominent advocate of a vision of cultural pluralism that remains especially salient in an age of globalization and technological homogenization. His influence was so great in persuading Woodrow Wilson and the British government to recognize a Jewish homeland in Palestine that Jacob de Haas, Theodor Herzl's American secretary, wrote that "the most consistent contribution to American Jewish history in the twentieth century has been that of Louis Dembitz Brandeis."[10]

Brandeis, who served on the Supreme Court from 1916 to 1939, was the leader of a Jeffersonian tradition that is as distinctive in the twenty-first century as it was during the New Deal era: a progressive champion of federalism and the autonomy of the states. (He was the first to characterize the states as "laboratories of democracy,"[11] a phrase that has become the touchstone of libertarian and conservative defenders of federalism today.) At the same time, Brandeis embodies a bipartisan constitutional tradition that is once again gaining broad adherents on both sides of the political spectrum, from Tea Party libertarians to progressive civil libertarians: a defender of personal and economic liberty and a foe of centralization in government or business. The states fulfilled his Jeffersonian belief that small-scale communities were most likely to satisfy human needs and to allow citizens to develop their faculties of reason through the rigorous self-education that Brandeis believed was necessary for full participation in American democracy.

At a time of intense polarization between conservatives and libertarians, who prefer small government and free enterprise, and liberals and progressives, who advocate a more energetic social welfare state, Brandeis is the historical figure who represents and blends the ideals of both sides of this crucial debate. He endorsed Jeffersonian ideals of small government and local democracy but applied those ideals to uphold state regulations that tamed the excesses of big business and monopoly. He offers, therefore, a unifying vision of liberty and democracy for our divided age.

Like Jefferson, Brandeis believed that the greatest threat to our constitutional liberties was an uneducated citizenry, and that democracy could not survive both ignorant and free. And because of Brandeis's pragmatic sense of human limitations, he believed that only in small-scale businesses and communities could individuals master the facts that were necessary for personal and political self-government. For this reason, as a Supreme Court justice, he generally championed judicial deference to state legislation—except when it clashed with protections for freedoms explicitly enumerated in the Constitution, such as the First Amendment's protections for free speech or the Fourth Amendment's protections against unreasonable searches and seizures. In those cases, he became the most prescient defender of civil liberties of the twentieth century.

There is, at the same time, a crucial difference between Brandeis's vision of judicial restraint and that of his contemporaries. He fervently believed in the economic justice of the legislation he voted to uphold. This distinguished him from Oliver Wendell Holmes, for example, who was even more rigidly committed to judicial deference because of his radical skepticism about the ability of judges or legislators to discern the truth, but who also had contempt for democracy and for progressive legislation. "I am so skeptical as to our knowledge about the goodness or badness of laws that I have no practical criticism except what the crowd wants," Holmes wrote in 1910, having told his sister nearly fifty years earlier that he "loathe[d] the thick-fingered clowns we call the people."[12] Brandeis, by contrast, never condescended to the people or to democracy: he was idealistic about the possibility of citizens engaging in serious deliberation in communities so as to pass laws that would meet human needs and promote economic justice. For this reason, Brandeis never professed agnosticism about the economic regulations he criticized his colleagues for striking down. Quite the contrary. Many of his dissents include a passionate defense of why legislators properly viewed those laws as reasonable and necessary. Brandeis's tendency to uphold laws he admired and to strike down those he deplored calls into question whether he had an independent commitment to judicial restraint that transcended his passionately held views on liberty and political economy. But the Jeffersonian consistency of his constitutional vision gave his opinions a prophetic force that continues to shape the court's understanding of the Constitution today.

Brandeis famously invented the Brandeis brief—a comprehensive collection of empirical studies designed to persuade judges about the importance of facts on the ground. The Brandeis brief transformed civil rights litigation—and inspired both Thurgood Marshall and Ruth Bader Ginsburg in their arguments for equal rights for African Americans and women—by introducing the idea that constitutional decisions should be informed by facts and evidence rather than purely deductive analysis. (Brandeis himself once declared that his own "Brandeis brief" should have been called "What Every Fool Knows"; he believed that "nobody can form a judgment that is worth having without a fairly detailed and intimate knowledge of the facts.")[13] And Brandeis's opinions and dissents read like Brandeis briefs: in case after case, he amassed facts and legislative history to demonstrate why the people of a state were amply justified in passing the progressive reforms that the court, which preferred abstractions about liberty to the realities of economic reform, considered arbitrary and unreasonable. Brandeis's prose is simple and direct, combining detailed attention to facts with a bold expression of basic principles of democracy and political economy. He took seriously his role as a craftsman and teacher, laboring with his clerks over many drafts to make his prose as accessible as possible. (After what seemed like the ultimate revision of an opinion, he asked his law clerk Paul Freund: "The opinion is now convincing, but what can we do . . . to make it more instructive?")[14] As a result, Brandeis's judicial opinions, like his speeches, books, and briefs, seem fresh and modern in the twenty-first century. By contrast, the prose of justices more celebrated in their day as judicial stylists, such as Oliver Wendell Holmes and Benjamin Cardozo, can seem dated and mannered, self-consciously striving for showy aphorisms and philosophical abstractions rather than trying to communicate with the reader on equal terms. In his prose, as in his politics, Brandeis was a democrat.

This short book is designed to introduce readers to what Brandeis thought and why he matters today, quoting extensively from his own powerful words. It is not intended to be a comprehensive biography: Brandeis has been fortunate in his biographers, and those seeking a full account of his extraordinary life have a variety of superb options, including Alpheus Thomas Mason's *Brandeis: A Free Man's Life* (1946), Philippa Strum's *Louis D. Brandeis: Justice for the People* (1984), Melvin I. Urofsky's *Louis D. Brandeis: A Life* (2009), and many others. Instead, I have drawn on what Brandeis wrote and also what he read to offer a condensed study of his thought and character.

Throughout this book, I argue that Brandeis, who was content to be called a Jeffersonian,[15] is the Jeffersonian who has most to teach us about our contemporary vexations involving political economy, civil liberties, and Zionism: the Jewish Jefferson! But it was a particular vision of Jefferson—the sage of Monticello as the scourge of corporations, monopolies, and financiers, the defender of farmers and producers—who most inspired the mature Brandeis. As Philippa Strum notes, Brandeis quoted Jefferson as early as 1904, but he read and invoked him more frequently in his later years.[16] After reading Francis W. Hirst's *The Life and Letters of Thomas Jefferson* in 1926, Brandeis issued his greatest free speech opinion, *Whitney v. California*, which cited Jefferson's letters and his First Inaugural. Two months after *Whitney* came down in May 1927, he read Jefferson's *Works*, followed by *The Federalist* and Charles Beard's *The Rise of American Civilization*.[17] He then traveled to Monticello in September "to pay homage . . . to Thomas Jefferson," and returned "with deepest conviction of T.J.'s greatness. He was a civilized man."[18] Brandeis finished off his Jeffersonian year in December 1927 by reading Albert Jay Nock's *Jefferson*. He called the book "the worthiest account of our most civilized American and true Democrat."[19]

Brandeis was so captivated by Nock's *Jefferson* that he persuaded the National Home Library Foundation to issue a reprint edition, which was published on his eighty-fourth birthday.[20] The edition is "dedicated with esteem and affection to MR. JUSTICE LOUIS BRANDEIS, *Friend of all just men and a lover of the Right*." Brandeis reciprocated this tribute by suggesting "that one copy shall go to every high school (and similar institution) in Kentucky. So far as teachers and students may be led to read the book something important may be done for the education—the culture—of the State."[21] Nock's vision of Jefferson—and of American constitutionalism—is, therefore, worth close attention as a window onto Brandeis's philosophy. And Nock does not hide his views or his intellectual influences. He acknowledges that he has "helped himself wholesale to the contents" of his "old friend" Charles Beard's "work on the Constitution and on the economic origins of Jeffersonian democracy," which had been published five years earlier. Channeling Beard, Nock writes that the framers of the Constitution (Jefferson was in Paris) represented capitalists and financiers rather than farmers, debtors, and small producers.[22]

Nock views Jefferson, whom he calls "the great libertarian,"[23] as a defender of the small producers and farmers against the predations of the large capitalists, monopolists, and financiers. Unlike Beard, Nock was no progressive, although in his day, as in ours, libertarian conservatives and civil libertarian liberals converged in their opposition to monopoly power. When he called Jefferson the "libertarian practitioner of taste and manners,"[24] Nock was also describing himself. In addition to founding the *Freeman*, a journal that opposed the growth of the state in all of its forms, Nock shuddered at the excesses of popular culture and defended classical education; his 1935 book *Our Enemy, the State* denounced welfare, the New Deal, and consolidated federal power. Nock's Jefferson, like Brandeis, exemplifies the same libertarian, classical, and agrarian values; it also impressed Brandeis with its depictions of Jefferson's aesthetic refinement. Thanking his sister-in-law, Pauline Goldmark, for sending another book on Jefferson on his birthday in 1929, Brandeis once again emphasized that "Jefferson has been properly painted for many achievements and qualities—without enough emphasis on the fact that he was the most civilized of our presidents."[25] The fact that Brandeis stressed three times that Jefferson was "civilized" without noting that his civilized lifestyle was supported by slavery can only be considered a blind spot for this tribune of liberty. But it was, of course, a blind spot that Jefferson shared.

The personal and philosophical affinities between Jefferson and Brandeis are striking. Jefferson was, according to Nock, "always the most abstemious of men, practically a vegetarian

. . . he drank little, using 'the weak wines only.'"[26] (By "the weak wines," Nock must have meant claret and hock as opposed to Madeira and port; as Jefferson recalled in 1817: "The taste of this country [was] artificially created by our long restraint under the English government to the strong wines of Portugal and Spain.") Brandeis, too, drank little as he grew older, although he indulged in an occasional beer with the Jewish garment workers he represented during a 1910 strike; and his table was infamous for its austerity. (Before Prohibition, however, Brandeis's brother Alfred sent him bottles of good Kentucky bourbon, which Brandeis enjoyed in moderation.) Jefferson was a devotee of physical exercise, having bought in Paris a "pedometer, which shall render you an exact account of the distances you walk"—a kind of eighteenth-century Fitbit.[27] Brandeis, who also loved the outdoors, remained fit throughout his life with regular horseback riding, camping, and canoeing, at which he excelled. (His balance was so sure, apparently, that he once fell out of the back of a canoe without rocking the boat.)[28] Jefferson was a lawyer who resolved "never . . . to wear any other character than that of a farmer";[29] he listed among his greatest accomplishments the importation of "heavy upland rice from Africa in 1790," which he promptly sent to Charleston.[30] "The greatest service which can be rendered to any country," Jefferson insisted, "is to add a useful plant to its culture."[31]

Brandeis, a lawyer whose father was a successful grain merchant and a less successful gentleman farmer, also exalted agrarian values throughout his life, and his vision of political economy was rooted in the cultivation of land. When Brandeis met a young Zionist who had discovered "wild rice" that could grow in the dry soil of Palestine, he called this the most important discovery he had ever encountered. Brandeis constantly urged his law clerks and acolytes to return to the communities that shaped them. (He was disappointed when one clerk confessed to have been brought up in Manhattan; and when a young journalist who later became a U.S. senator wrote to him for career advice, he responded, in full: "Stay in Oregon.") Brandeis ultimately found in Palestine the fulfillment of Jefferson's ideal of economic and personal development rooted in small communal farms. Jefferson was fascinated by "efficiency studies" in farming,[32] and his agricultural journals calculating the time farmers took to fill wheelbarrows anticipated the southern planters who made "studies in industrial efficiency, and developed a highly effective technique in scientific management."[33] Brandeis became an enthusiastic Taylorite, applying Frederick W. Taylor's principles of scientific management to industrial organization in order to give farmers and industrial workers the leisure time necessary for self-improvement and education.

In their personal economies, however, Jefferson and Brandeis diverged. Jefferson never managed to make farming pay or to balance his accounts; according to Garry Wills, he was an aestheticized elitist and shopaholic who "went on a buying spree in France that was staggering in its intensity," cluttering Monticello with Houdon busts and a fauteuil from Marie Antoinette's preferred *ébéniste*.[34] He left the presidency $20,000 in debt and was temporarily rescued from bankruptcy only by unsolicited emergency contributions from cities across the East; within six months of his death, most of his property had been sold and his daughter and her family were turned out of Monticello.[35] Brandeis, by contrast, embodied fiscal responsibility and frugality, having resolved to provide for the needs of his wife and daughters while devoting himself to public service. His income as a lawyer was nearly $100,000 a year—the relative purchasing power in today's dollars would be more than $2.5 million—and he spent only $10,000 on annual living expenses.[36] As a result, he made his first million by 1907 and, through conservative investing and simple living, he had saved $2 million by the time he joined the court in 1916.[37] When he died, his estate totaled more than $3 million, an amount that surprised and discomfited some of his progressive acolytes. But Brandeis never sought money as an end in itself. He considered financial stability to be a prerequisite for personal freedom, and once his fortune was secure, he refused to accept payment for his pro bono activities, viewing his surplus time as an asset to be invested on the public's behalf.

Jefferson viewed American history as a battle between the forces of consolidation and decentralization, between agrarian producers and monopolistic financiers. "The trouble with government in Europe as [Jefferson] saw it, was its complete centralization in the hands of the relatively few non-producers," Nock writes. "For America, Mr. Jefferson was convinced that republicanism was a better system because it lent itself less easily to centralization."[38] In responding to the proposed Constitution, Jefferson expected that America would be divided into self-governing agricultural units of the smallest scale possible. According to Nock, "His own private view went far beyond the idea of the State as the self-governing unit; he was for making the smallest political unit self-governing, in order to keep the producer alert and interested."[39] Brandeis, too, insisted that decentralization in government and economics was the only way to protect the liberty of farmers, industrial workers, and small producers. "When you talk on 'Curse of Bigness,'" he wrote to Norman Hapgood, who wrote the introduction to the reprint edition of Brandeis's great book *Other People's Money*, "stress 'No man more than one job' as the correlative of 'Every Man a Job.' That is demanded by democracy as well as efficiency. And the job must not be too big a one. The proposition is applicable to government as well as to private business. Hence beware of centralization; and beware also of the mania of consolidating bureaus."[40]

Brandeis, like Jefferson, was a foe not of capitalism but of monopoly. "Mr. Jefferson always had a sound and clear view of the function of capital as a factor in production, always drawing a sharp distinction between capitalism and monopoly," as Nock puts it. "It was the monopoly-feature, the element of law-created economic privilege, to which he objected."[41] In this hatred of monopolies, Jefferson was not alone among the American founders. The Boston Tea Party, which sparked the American Revolution, was a rebellion against the government-granted monopoly held by the East India Company. After the Constitutional Convention, Jefferson expressed grave concern about government-granted monopolies of trade. He complained to James Madison that the Constitution contained no Bill of Rights protecting, among other basic liberties, "restrictions against monopolies,"[42] and he supported the following consti-tutional amendment: "Monopolies may be allowed to persons for their own productions in literature and their own inven-tions in the arts for a term not exceeding —— years but for no longer term and for no other purpose."[43]

Madison responded that the federal government should have the power to grant "charters of incorporation," but his proposal was voted down on the grounds that it might lead to "monopolies of every sort,"[44] as George Mason put it. Madi-son also resisted the constitutional amendments proposed by six states that would have provided "[t]hat the congress do not grant monopolies, or erect any company with exclusive advan-tages of commerce."[45] In his argument justifying the constitu-tionality of the Bank of the United States, Alexander Hamilton invoked the argument that these states believed Congress had inherent power to create trade companies or corporations but believed that the power should not be used to grant exclusive privileges.[46] Nevertheless, Jefferson insisted that Hamilton's Bank of the United States violated the Constitution because the notion that Congress had "implied powers" to charter cor-porations clashed with the Tenth Amendment,[47] which says that powers not delegated to the United States are reserved to the states or the people.

Brandeis was not a strict constructionist and did not share Jefferson's belief that Congress could only exercise powers explicitly enumerated in the original Constitution. He insisted that the "living law" had to adapt to social change and attempted to translate the values of the framers of the Constitution into an age of technologies and mass-production methods they could not have imagined. Still, Brandeis was sympathetic to Jefferson's views on political economy; and he developed Jefferson's distinction between merchant bankers, who lent their own capital for productive enterprises, and monopolists, who underwrote risky instruments with what Brandeis unforgettably called "other people's money." The monopolies of Brandeis's day were not government-chartered banks, like the Bank of the United States, but the web of private investment banks and railroads controlled by Brandeis's nemesis, J. P. Morgan. In *Other People's Money*, Brandeis denounced Morgan for the oligarchic economic and political power that his control over the "quick capital" of others allowed him to wield. Morgan and other oligarchs made reckless bets on complicated instruments whose value they couldn't possibly understand, Brandeis believed; and in this sense, his opposition to bigness, in business and government, was connected to his pragmatic understanding of the limitations of human knowledge.

Brandeis's friend and acolyte Jacob de Haas, the Zionist journalist and representative of Herzl, concisely summed up the connection between Brandeis's theory of political economy and his theory of knowledge:

> He not only disesteems bigness but the characteristic worship of great aggregations appals him. He puts efficiency in the first place and believes no man is big enough to run the world, no corporation efficient enough to monopolize an industry. He has a keen sense of the natural limitations of human effort and he distrusts operations that grow beyond the intimate contact of a conceiving and directing mind.

Many men have gone from him disappointed because he has by his simple advice crushed their gorgeous dreams. In legislation, in organization, or in commonplace business he is apt to advise, "Go home, select a little thing and do that thing well; the rest will follow." If he has a motto it is Goethe's line "In der Beschränkung zeigt sich erst der Meister."[48]

Brandeis would quote, and helpfully translate, this motto in *Other People's Money:* "It is only . . . when working within limitations, that the master is disclosed."[49]

Jefferson attacked the increasingly powerful federal judiciary as a haven for monopolists and the exploiting classes. He saw the Supreme Court under the leadership of his distant cousin Chief Justice John Marshall as an instrument of centralization; he wrote to William Johnson in 1823 that he feared no danger more "than the consolidation of our Government by the noiseless and therefore unalarming instrumentality of the Supreme Court."[50] Jefferson deplored Marshall as "a crafty chief judge who sophisticates the law to his mind by the turn of his own reasoning . . . construing our Constitution from a co-ordination of a general and special government to a general and supreme one alone."[51]

In the old Jeffersonian spirit, Brandeis voted to strike down the most centralizing aspects of the New Deal, on the grounds that the framers of the original Constitution had intended to protect liberty rather than efficiency. (Brandeis favored efficiency in small enterprises, not large ones.) But Brandeis more often than not defended judicial restraint rather than judicial engagement: state legislatures in Brandeis's day were friends rather than enemies of the producing classes, and Brandeis frequently denounced his more activist colleagues on the court for their tendency to strike down maximum hour, minimum wage, and price maintenance laws, which he considered shields that protected small workers and small businesses from economic exploitation.

Brandeis was a hero of the Progressive movement, and one of its shining lights. His career is a reminder that judges do not create themselves out of nothing, but that their views reflect those of political coalitions that begin with grassroots activism. The populist crusade against big business gained steam in the 1890s, and by the turn of the century a coalition of industrial workers, urban social reformers, small business, and farmers began to lobby state legislatures to pass laws to curb corporate excesses in an industrial age. In the first decade of the twentieth century, state legislatures responded by enacting antitrust laws, maximum hour and minimum wage laws, and workmen's compensation laws.[52] But the American judiciary in those momentous years cast itself as a pro-business conservative force, defending property rights and corporate interests against progressive regulation. As a result, Progressivism, as Learned Hand put it, "reflects a suspicion of courts."[53]

Although Brandeis worked with the Progressives, and although he voted enthusiastically to uphold progressive legislation, he did not share the Progressive faith in government by experts who would evaluate facts on the people's behalf and could spare workers the need to think for themselves. Instead, like Jefferson, he believed passionately that citizens have a duty to educate themselves so that they are capable of self-government, both personal and political, and of defending their liberties against overreaching corporate and federal power. As his biographer Alfred Lief observed in 1936, "Brandeis had little faith in what passed for good government, the paternalistic hand which stunted growth. Ancient history was studded with instances of the demoralizing effects of benevolence; in Rome, after a period of benevolent emperors, the populace stagnated. America's need was not more government but a greater development of her citizens."[54] As a result, Lief suggests, Brandeis especially admired Jefferson's notion of limited government, his vision in foreseeing "the conservation problem, which would come up after the disappearance of free land," his far-reaching mind, which Brandeis considered more cultivated than the comparatively unlearned Lincoln, and his conviction that, with time and education, "citizens would have as little need of government as possible."[55]

Jefferson, of course, has a blemish on his legacy, and that blemish is slavery. In 1791, Benjamin Banneker, an African American surveyor and astronomer, wrote to Jefferson, then secretary of state, criticizing the author of the Declaration of Independence for hypocrisy in declaring that all men are created equal while at the same time owning slaves. "Sir how pitiable is it to reflect, that altho you were so fully convinced of the benevolence of the Father of mankind, and of his equal and impartial distribution of those rights and privileges which he had conferred upon them, that you should at the Same time counteract his mercies, in detaining by fraud and violence so numerous a part of my brethren under groaning captivity and cruel oppression," Banneker wrote.[56] Jefferson's polite reply was unsatisfying: "No body wishes more than I do to see such proofs as you exhibit, that nature has given to our black brethren, talents equal to those of the other colours of men, and that the appearance of a want of them is owing merely to the degraded condition of their existence both in Africa and America."[57]

Brandeis, too, had a blind spot on race. Unlike his abolitionist uncle, and unlike other Jewish lawyers who were early members of the NAACP, such as Louis Marshall, president of the American Jewish Committee, Brandeis was never a crusader for racial equality. On July 4, 1915, at Faneuil Hall in Boston, he delivered an inspiring speech, "True Americanism," that evoked the Declaration of Independence in denouncing the persecution of Jews in Russia and seemed to include African Americans in his vision of the pluralistic American ideal. "Other countries, while developing the individual man, have assumed that their common good would be attained only if the privileges of their citizenship could be limited practically to natives or to persons of a particular nationality," Brandeis argued. "America, on the other hand, has always declared herself for equality of nationalities as well as full equality for individuals. It recognizes racial equality as an essential of full human liberty and true brotherhood, and that racial equality is the complement of democracy."[58]

On the Supreme Court, however, Brandeis settled into what one critic has described as "an extended period of racial ambivalence," silently joining the majority in every race case that came before the court during his tenure.[59] Some of these cases advanced the cause of racial equality and others did not, but Brandeis took a leadership role in none of them, neither writing for the majority nor filing separate dissents or concurrences. Brandeis was no more or less supportive of racial equality than the other progressive justices of his era, and in his personal relations, he treated African Americans with respect.[60] Before joining the court, moreover, he privately advised lawyers seeking racial equality on at least two occasions.[61] But his public silence on racial issues contrasts with public crusades not only for industrial democracy but also for women's suffrage, which he had initially opposed but came enthusiastically to support. As he explained in a speech during the 1912 presidential campaign:

> I came to the conclusion after a good deal of effort in that direction that if we were to improve the working condition of the people, it would have to be done by the people themselves, and in the effort to give the people this opportunity I found that the large part of those who needed it most were women workers, because they were less experienced, less protected by organization and because the demands of industry bore more heavily on them. I saw they needed not only protection but knowledge of affairs. They needed much to uplift them out of the smallness and trivialities of life, and

I saw that nothing would be more potent in that direction than the privilege of the ballot. Women often have greater opportunities than men to bring about social reform, for which all of us are working. They have the desire, enthusiasm and understanding. I learned much from them in my work. So having been of the opinion that we would advance best by leaving the voting to the men, I became convinced that we needed all the forces of the community to bring about this advance.[62]

Brandeis changed his mind about women's suffrage after having worked with remarkable women in the Progressive movement to defend the constitutionality of maximum working hours for women, including his sister-in-law, Josephine Goldmark, and the women leaders of the National Consumers League, who impressed him with their formidable research skills. By contrast, Brandeis, a southern Democrat at a time when both parties supported segregation, never worked closely with African American lawyers, although he did support the development of the newly created Howard University Law School because of his belief in the importance of education for African Americans. In the 1920s, he told Mordecai Johnson, the dynamic new African American president of Howard, that the standards of the law school had to be improved in the same way that Johnson was improving the standards of the university as a whole. "I can tell most of the time when I'm reading a brief by a Negro attorney," Brandeis told Johnson. "You've got to get yourself a real faculty out there or you're always going to have a fifth-rate law school. And it's got to be full-time and a day school."[63] Despite Brandeis's tone of intellectual condescension, Johnson took the justice's advice and hired as dean of Howard a thirty-four-year-old Harvard Law School graduate, Charles Hamilton Houston, who also became the litigation director of the NAACP. And, inspired by Brandeis's insistence on the importance of facts, Houston and the Howard-educated

Thurgood Marshall filed a series of briefs collecting empirical evidence about the effects of segregation that eventually persuaded the Supreme Court to strike down segregation in *Brown v. Board of Education.*

Jefferson's faith in the importance of education for all was similarly profound. In his inadequate response to Benjamin Banneker, he wrote of African Americans: "I can add with truth that no body wishes more ardently to see a good system commenced for raising the condition both of their body and mind to what it ought to be, as fast as the imbecillity of their present existence, and other circumstances which cannot be neglected, will admit."[64] And at the end of his life, Jefferson supported two public measures to resist the tyrannies of centralization and to promote local self-government. One proposed to divide Virginia into small wards; the other, as Jefferson put it, was a program of "general education, to enable every man to judge for himself what will secure or endanger his freedom."[65] Jefferson had long been interested in public education, maintaining that "the most effectual means of preventing the perversion of power into tyranny are to illuminate as far as possible the minds of the people."[66] In the Virginia Assembly, which he joined in October 1776, he proposed a system of popular education, to allow citizens "to understand their rights, to maintain them, and to exercise with intelligence their parts in self-government."[67] In 1797, he proposed that each ward should have public elementary schools, but that the twenty boys (and they were only boys) "of best genius" in the state should be promoted to the public grammar school.[68] As president, Jefferson proposed the creation of a national university, open to the best students across America; when Congress declined to fund the project, he focused his attentions on creating an elite university in his home state.

Brandeis shared Jefferson's belief that a democracy could not remain free without educated citizens who were capable of understanding and defending their liberties. But he was more democratic in his belief that all men and women had the potential and the duty to "develop their faculties," as he put it in his concurring opinion in *Whitney v. California* (1927), the most important defense of the value of free speech in the twentieth century. In *Whitney*, Brandeis cites Jefferson's First Inaugural ("We are all Republicans, we are all Federalists") in drawing a connection between the importance of self-education and reasoned discussion. Here are his beautiful words:

> Those who won our independence believed that the final end of the state was to make men free to develop their faculties, and that in its government the deliberative forces should prevail over the arbitrary. They valued liberty both as an end and as a means. They believed liberty to be the secret of happiness and courage to be the secret of liberty. They believed that freedom to think as you will and to speak as you think are means indispensable to the discovery and spread of political truth; that without free speech and assembly discussion would be futile; that with them, discussion affords ordinarily adequate protection against the dissemination of noxious doctrine; that the greatest menace to freedom is an inert people; that public discussion is a political duty; and that this should be a fundamental principle of the American government.[69]

Jefferson was not Brandeis's only model in connecting the survival of democratic liberty with the importance of lifelong self-education. One of Brandeis's favorite books, as Philippa Strum notes, was Alfred Zimmern's *The Greek Commonwealth*, which he read in the winter of 1913.[70] Zimmern, like Brandeis, viewed Periclean Athens as a model for modern democracies (although he acknowledged that it was a slave society), and insisted that only active and serious face-to-face deliberation by engaged citizens in small groups could safeguard democratic virtue. Rejecting Holmes's cynical view that majority will had to be accepted even when it was brutally misguided, Brandeis worried, with Jefferson, that governing majorities could become occasionally tyrannical, and that democratic liberty would falter if citizens ceased to be engaged. But he also had faith that a virtuous and engaged citizenry—grounded in small communities— could, through deliberation, achieve a good in common that they could not know alone.

Brandeis was especially struck by Zimmern's definition of the Greek conception of leisure: namely, the time away from business when the citizens could develop their faculties through the art and contemplation that were indispensable for full participation in public affairs. "The Greek word for unemployment is 'scholê,' which means 'leisure': while for business he has no better word than the negative 'ascholia,' which means 'absence of leisure.' The hours and weeks of unemployment he regards as the best and most natural part of his life," Zimmern wrote. "Leisure is the mother of art and contemplation, as necessity is the mother of the technical devices we call 'inventions.'"[71]

Brandeis paid close attention to Zimmern's definition: "The Greek word for 'unemployment' is 'leisure,'" he wrote to his wife, Alice, in 1914, citing Zimmern. "[W]hat a happy land that."[72] And he developed a similarly strenuous conception of leisure as a requirement for the lifelong education that he believed essential to American citizenship. "Whether the education of the citizen in later years is to be given in classes or from the public platform, or is to be supplied through discussion in the lodges and the trade unions, or is to be gained from the reading of papers, periodicals and books, in any case, freshness of the mind is indispensable to its attainment,"[73] he wrote in "True Americanism," the 1915 Fourth of July oration, which was clearly influenced by Zimmern: "And to the preservation of freshness of mind a short workday is as essential as adequate food and proper conditions of working and of living. The worker must, in other words, have leisure. But leisure does not imply idleness. It means ability to work not less but more, ability to work at something besides breadwinning, ability to work harder while working at breadwinning, and ability to work more years at breadwinning. Leisure, so defined, is an essential of successful democracy."[74]

Just as Brandeis insisted that industrial workers and farmers had the capacity for self-education throughout their lives, so he, like Jefferson, supported the development of his local university. Starting in 1924, Brandeis devoted himself to improving the University of Louisville—in particular its library, its art collection (to increase appreciation of the contributions of the Greeks and Romans to ancient and modern civilization), and its law school (which was officially renamed for him in 1997). "History teaches, I believe, that the present tendency toward centralization must be arrested if we are to attain the American ideals, and that for it must be substituted intense development of life through activities in the several states and localities," Brandeis wrote to his brother Alfred in 1925. "The problem is a very difficult one; but the local university is the most hopeful instrument for any attempt at solution."[75] Brandeis was even more Jeffersonian than Jefferson in his insistence that the University of Louisville should be entirely local in its focus. "Our university can become great, and serve this end, only if it is essentially Kentuckian—an institution for Kentuckians, developed by Kentuckians."[76] But he was more democratic than Jefferson in his belief that all workers, from farmers to garment workers, had the capacity for the self-education he believed was necessary for the survival of democracy and liberty. "No doubt my standards seem to some exacting," he wrote to his daughter Susan the same year. "But my insistence results largely from my faith in man's possibilities and in his perfectibility."[77]

In 1922, Brandeis summed up what Alpheus Mason, his approved biographer, calls "his creed in essence."[78] His friend

Robert W. Bruère had convinced him to speak to the Federal Council of Churches in America, and Brandeis wrote to Bruère distilling his position:

> Refuse to accept as inevitable any evil in business (e.g., irregularity of employment). Refuse to tolerate any immoral practice (e.g., espionage). But do not believe that you can find a universal remedy for evil conditions or immoral practices in effecting a fundamental change in society (as by State Socialism). And do not pin too much faith in legislation. Remedial institutions are apt to fall under the control of the enemy and to become instruments of oppression.
>
> Seek for betterment within the broad lines of existing institutions. Do so by attacking evil *in situ;* and proceed from the individual to the general. Remember that progress is necessarily slow; that remedies are necessarily tentative; that because of varying conditions there must be much and constant enquiry into facts . . . and much experimentation; and that always and everywhere the intellectual, moral and spiritual development of those concerned will remain an essential—and the main factor—in real betterment.
>
> This development of the individual is, thus, both a necessary means and the end sought. For our objective is the making of men and women who shall be free, self-respecting members of a democracy—and who shall be worthy of respect. Improvement in material conditions of the worker and ease are the incidents of better conditions—valuable mainly as they may ever increase opportunities for development.
>
> The great developer is responsibility. Hence no remedy can be hopeful which does not devolve upon the workers' participation in, responsibility for, the conduct of business: and their aim should be the eventual assumption of full responsibility—as in co-operative enterprises. This participation in, and eventual control of, industry is likewise an essential of obtaining justice in distributing the fruits of industry.
>
> But democracy in any sphere is a serious undertaking. It substitutes self-restraint for external restraint. It is more dif-

ficult to maintain than to achieve. It demands continuous sacrifice by the individual and more exigent obedience to the moral law than any other form of government. Success in any democratic undertaking must proceed from the individual. It is possible only where the process of perfecting the individual is pursued. His development is attained mainly in the processes of common living. Hence the industrial struggle is essentially an affair of the Church and is its imperative task.[79]

Brandeis believed, in other words, that religion could prepare citizens for democratic citizenship, not by imposing sectarian dogma but by inculcating the habits of personal discipline and self-restraint that made possible the self-education on which democracy relies. It was a Jeffersonian and Periclean vision of religion, and he would eventually look to the secular and agrarian kibbutzim of Palestine as the best laboratory for the small-scale democracy he idealized. But he also absorbed his strenuous vision of morality and ethics from his beloved mother, who taught him to hold himself and others to the highest moral standards without embracing organized religion. This was the paradox that allowed a secular Jew who had not previously embraced his Jewish identity to become, at the age of fifty-seven, the leader of the American Zionist movement. It also led him to organize both his personal life and his political philosophy to maximize individual liberty and to emphasize the collective responsibility of all citizens to protect freedom against incursions by big government and big corporations. As he put it in his most eloquent defense of free speech, "[T]he greatest menace to freedom is an inert people."

Jefferson chose three accomplishments for his own epitaph: "author of the Declaration of American Independence, of the statute of Virginia for religious freedom, and father of the University of Virginia."[80] Brandeis never presumed to write his own epitaph, but his accomplishments were similarly inspiring:

author of *Other People's Money* and of the greatest defenses of privacy and free speech in the twentieth century, champion of the University of Louisville and of the Jewish homeland in Palestine. To understand the forces that shaped this great American prophet, let's begin at the beginning.

1

The Curse of Bigness

As LIBERAL REVOLUTIONS were crushed across Europe, the pilgrims of 1848 set off for liberty and America. They included Louis Brandeis's father, Adolph Brandeis, who burned with a revolutionary passion for freedom: as soon as he heard about the uprising against the Austrian imperial government in Prague, he rushed to join the rebels; only an attack of typhoid fever thwarted his plan. The illness proved to be a blessing in disguise; because he missed the revolution, the twenty-six-year-old Brandeis avoided being placed on a list of those "proscribed" by the emperor and was able to leave Prague for the New World. This combination of a devotion to liberty and an ability to turn setbacks into opportunities was characteristic of Adolph Brandeis's career, and his sense of revolutionary optimism inspired his son for a lifetime. At the outbreak of World War I, Louis Brandeis wrote to his daughter, "To me the world seems more full of hope and promise than at any time since the joyous

days of '48, when liberalism came with its manifold proposals."[1] From his father, Brandeis absorbed the inspiring example
of a small businessman who, through hard work on a human
scale, could develop his intellectual faculties and dedicate himself to personal and economic freedom while providing for the
needs of his family and his community.

Born in Prague in 1822, Adolph Brandeis had hoped to become a chemist but, faced with the immediate need to earn
a living, joined the mill his father owned for printing cotton.
This was the first of the many small businesses that he would
manage effectively over the coming decades. But Brandeis's
chances for advancement in the Austro-Hungarian Empire were
limited by anti-Semitic laws and discriminatory taxes as well as
by a new technology that threatened to make the family's hand-
block textile printer obsolete. Failing to find work after gradu-
ating with distinction from the local technical school, he set off
for Hamburg, where he worked as a grocer; but this kept him
apart from his next-door neighbor, with whom he had fallen
in love.

When she met the charming, witty, and optimistic Adolph,
Frederika Wehle Dembitz was living with her uncle and aunt
across the street from the Brandeis cotton-print mill; like
Adolph, she came from a Jewish family that traced its history
back to the fifteenth century. Both the Brandeis and Dembitz
families belonged to a persecuted sect of Judaism that professed allegiance to Jacob Frank, an eighteenth-century self-
proclaimed messiah who emphasized the cultivation of inner
freedom and the radical transgression of doctrinal boundaries.
By rejecting the yoke of tradition, Frankism led to the Reform
Judaism of the nineteenth century and opened up its adherents,
including Brandeis's ancestors, to new political and cultural
trends.[2] Perhaps as a result, Frederika, born in 1829, grew up in
a secular home—the family had a Christmas tree every year—
in Poland, where her father was the court physician. From tu-

tors and her father, she learned French, dancing, music, history, and literature: she became a passionate reader, a devotee of Schiller and Goethe. Putting music and reading at the center of her life, she passed the same values along to her children. But because her uncle's family, too, was in the economically embattled textile trade, the Wehles and the Brandeises looked to America and to agriculture to revive their fortunes. In the same Jeffersonian spirit, Louis Brandeis throughout his life viewed yeomen farming—from the American South of his boyhood, which was sustained by slavery, to the kibbutzim of Israel—as the path to freedom and the ideal of democratic self-government.

In 1848, when Adolph Brandeis left Prague to search for farmland in America, he was a scout for the Brandeis, Dembitz, and Wehle families, arriving in New York and then heading west. He worked as a farmhand in Ohio, and wrote letters to Frederika quoting the poet Heinrich Heine and praising the independence of farmers and the leisure they had to improve themselves in the evening through reading and convivial conversation. Having identified a promising destination in Madison, Indiana—between Cincinnati and Louisville—Adolph sent for his family, and twenty-six members of the Brandeis, Dembitz, and Wehle clans embarked at Hamburg on the steamer *Washington*, accompanied by twenty-seven trunks and two grand pianos.

The families arrived in America in May 1849, and Adolph and Frederika were married the following September, joined in a double ceremony by Adolph's brother Samuel, a doctor, who married Frederika's cousin Lotti Wehle. The two couples set up a joint household in a small house in Madison, and the Brandeises had their first child, Fannie, in 1851. Concluding that farming was impractical, Adolph set up a grocery and corn-starch factory instead. The grocery thrived, but the starch factory did not, and so he moved his growing family down the Ohio River to Louisville, Kentucky. There he set up a whole-sale wheat shipping business that flourished in response to demand for wheat from the East Coast; his ventures then ex-panded to include a flour mill, a tobacco factory, and, at last, an eleven-hundred-acre farm, and he and Frederika had three more children: Amy, born in 1852, Alfred, born in 1854, and Louis, born on November 13, 1856.

Louis Brandeis's childhood was marked by emotional secu-rity, reflecting his reciprocated love for his siblings and his high-minded, civilized, and affectionate parents. His older sis-ters doted on him: Amy would name her son after her admired brother. Louis was especially close to his brother Alfred, with whom he took camping and canoe trips throughout his life: although studious, both boys also enjoyed youthful pranks—in 1864, they almost blew each other up while experimenting with fireworks on the Fourth of July. From his father, Louis ab-sorbed wit and a talent for motivating others to do their best work. Most of all, Louis was close to his adoring mother, Frederika, the dominant figure in the household, who kept a close eye on his academic and moral progress. Frederika was a committed abolitionist, not a popular position in the pro-Union but hardly antislavery Kentucky, and Brandeis's earliest memories included "a licking I got in school on the morning after Bull Run." (He would have been just over five years and nine months old after the second battle of Bull Run, where Robert E. Lee soundly defeated the Union army at Manassas, Virginia, in August 1862.) He also remembered "helping my mother carry out food and coffee to the men from the North," as he told an interviewer in 1911. "The streets seemed full of them always. But there were times when the rebels came so near that we could hear the firing."[3] After the Civil War, Brandeis's mother, like other liberal whites, sympathized with Louisville's

African American community rather than the former slaveholders, and Brandeis, recalling his childhood, emphasized that his family had servants, not slaves.[4]

Frederika forbade the children to talk about business, finance, or personal gossip at the dinner table, encouraging them instead to discuss music, art, and literature. Brandeis later attributed his reformer's zeal for public service to her example and observed that "the greatest combination of good fortune any man can have is a parentage unusual for both brains and character."[5]

Frederika insisted on rigorous moral standards but not on organized religion. Although they never denied their Jewish heritage, the Brandeises were not observant Jews: they exchanged Christmas cards and the children were criticized by their neighbors for riding on Yom Kippur. In her *Reminiscences*, Frederika explained why she raised her children without organized religion: "Love, virtue, and truth are the foundation upon which the education of the child must be based. They endure forever. . . . And this is my justification for bringing up children without any definite religious belief: I wanted to give them something that neither could be argued away nor would have to be given up as untenable, namely a pure spirit and the highest ideals as to morals and love. God has blessed my endeavors."[6] Nevertheless, Brandeis had one important religious role model: his uncle, Lewis N. Dembitz, an orthodox Jew and fervent Zionist, whose Sabbath table Brandeis vividly remembered. Dembitz was also one of the three Jewish delegates to the Republican convention of 1860 who voted to nominate Abraham Lincoln.[7]

Brandeis admired his uncle intensely for his accomplishments as a lawyer and Talmudic scholar—he would play a role in establishing Hebrew Union College and the Jewish Theological Seminary—so much so that he would eventually substitute his uncle's name, Dembitz, for his own middle name, David. His uncle reciprocated Brandeis's admiration, although he appears to have set a high bar: when Brandeis was appointed to teach at Harvard Law School, Dembitz wrote to his nephew, "It's the first time that I felt glad at your changing your middle name from 'David' to 'Dembitz.'"[8] After his uncle's death, a passing comment from Theodor Herzl's American representative, who recalled that Lewis Dembitz was a "noble Jew," helped to persuade Brandeis, in his fifties, to assume the leadership of the American Zionist movement. Years later, Brandeis wrote to Lewis Dembitz's daughters a moving tribute to his revered uncle: "To those of my generation he was a living university. . . . In the diversity of his intellectual interests, in his longing to discover truths, in his pleasure in argumentation and in the process of thinking, he reminded of the Athenians. . . . It was natural that he should have been among the first in America to support Herzl in his efforts to build a New Palestine."[9] To compare someone to an Athenian was Brandeis's highest praise.

At the age of seventeen, Brandeis learned about the dangers of big banks that gambled with what he would later call "other people's money": his father's business was wiped out in the Panic of 1873 after the collapse of eastern banks left several of his clients bankrupt. Apparently unrattled by this reversal of fortune, Alfred Brandeis then took the family to Europe for three years to show his children their roots. Although he had been a prize-winning and precocious student in Louisville, Louis failed the entrance exam for the gymnasium in Vienna and spent his first months in the city attending university lectures as well as concerts and the theater. He then persuaded the rector of the Annen-Realschule in Dresden to admit him without the entrance exam and excelled at his studies, which he credited with teaching him the importance of inductive reasoning, of developing new ideas by rigorously mastering facts. Years later he told his clerk Paul Freund "that although he did well in his studies theretofore, it was not until he went to Dresden that he really learned to think. He said that in preparing an essay on a subject about which he had known nothing, it dawned on him that ideas could be evolved by reflecting on your material. This was a new discovery for him."[10] Throughout his life, he proved willing to change his mind on important issues, from free speech to Zionism to women's suffrage. Critics accused him of inconsistency, but admirers detected an impressive willingness to adjust his opinions after mastering new facts. ("It has been one of the rules of my life," he once told an interviewer, "that no one shall ever trip me on a question of fact.")[11] And although Brandeis changed his opinions about particular policy issues, he did not alter his basic principles— about the dangers of size in business and government, the importance of industrial and political democracy, the importance of liberty in creating independent, self-reliant citizens who were capable of self-mastery, and the duty of all citizens to educate themselves to develop the faculties of character, reason, and judgment that made self-government possible.

Despite his intellectual awakening in Germany, he recalled in the 1911 interview that "I was a terrible little individualist in those days" and "the German paternalism got on my nerves. One night, for instance, coming home late and finding I had forgotten my key, I whistled up to awaken my roommate; and for this I was reprimanded by the police. This made me homesick. In Kentucky you could whistle. . . . I wanted to go back to America, and I wanted to study law. My uncle, the abolitionist, was a lawyer; and to me nothing else seemed really worth while."[12]

Inspired by his uncle to take up law, Brandeis returned to America in 1875 and enrolled at Harvard Law School. A fine description of Brandeis at Harvard in 1878 comes to us in a letter by a classmate, William Cushing, to his mother: "My friend Brandeis is a character in his way—one of the most brilliant legal minds they have ever had here. . . . Hails from Louisville, is not a college graduate, but has spent some years in Europe, has a rather foreign look and is currently believed to have some Jew blood in him, though you would not suppose it from his appearance—tall, well-made, dark, beardless, and with the brightest eyes I ever saw. Is supposed to know everything and to have it always in mind. The professors listen to his opinions with the greatest deference. And it is generally correct."[13]

His closest friend on the faculty was James Bradley Thayer, the champion of strenuous judicial deference; at Thayer's home in Cambridge on Phillips Place, he heard a lecture by his favorite author, Ralph Waldo Emerson. He also heard the last Harvard lectures of Henry Adams and kept a commonplace book filled with quotations from Emerson, Shakespeare, Matthew Arnold, Stevenson, Swinburne, and Lowell, who seem to have fired his polemical fervor: "The masses of any people, however intelligent, are very little moved by abstract principles of humanity and justice, until those principles are interpreted for them by the stinging commentary of some infringement upon their own rights."[14] Because of his father's continued financial challenges, Brandeis borrowed funds for his law school tuition from his brother Alfred, and made additional money by tutoring his classmates. He lived so frugally and invested so well that at the end of his studies he had saved nearly $1,500, which he used to buy a railroad bond—the beginning of a lifelong practice of conservative investing in safe instruments with low returns that he continued even after he had become a millionaire.

Although he rationed his time rigorously during law school —giving up the violin after concluding he could never excel and his time would be better spent on other pursuits—Brandeis's academic exertions exhausted him, and he developed eye strain that required him to ask his friends to read his law books to him. A letter to his sister at the end of 1877 conveys his Stakhanovite work schedule and his ability to enlist classmates in reading to him. "Wednesday evening I went to the Richards[,] studied about two hours & a half, then talked for about three quarters of an hour to Mother & daughter, and from eleven to o'clock [sic] listened to an article from the 'New Quarterly' on the 'Lord Chancellors & Chief Justices since Lord Campbell.'"[15] And having concluded that "reading, equivalent to drinking maketh a full man," he set aside time in Cambridge and throughout his life to read classic works of literature as well as law. In letter from 1878, he wrote, "The whole of every Sunday morning is spent with my friend [Philippe] Marcou in reading (listening to—on my part) the German Classics—Goethe, Schiller, Lessing, Grillparzer."[16] Despite his eye ailment, which later cleared up, he surpassed his older classmates and graduated first in his class, with the highest marks in the history of the school. (His two-year average was 97, including two marks of 99 and three of 100).[17] Because he was not yet twenty-one, the faculty had to grant a special dispensation to allow him to receive his law degree with the rest of his class.

In 1879, he returned briefly to the Midwest to practice law in St. Louis with the encouragement of his mother and brother-in-law, but soon accepted an invitation from his law school friend Samuel Warren to return to Boston to form a law partnership and to clerk for Horace Gray, the chief justice of the Massachusetts Supreme Court and future justice of the U.S. Supreme Court. "I am treated in every respect as a person of co-ordinate position," he wrote of his clerkship to his brother-in-law, Charles Nagel, who would go on to serve in President Taft's cabinet. "[The chief justice] asks me what I think of his line of argument and I answer candidly."[18]

In a letter to his mother, Brandeis gives us a sense of his daily schedule, which always included time for focused leisure: "You want to know how I pass my days: then read: I get up shortly after seven o'clock, have breakfast, go for a walk usually till nine o'clock. Then (every day this week) I stayed at the C.J. [chief justice's] till 2 o'clock. After lunch I go to our office, talk over business affairs with Warren, work there or in the Law-library according as business requires, and shortly after six o'clock I have dinner." He then describes evenings rowing, swimming, and "shouting for joy in the full enjoyment of a bath in the lake. . . . Oh, how beautiful are heaven and earth here, hills and water, nature and art!"[19]

Despite his reputation as austere in public (his clerks would recall sliding copies of opinions under the door of his apartment at the crack of dawn and his silently retrieving the draft without opening the door), Brandeis revealed a loving and tender side in his letters to his family. His filial devotion was certainly moving: he said good night to his mother every evening until he left for law school and wrote her affectionate letters throughout his life. "I must send you another birthday greeting and tell you how much I love you," he wrote to his mother in 1888, when he was thirty-two. "[W]ith each day I learn to extol your love and your worth more—and that when I look back over my life, I can find nothing in your treatment of me that I would alter. . . . I believe, most beloved mother, that the improvement of the world, reform, can only arise when mothers like you are increased thousands of times and have more children."[20]

Brandeis was similarly demonstrative in his courtship of his second cousin, Alice Goldmark, whom he had first met as a child. Brandeis became emotionally intimate with Alice in Louisville in March 1890, when he visited for the funeral of his sister Fannie, who had committed suicide in the wake of a depression that followed the death of her son and the birth of her daughter. Several months after the funeral, Alice invited Brandeis to join her family on their annual summer vacation in New Hampshire, and Brandeis's letters soon became ardent. "My Dear, Sweet Alice," Brandeis wrote in September of the same year. "How I long to be with you, to ask and to tell all that concerns us both. . . . To think you are mine and that I should know so little of my treasure—so little except its vastness, except that it is illimitable."[21] Later that month, he continued in the same vein. "My dear Alice, I see the future so beautiful, so rich in the blessings which your love will bring, there is a new point of view to every trivial circumstance of life. I have found the much longed for New Dimension. It must be depth. I looked into your eyes and beheld the infinite."[22]

The courtship was swift: Brandeis and Alice were engaged in October and married in March 1891, a year after their romance began. Alice's brother-in-law, Felix Adler, the founder of the New York Society for Ethical Culture, performed the civil ceremony, which included no hints of Judaism. And the marriage was long and happy: Brandeis's letters to Alice continued to be tender until the end. On her birthday in 1908, Brandeis wrote: "Only a word of love for tomorrow, and all time. I should regret more being absent on this day, were not all the year fete days."[23] And he was still joking with her in 1911: "Having left my pajamas at home, I have purchased some flannelettes of dazzling beauty."[24] When Melvin Urofsky published an article about Brandeis's letters to his family in the 1980s, David Riesman, one of Brandeis's last law clerks, who would go on to become the leading sociologist of his era (and one of my college teachers), wrote to me to express surprise. "For me, the most interesting news in the article on Brandeis was his writing daily to his wife when he was away," Riesman wrote. "When I was his clerk, his wife seemed only to play a role of chaperon, sending guests away lest the Justice become over-tired."[25]

Alice remained involved in progressive political causes—supporting the campaign, for example, of Robert M. La Follette, the Progressive senator from Wisconsin. And during the austere Sunday afternoon teas the couple held in Washington during Brandeis's Supreme Court years, she ensured that each guest had ten or fifteen minutes in the seat of honor next to her husband, her intent to minimize the strain and maximize the facts and informed opinion he received. Marquis Childs described the hour-and-a-half teas as a "slightly awesome institution" where guests would sit in stiff, high-backed chairs in the Brandeis's living room on California Street, gazing at the prints of classical ruins. One of the guests to whom Brandeis took a liking was the young Harry Truman, who wrote that he and Brandeis "were certainly in agreement on the curse of bigness."[26] Riesman recalled that Mrs. Brandeis "was glad to have me arrange to invite people for Sunday tea who would be interesting for the Justice."[27]

Alice also supported his Supreme Court nomination as a welcome change from the exertion of his political activities; when he returned home on the day of his confirmation on June 1, 1916, she greeted him with a warm "Good evening, Mr. Justice Brandeis,"[28] as opposed to her habitual endearment, "Demby." Still, throughout their fifty-year marriage, Alice suffered neurasthenic ailments that prevented her from participating in Brandeis's vigorous exercise regimen of hiking and canoeing or in household management; from the beginning of their marriage, Brandeis took charge of practical domestic affairs, ranging from paying bills (with an eagle eye on expenses, which he carefully enumerated) to buying furniture, in order to relieve his wife of strain.

In 1893 and 1896, respectively, Brandeis's two daughters, Susan and Elizabeth, were born. Brandeis devoted himself to the education of both, reading to them for an hour every morning during his 7:00 breakfast from literature, history, philosophy, or math. Making time for his family was part of Brandeis's philosophy of setting aside time for rest, vacations, and leisure, rather than working day and night.[29] Both daughters had distinguished careers in public service, with their father's loving but watchful support: Susan, who graduated from Bryn Mawr and the University of Chicago Law School, practiced law with her husband, Jacob H. Gilbert. She helped to oversee New York schools as a member of the state board of regents and was a lifelong member of Hadassah.[30] Elizabeth graduated from Radcliffe and received her PhD in economics from the University of Wisconsin; she later taught at Wisconsin and contributed to the series *History of Labor in the United States*, focusing on the period from 1896 to 1932. With her husband, Paul Raushenbush, she fought for federal and state laws guaranteeing unemployment compensation.[31] Brandeis was proud of both daughters for advancing his own passionate devotion to Zionism and social justice for the unemployed.

After law school, he set up a law practice in Boston with his Brahmin classmate Samuel Warren, with whom he wrote in 1890 "The Right to Privacy," one of the most famous law review articles in American legal history. Published in the *Harvard Law Review*, it was inspired, according to Brandeis, by Warren's "deep-seated abhorrence of the invasions of social privacy"[32] by new media technologies such as the instant camera and the tabloid press. In particular, Warren and his patrician wife were upset about gossip items in the Boston society pages—including stories about Mrs. Warren's friendship with President Grover Cleveland's young bride, which they somehow perceived as an indignity. (Another account says that Warren was "outraged when photographers invaded his babies' privacy and snapped perambulator pictures.")[33] Despite the fact that Louis and Samuel were close friends in law school—Samuel ranked second in the class after Brandeis and read to him to conserve his vision—Mabel Warren's anti-Semitism led her to exclude Brandeis from her wedding and her home. That didn't prevent her, however, from urging her husband to seek out Brandeis to propose a remedy for what she considered the indignities of the society pages, in which she and her husband appeared more than sixty times in the 1880s.[34]

In their article, Warren and Brandeis began by decrying new media technologies that menaced the privacy of celebrities and aristocrats. "Instantaneous photographs and newspaper enterprise have invaded the sacred precincts of private and domestic life; and numerous mechanical devices threaten to make good the prediction that 'what is whispered in the closet shall be proclaimed from the house-tops,'" they wrote.[35] "To satisfy a prurient taste the details of sexual relations are spread broadcast in the columns of the daily papers. To occupy the indolent, column upon column is filled with idle gossip, which can only be procured by intrusion upon the domestic circle."[36]

Warren and Brandeis set out to identify a legal principle that might protect celebrities and other objects of tabloid gossip from emotional injury. Here, however, they faced a challenge. Unlike European law, American law had not, historically, protected individuals from the hurt feelings that resulted from what they called offenses against "honor." Instead, American law had protected liberty rather than dignity. So Warren and Brandeis set out radically to transform American law by proposing an entirely new legal right, which they called "the right to be let alone." The right they proposed had three elements: it allowed celebrities to sue the press for emotional injury; it allowed citizens to remove true but embarrassing information from public debate; and it required courts to distinguish between what truthful information was fit for the public to know and what was none of the public's business.[37] There was just one problem with the new right that Brandeis and Warren proposed: it clashed directly with the First Amendment's protections for free speech and public debate. Although Brandeis's article attempted to preserve free speech by treating public figures differently than private figures, the distinction still required judges to decide when emotional injury should trump the public's interest in truthful facts or opinions. Even when he received the page proofs of the privacy article in November 1890, he wrote to Alice Goldmark: "[T]he little I read did not strike me as being as good as I had thought it was."[38]

In his later opinions on the Supreme Court, Brandeis came

to believe, as the scholar Neil Richards put it in describing Brandeis's evolution, that "when free speech and traditional notions of privacy conflict, free speech should almost always win."[39] And Brandeis also came to embrace a different vision of privacy—Richards calls it "intellectual privacy," which he defines as "protection from surveillance or interference when we are engaged in the processes of generating ideas."[40] In other words, Brandeis came to believe that we don't need to choose between privacy and free speech because far from clashing with democratic values of public debate, intellectual privacy is essential to it.

One of the experiences that may have changed Brandeis's mind about the right to privacy was his growing interest in what he called the "Duty of Publicity" as a way of countering economic fraud. As he wrote to Alice in 1891, writing "an article on 'the Duty of Publicity'—a sort of companion piece to the last one" (that is, his article on the right to privacy) "would really interest me more." His imagination was fired, he said, by examples of "the wickedness of people shielding wrongdoers & passing them off . . . as honest men." His conclusion: "If the broad light of day could be let in upon men's actions, it would purify them as the sun disinfects."[41] Over the course of the decade, Brandeis would develop this metaphor as he became increasingly focused on the idea that citizens could protect themselves from the greed and predations of unscrupulous capitalists if they understood the complicated financial instruments in which they were being asked to invest, and this led to one of the most memorable aphorisms in his 1914 book *Other People's Money:* "Publicity is justly commended as a remedy for social and industrial diseases. Sunlight is said to be the best of disinfectants; electric light the most efficient policeman."

In thirty-seven years of law practice, Brandeis became one of the most successful lawyers in America, hailed as "the people's lawyer" for representing the interests of family businesses and minority stockholders in fights against the rapacious monopolies of the Gilded Age. Early in his career, Brandeis had defended corporations for contributing to "the great industrial development of the present century," including the construction of the railroads and telegraph; but Andrew Carnegie's decision in 1893 to mobilize Pinkerton guards, who opened fire on the striking union workers at the Carnegie plant in Homestead, Pennsylvania, convinced him that management and labor unions were not competing on equal terms. As a result, Brandeis told an early biographer, he threw away the notes he had drafted for a series of lectures on business law at MIT and, rather than criticizing social legislation designed to help workers and unions, as he had planned, he defended them instead. "Those talks at the Tech marked an epoch in my own career," Brandeis recalled.[42] (The notes of Brandeis's MIT lectures themselves, however, suggest that he scarcely mentioned the Homestead crisis, so he may have increased its significance in retrospect.)[43] Rejecting both radical socialism and radical laissez-faire, Brandeis came to believe that vital unions were as necessary as vital manufacturers, so that labor and capital could negotiate on equal terms. The foe of excessive capitalism was also a foe of excessive government regulation and above all relied on elevating the educational standard of workers to allow them time to think for themselves, at home and at work.

Brandeis was also influenced by the political success of the People's Party, also known as the Populists, a coalition of Grangers, or aggrieved farmers, and Greenbacks, who demanded currency reform. He closely read muckraking attacks on plutocracy such as "The Story of a Great Monopoly," the *Atlantic Monthly*'s exposé of Standard Oil, by Brandeis's acquaintance Henry Demarest Lloyd, who called himself "the people's attorney."[44] As the Progressive movement gained momentum, Congress regulated the railroads with the Interstate Commerce Commission and passed the Sherman Antitrust Act to break up monopolies. After Cleveland defeated Harrison in 1892 with the help of the People's Party, Congress passed a federal income tax in 1894. The Supreme Court would later strike down or hobble some of these early reforms. Brandeis increasingly challenged lawyers to defend the interests of the people rather than the corporations. "Instead of holding a position of independence, between the wealthy and the people, *prepared to curb the excesses of either*, able lawyers have, to a large extent, allowed themselves to become adjuncts of great corporations and have neglected the obligation to use their powers for the protection of the people," he told the Harvard Ethical Society in 1905.[45]

Although Brandeis came to be a leader of the Progressive movement, and although others would call him "the people's lawyer," he saw himself as fighting for what Melvin Urofsky calls the traditional view of the relationship between the commonwealth and private businesses, in which the state defended the public interest, financial probity, and the accurate valuation of corporate property. By the turn of the century, however, this view was under siege by the modern view, championed by Wall Street bankers, that saw stock as a commodity that investors bought at their own risk. According to this view, widespread in the Gilded Age, the state had no role in regulating corporations beyond preventing outright fraud.[46]

Brandeis cast himself as "counsel to the situation," a kind of Jeffersonian McKinsey consultant, representing the interests of both labor and management. Immersing himself in the facts, he attempted to identify what both sides wanted and to propose creative solutions that balanced all of the interests concerned.[47] (Later, during his confirmation hearings for the Supreme Court, critics charged him with conflict of interest for representing both sides; in the American Bar Association and elsewhere, debate continues about whether Brandeis acted ethically).[48] Still, Brandeis's clients valued him for using facts to solve problems. In 1902, for example, William H. McElwain, the head of a large New England shoe-making company, asked Brandeis's help in persuading his workers to accept a cut in wages without going on strike. Although McElwain prided himself on paying his workers well, Brandeis discovered they were laid off during slow periods and, over the course of a year, made less than a living wage. By persuading McElwain to reorganize his business so he could plan ahead rather than accepting rush orders, Brandeis was able to guarantee the workers around three hundred days of a work a year.[49] The reform fueled his lifelong belief that "regularity of employment" was a key component of industrial democracy and economic opportunity.

At the same time, Brandeis managed to do well by doing good: he earned his first million by frugal living and investing in government or municipal bonds rather than stocks, which he considered a form of legalized gambling. He chastised his brother Alfred for buying stocks—"I feel very sure that unser eins [our kind of people] ought not to buy and sell stocks. We don't know much about the business—and beware of people who think they do."[50] Consistent with his philosophy that people should only assume risks they understand, he continued: "[D]on't try to make your money out of investments. Make it out of your business. Of that you understand as much as anybody."[51]

Brandeis sought financial independence in order to achieve spiritual independence—providing for his family and investing his extra time and income in the public causes that his parents and upbringing had inspired him to champion. He resolved to give an hour a day of his time to pro bono legal activity, and in 1905 he told Edward Filene, the civic-minded Boston merchant who owned Filene's Department Store, that he eventually hoped to give half his time.[52] "Some men buy diamonds and other works of art; others delight in automobiles and yachts," he told a reporter in 1911. "My luxury is to invest my surplus effort, beyond that required for the proper support of my family, to the pleasure of taking up a problem and solving, or helping to solve, it for the people without receiving any compensation."[53] He insisted in another interview that, although he believed in property rights, courts were wrong to view them as an end in themselves. "I don't want money or property most," he declared. "I want to be free."[54]

Brandeis's first crusade against public corruption came in 1904 when he attacked the planned reorganization of the Boston gas system. Under a proposed merger, eight Boston gas companies proposed to consolidate their assets and to raise rates. Brandeis, representing the Public Franchise League of Boston, navigated between conservatives, who wanted as much consolidation and profit as possible, even at the cost of buying off regulators, and reformers, who preferred to take over the utilities under municipal ownership. He persuaded the Boston legislature and the executives of the aptly named Boston Consolidated Gas Company to adopt a "sliding scale" of rates that allowed the company to raise dividends in exchange for lower rates.[55] Brandeis's sliding scale reduced the price of gas from 90¢ to 80¢ within a year and resulted in higher dividends and public savings of up to $800,000. The greatest benefit, Brandeis wrote in an essay called "How Boston Solved the Gas Problem," was that "the officers and employees of the gas company now devote themselves strictly to the business of making and distributing gas, instead of . . . in lobbying and political intrigue."

Concluding that "neither private nor public ownership" of public utilities "is wholly satisfactory," he praised the moderate compromise as "a partnership between the public and the stockholders of the gas company—a partnership in which the public will secure an ever-increasing share of the profits of the business."[56] For him, the price of gas was less important than fairness both to investors, who deserved a reasonable rate of return, and consumers, who deserved reasonable prices. Denouncing his opponents on the left and the right as "fanatics" who were "as ready to do injustice to capital as the capitalists have been ready to do injustice to the people," Brandeis wrote to his brother Alfred, "I consider this a most important step in public economics & government—an alternative for municipal ownership, which will keep the Gas Co. out of politics."[57] In other words, Brandeis advocated what he would call "regulated competition" as an alternative to government takeover of the utilities or to unregulated monopolies, both of which he abhorred. He said repeatedly that he wanted to keep business out of government and government out of business.

In 1905, Brandeis began to collect his ideas about "Industrial-Cooperation" in an address to the Filene Cooperative Association. Founded by Edward Filene and his brother Lincoln, both of whom had taken over Filene's Department Store from their father, William, a German Jewish immigrant, the FCA was an employees' union based on the principle of industrial democracy, the notion that if workers could argue for better work conditions, their personal investment in the success of the business and the quality of their work would improve. (Brandeis also joined the Filene brothers in forming the Industrial League, which encouraged Boston employers to take a progressive approach to employee relations.) In his speech, Brandeis praised the members of the FCA for "aiding in the solution of the greatest problem which is before the American people in this generation—the problem of reconciling our industrial system with the political democracy in which we live." Brandeis identified three preconditions for the "self-government" that he believed to be as essential in industry as in politics. Workers had to be "master of themselves"; "they must work with and for others, for the institution of which they are part"; and, above all, "they must think." He continued, "Democracy is only possible, industrial democracy, among people who think; among people who are above the average intelligence." But he stressed that "intelligence is not a gift that merely comes. It is a gift men make and women make for themselves. It is earned, and it is earned by effort."[58]

This strenuous notion of industrial and political democracy —based on the idea that workers and citizens had an obligation to educate themselves to be capable of self-government— suffused Brandeis's thinking about the Constitution as well as the workplace. In a 1913 interview, "Efficiency and Social Ideals," Brandeis declared that "in order to live men must have the opportunity of developing their faculties; and they must live under conditions in which their faculties may develop naturally and healthily."[59] That resonant phrase "develop their faculties" would reemerge more than two decades later in Brandeis's greatest Supreme Court opinion about free speech, in which he declared that "the final end of the State was to make men free to develop their faculties."[60] Brandeis's faith in the duty of education for self-government was vindicated in 1910 when he represented immigrant garment workers during a strike in New York City. Both the workers and management involved in the strike were Russian Jews, and Brandeis later recalled how impressed he had been by the intellectualism, idealism, and empathy of the immigrant Jewish workers. The experience gave him respect for their support for Zionism and their concerns about European anti-Semitism.[61] It also helped convert Brandeis to the Zionist cause.

On the industrial level, Brandeis maintained, "men and women must have leisure, which the Athenians called 'freedom' or liberty."[62] (He issued his statement in November 1913, just after reading Alfred Zimmern's *Greek Commonwealth*.) And this leisure could be achieved by the "abolition of child labor, shorter hours of labor, and regular days of rest" as well as greater earnings. Moreover, "these demands for shorter working time, for higher earnings and for better conditions cannot conceivably be met unless the productivity of man is increased."[63] This was one reason Brandeis became an enthusiastic promoter of Taylorism, or scientific management to maximize efficiency in the workplace. Brandeis discovered scientific management after reading Frederick Taylor's 1903 paper "Shop Management."[64] Taylor set out to use scientific techniques to determine the best time and manner to perform any task in the production process. The idea appealed to Brandeis's notion of bringing both sides in labor disputes together for face-to-face discussions to iron out their differences; scientific management promised the efficiency and prosperity that could achieve this goal.[65] Unlike Taylor, however, who insisted on a set of rigid procedures to achieve efficiency, such as the elimination of guesswork by workers, Brandeis embraced a more humanistic approach to scientific management. In determining the proper time to perform a task, he insisted that "representatives of the workers ought surely to have a voice."[66] He went on to set out a vision of scientific management, negotiated by unions and management, that he believed would create better citizens as well as better workers: "Scientific management does not mean making men work harder. Its every effort is to make them work less hard; to accomplish more by the same amount of effort, and to eliminate all unnecessary motions; to educate them so as to make them more effective; to give special assistance to those who when entering upon their work are most in need of assistance, because they are least competent."[67]

Brandeis made national headlines in a 1910 hearing at the Waldorf-Astoria before the Interstate Commerce Commission by insisting that the railroads, by adopting scientific management techniques, could save "a million dollars a day"![68] (Some railroads, deciding to challenge Brandeis, adopted scientific management and did indeed save millions.) But Brandeis did not believe that most corporations would voluntarily adopt scientific management on their own. To guarantee industrial democracy, he insisted, the power of employers had to be countered by the power of unions. Testifying before Congress on industrial relations in 1915, he noted "the contrast between our political liberty and our industrial absolutism." Although in politics "every male has his voice and vote," in the workplace "the individual employee has no effective voice or vote" and "the result, in the cases of these large corporations, may be to develop a benevolent absolutism."[69]

Brandeis recognized the importance of convincing workers that his humanistic vision of Taylorism was in their interest. "Those who undertake to apply the truths which Taylor disclosed must remember that in a democracy it is not sufficient to have discovered an industrial truth, or even the whole truth. Such truth can rule only when accompanied by the consent of men," he wrote in *Business—A Profession*, the collection of essays he published in 1914. Calling the hostility of labor to scientific management a "misunderstanding," he said that labor had to be convinced that "industrial truths" are consistent with "human truths," promising that "the greater productivity attained [is] clearly consistent with the health of the body, the mind, and the soul of the worker . . . with industrial freedom . . . [and with] greater joy in work, and generally in living."[70] In the end, however, unions remained suspicious of, or actively hostile to, the scientific management that Brandeis advocated, fearing that increased efficiency would result in layoffs.[71] For this reason Brandeis's idealistic embrace of scientific management has been criticized by modern scholars, who suggest that his fixation on rationality, logic, individual fulfillment of workers, and altruistic collaboration between management and unions blinded him to the reality of industrial politics.[72]

Brandeis anticipated, however, that unions might not be powerful enough to bring about industrial democracy on their own. What "makes the great corporation so dangerous" is the unchecked power it possesses, he testified.[73] Applying constitutional principles to industrial challenges, Brandeis insisted: "I think all of our human experience shows that no one with absolute power can be trusted to give it up even in part. That has been the experience with political absolutism; it must prove the same with industrial absolutism."[74] Anticipating his concern with "the curse of bigness," he insisted that the state might have to break up large corporations—imposing "a limit upon the size of corporate units"[75]—in order to guarantee industrial democracy: "Size may become such a danger in its results to the community that the community may have to set limits."[76]

In Brandeis's view, the various remedies for industrial unrest he endorsed—including scientific management, arbitration, mediation and conciliation, profit sharing, and the minimum wage—were subsidiary to the broader goal of "industrial democracy," which he defined as a system that gave the worker "not only a voice, but a vote; not merely a right to be heard, but a position through which labor may participate in management."[77] Concerned that bankers who served as directors of more than one large corporation didn't have time to master the facts required for understanding each of the businesses they oversaw, Brandeis believed that scientific management would make employers more invested in their employees and more willing to guarantee regularity of employment.[78]

Brandeis's concern with regularity of employment, the curse of bigness, and industrial democracy culminated in a series of public crusades following his attack on the consolidation of the Boston gas companies. In 1906, he organized the Massachusetts Savings Bank Insurance League to make life insurance more like a savings bank investment. Brandeis identified an evil— the exploitation of poor workers by rapacious insurance companies who sold policies at usurious prices—and a pragmatic, small-scale, legislative solution—selling insurance at fair prices through savings banks—that avoided heavy-handed federal regulation. Companies like the Equitable Life Assurance Company of New York Life provoked alarm by the corrupt behavior and lavish spending of their executives, who risked what Brandeis called the "quick capital" of policyholders by investing in unstable rail and shipping monopolies controlled by financiers such as Brandeis's nemesis, J. P. Morgan. To court the life insurance executives, Morgan and his cronies put them on the boards of directors of the railroad companies in which they were investing,[79] and an investigation by the New York State legislature found widespread abuses by insurance executives, including corrupt campaign contributions and falsified books.

Brandeis contrasted the risky behavior of the insurance companies with the stability of locally controlled savings banks, which were better capitalized and able to guarantee continued coverage even if workers missed insurance payments. Rejecting the uniform federal regulations that the insurance companies sought because they thought its one-size-fits-all approach would be easier to obey, Brandeis persuaded the Massachusetts legislature to pass a state regulation in 1907 by which savings banks sold life insurance to workers at rates they could afford.[80] The Massachusetts law became a model for life insurance regulation in New York, and Massachusetts Savings Bank Life Insurance celebrated its centennial in 2007, surviving recent financial crises because of conservative investments and strict regulations.[81] Brandeis considered the result "a perfect reform."[82]

The same year, Brandeis took on a transportation monopoly in New England. When the New Haven Railroad, once again controlled by J. P. Morgan, tried to buy one of its competitors, the Boston and Maine lines, public criticism in Massachusetts focused on the indignity of New York financiers controlling a local trolley company. Brandeis focused instead on the dangers of monopoly and the financial weakness of the New Haven line. Viewing the battle in characteristically moralistic terms, Brandeis wrote to his brother Alfred: "The enemy is still worrying us. . . . The merger is troublesome. . . . Our business-men fail to grasp to [*sic*] the evils of monopoly and are cowards besides. If we get time enough we may enlighten them, but it is too hot for much education."[83] Brandeis objected to the merger on the grounds that it would create a monopoly too large to be managed efficiently, with corresponding "political dangers surrounding a monster corporation controlling all transportation facilities of New England." As he wrote in a 1908 address, "The New England Transportation Monopoly": "For every business concern there must be a limit of greatest efficiency. . . . The disadvantages attendant upon size may outweigh the advantages. Man's works have outgrown the capacity of the individual man. . . . Any transportation system which is called upon not merely to operate, but to develop its facilities, makes heavy demands upon its executive officers for initiative and for the exercise of sound judgment."[84]

Brandeis's conclusion about the dangers of size was both political and moral: "There is no way in which to safeguard people from despotism except to prevent despotism. There is no way to safeguard the people from the evils of a private transportation monopoly except to prevent the monopoly. The objections to despotism and to monopoly are fundamental in human nature. They rest upon the innate and ineradicable selfishness of man. They rest upon the fact that absolute power inevitably leads to abuse."[85] In the end, the Massachusetts legislature and governor approved the merger in the face of intense lobbying. ("Amidst innumerable broken promises of support we got unmercifully licked but it took all the power of the Republican machine & of the Bankers' money to do it, and I am well content with the fight made," Brandeis wrote to Alfred.)[86] Eventually, however, the New Haven line collapsed, thanks to the profligate borrowing of its head, Charles Sanger Mellen, who was forced to resign in 1913.[87]

In January 1908, Brandeis argued before the Supreme Court the landmark case of *Muller v. Oregon*.[88] Three years earlier, in the landmark *Lochner* case, the court had struck down New York's law setting maximum hours for male bakers on the grounds that it interfered with the employers' freedom of contract.[89] In *Muller*, however, Brandeis persuaded the court to uphold a similar law setting maximum hours for women. And he did so with a pioneering and exhaustive compilation of facts and "sociological" data. With the help of his sister-in-law, Josephine Goldmark, he amassed more than one hundred pages of American and European labor studies showing that long working hours affected the health, safety, and morals of women.[90] The Supreme Court unanimously upheld the law, in an opinion that sounds paternalistic today. "That woman's physical structure and the performance of maternal functions place her at a disadvantage in the struggle for subsistence is obvious," Justice Brewer wrote for the court. "[H]istory discloses the fact that woman has always been dependent upon man."[91] Brewer also took the unusual step of acknowledging Brandeis's influence in his opinion. "In the brief filed by Mr. Louis D. Brandeis for the defendant in error is a very copious collection of all these matters," he wrote, singling out Brandeis's data about "the course of legislation, as well as expressions of opinion from other than judicial sources." And the brief, which emphasized facts rather than legal citations, became a model for the so-called Brandeis brief, which urges judges to immerse themselves in the factual background of a case. The brief influenced Thurgood Marshall's brief in *Brown v. Board of Education*, which persuaded the Supreme Court to cite hotly contested sociological data about the effects of segregation on African American schoolchildren.[92]

Brandeis's brief in *Muller* began with a list of laws passed by twenty U.S. states and "the leading countries of Europe" restricting the working hours of women. It then included a discussion of "the world's experience upon which the legislation limiting the hours of labor for women is based," ranging from a report from a British physician about the physical differences between men and women to an 1895 report of the German Imperial Factory Inspectors.[93] Brandeis offered another defense of progressive economic legislation in a 1915 brief in a Supreme Court case called *Stettler v. O'Hara*, where the court upheld, by a 4–4 vote, Oregon's minimum wage law.[94] (Brandeis, by then on the court, did not participate.) Published as an essay entitled "The Constitution and the Minimum Wage," Brandeis gave us a sense of the rhetorical approach he would refine in his Supreme Court opinions, first presenting the justifications that led the Oregon legislature to pass the law; then surveying the exhaustive data that the legislature considered in reaching its conclusions; then presenting still more evidence ("three hundred and sixty-nine extracts") from outside the record; and then asking whether the legislature was unreasonable to reach its conclusion: "Does that seem a revolutionary doctrine? Does it seem revolutionary for the legislature of Oregon to pass a minimum-wage law when it knows the conditions in Oregon to be such that degeneration of the people, and heavy burdens upon the taxpayer and upon the industry of the commonwealth, must necessarily result if women are permitted to continue to be employed at less than living-wages? The Supreme Court of Oregon, likewise knowing something of local conditions, held that it was not."[95]

Brandeis then performed a rhetorical arabesque, suggesting that although the Oregon legislature was entirely correct in passing a minimum wage law, judges should uphold the law unless they concluded that the legislature was completely irrational.

> I conceive the only question before the court to be this: Is this particular restriction upon the liberty of the individual one which can be said to be arbitrary, to have no relation to the ends sought to be accomplished? Whether or not it is arbitrary, whether it is reasonable, must be determined largely

by results where it has been tried out. Can this court say that the legislature in Oregon, knowing local conditions in Oregon, supported by the Supreme Court of Oregon (supposed also to have some special knowledge of local conditions in Oregon), was so absolutely and inexcusably mistaken in their belief that the evils exist and that the measures proposed would lessen those evils, as to justify this court in holding the restrictions upon the liberty of contract involved cannot be permitted?[96]

Brandeis concluded with an idea that he would later develop on the Supreme Court—the idea of giving the states wide latitude to experiment as "laboratories of democracy." He wrote: "When we know that the evil exists which it is sought to remedy, the legislature must be given latitude in experimentation.[97] . . . Nothing could be more revolutionary than to close the door to social experimentation. The whole subject of women's entry into industry is an experiment. And surely the federal constitution—itself perhaps the greatest of human experiments—does not prohibit such modest attempts as the women's minimum wage act to reconcile the existing industrial system with our striving for social justice and the preservation of the race."[98] Despite the jarring note of eugenics in the final clause, the brief reminds us that for Brandeis, a commitment to judicial restraint was fused with a passionate devotion to the moral correctness of the laws he defended.

For David Riesman, the only one of Brandeis's law clerks who expressed criticism of Brandeis after the clerkship,[99] Brandeis's moral commitments, including his devotion to states' rights, trumped his devotion to the facts. In a 1996 letter, Riesman wrote to me that Brandeis would have been "horrified" by the Supreme Court decision striking down the Virginia Military Institute's all-male admissions policy because "it is hard to overstate Justice Brandeis's dedication to states' rights." Riesman recalled that when he was Brandeis's clerk in the 1935–36 court term, the first case he worked on involved an Oregon law requiring berry boxes to be of a specified size and shape. As Riesman recalled, "Justice Brandeis sent me in characteristic 'Brandeis Brief' fashion to find out what lay behind the law. I went to the Interstate Commerce Commission, and to the railroads. I quickly found that the Oregon law had been passed to keep out berry boxes made from California redwoods, something clearly understood at the ICC and also by the commercial interests, railroads and box makers, involved." Riesman reported all this to Justice Brandeis, emphasizing that the California redwood boxes were clearly superior to the Oregon boxes, injuring fewer berries and carrying more.

To Riesman's disappointment, Brandeis wrote an opinion for a unanimous court upholding the protectionist Oregon law on the hypothetical grounds that the shape of the box might better preserve the berries and help consumers estimate their quality.[100] "Brandeis's political aim was to sustain states' rights as against the federal government,"[101] Riesman wrote, still frustrated sixty years later that the justice had ignored his factual investigation. A more charitable way of putting the same point is the one Brandeis expressed in his Brandeis briefs: even if state legislators pass laws for protectionist motives that sometimes clash with their stated public objectives, judicial deference to state economic experiments is such an overriding value that judges should uphold them unless the legislators are "absolutely and inexcusably" mistaken in their beliefs and the laws "have no relation to the ends sought to be accomplished."

During this busy period, which included Supreme Court arguments and the fights against the New Haven Railroad and Boston gas companies, Brandeis continued to make time for travel and exercise. Alice's health didn't allow her to travel with him: throughout the early years of their marriage, she suffered from exhaustion and required periods of recovery in rest homes. Brandeis took a cross-country trip with his friend Herbert

White that brought them over the Rockies through Wyoming and Nevada to California. He wrote to Alice, "DEAREST: We spent the night at Pasadena, amidst date palms and pepper and joyous flowers." Still, in the Athenian spirit of leisure, there was always time set aside for instruction as well as amusement: "The sun beats down, as it should in a desert. . . . I am learning a great deal of geography and much is made real of which we have vaguely heard."[102]

Brandeis's public crusades catapulted him into politics and contributed to a dramatic and consequential split in the Republican Party that would help decide the election of 1912. Brandeis was initially impressed with both Theodore Roosevelt and his handpicked successor William Howard Taft. He visited Roosevelt in 1908 and wrote to his brother that the president "impressed me most favorably in every way—manners included."[103] Brandeis added that "[Roosevelt] is a great man" and his recent radical speech "expressed just my sentiments" in urging Congress to regulate the railroads, strengthen the Sherman Antitrust Act, and favor labor over "predatory wealth."[104] Brandeis would go on in November to vote for Taft. "Taft is admirably qualified for the position & doubtless will—if he lives—prove a fine President, rather of the Cleveland type," he wrote to Alfred, "but I fear the Republican Party will be less manageable than under Roosevelt & that we shall see much of the moneybags we abhor."[105]

Brandeis's fears about Taft were soon vindicated. In 1910, *Collier's* magazine asked Brandeis to become involved in the Pinchot-Ballinger affair, which began as a fight over environmental policy, a topic that deeply interested Brandeis. With his Jeffersonian idealization of the farmer and agrarian democracy, Brandeis was an early environmentalist. He wanted the federal government, rather than the investment bankers, to oversee the development of virgin land in places like Alaska to ensure that profits would be retained by the people rather than the bankers and "that the opportunities of earnings of the settlers in Alaska will be the most liberal conceivable." He suggested to Senator Robert La Follette the following Progressive slogan:

> Alaska; the land of Opportunity.
> Develop it by the People, for the people.
> Do not let it be exploited by the Capitalists,
> for the Capitalists.[106]

Brandeis supported Roosevelt's fight for America's natural resources, which Roosevelt called the most important national issue aside from war. "Conservation is a great moral issue for it involves the patriotic duty of insuring the safety and continuance of the nation," Roosevelt declared in a 1910 speech, "The New Nationalism."[107] Still, Roosevelt's conservation effort, led by deputies such as the chief forester at the Department of Agriculture, Gifford Pinchot, differed from that of modern environmentalists: he aspired to allow experts to administer land development in the public interest.[108] But when William Howard Taft succeeded Roosevelt in 1909, he replaced Roosevelt's conservation-minded secretary of the interior, James R. Garfield, with Richard A. Ballinger, who had defended corporations in suits involving land use but who also wanted to allow land development by small entrepreneurs. Pinchot, a whistleblower, was concerned that Roosevelt's pro-environment policies would be repudiated, a fear he considered vindicated when Ballinger put up for sale coal deposits in Alaska that Roosevelt had protected. The charge was that the government was giving away the valuable Alaskan land to a syndicate of investment bankers headed by Brandeis's old enemy, J. P. Morgan. An interior official named Louis Glavis suspected that the sale involved breaking the law and presented formal charges against Ballinger to President Taft. After conferring with Ballinger and the attorney general, George W. Wickersham, Taft fired Glavis and urged Pinchot not to take up his case. Pinchot resisted and

Collier's magazine then published Glavis's report as a cover story with the headline "The Whitewashing of Ballinger."[109] In response to national demands for an investigation, Congress appointed six senators and six representatives to a joint investigating committee, and *Collier's* hired Brandeis as counsel for Pinchot and Glavis for a fee of $25,000.[110]

The climactic moment in the Pinchot-Ballinger hearings came when Brandeis, during a cross-examination, revealed that Wickersham's report, which Taft said had persuaded him to clear Ballinger, had been backdated by the attorney general to a date before the president's interview with his secretary of the interior. The goal was to give the impression that Taft had made his decision after reviewing the evidence. As was usual in Washington, the cover-up was worse than the crime: the Justice Department could have admitted to the backdating but instead lied about it. In April, Brandeis wrote to his wife: "Yesterday was a terrible day. I almost felt like an executioner . . . it was an awful thing for Wickersham to have done & unfortunately the President (whom we have not mentioned) is as guilty as W. To date back that Attorney General's report so as to make it appear that it was prepared before the President's letter . . . comes pretty near giving false testimony."[111] In the event, Taft confessed to the committee that the letter had been backdated.[112] Although some senators thought Brandeis's merciless investigation went too far—and although Ballinger himself was ultimately exonerated of wrongdoing—Brandeis continued to see the battle in Manichean and moralistic terms. "There is nothing for us to do but to follow the trail of evil wherever it extends. Fiat Iustitia. In the fight against special interest we shall receive no quarter and may as well make up our minds to give none. It is a hard fight. The man with the hatchet is the only one who has a chance of winning in the end."[113]

Despite his steely moralism, Brandeis was never personally vindictive: after Ballinger resigned in protest, Brandeis endorsed

Taft's chosen successor and also cleared Taft of new accusations of favoritism in Alaskan land sales after the Democratic House put him in charge of a follow-up investigation.[114] But the rift between Pinchot and Taft that Brandeis helped to precipitate led to an even more dramatic rift between Taft and Roosevelt that would transform American politics. In April, as the Ballinger hearings were boiling over, Gifford Pinchot took a steamship to the Italian Riviera to meet with his patron and friend Theodore Roosevelt, who had just concluded a year-long safari in Africa. The two men concluded that Taft had betrayed Roosevelt's progressive legacy by failing to protect the environment, to reduce tariffs, and to regulate the trusts. In particular, Taft's removal of Pinchot hardened Roosevelt's resolve against him.[115] Based on the conversation with Pinchot, Roosevelt wrote an anguished letter to the progressive Republican Henry Cabot Lodge declaring that since the Taft administration had "completely twisted round the policies I advocated and acted upon," it would be impossible for him to support Taft in the upcoming congressional elections.[116] The result of the split in the Republican Party between Roosevelt and Taft would elect Woodrow Wilson and put Brandeis on the Supreme Court.

2

◆·◆·◆

Other People's Money

IN THE PIVOTAL ELECTION of 1912, all three presidential candidates—Theodore Roosevelt, Woodrow Wilson, and William Howard Taft—agreed about the importance of restraining monopolies. But they disagreed about how, precisely, corporate power should be checked.[1] Taft, favoring a law enforcement model, insisted that the money trusts should be prosecuted if they violated the Sherman Antitrust Act. The Hamiltonian Theodore Roosevelt argued in his "New Nationalism" for "regulated monopoly," accepting the efficiencies of large corporations but countering them with strong federal oversight bodies such as the Interstate Commerce Commission. By contrast, for the Jeffersonian Woodrow Wilson, whose "New Freedom" Brandeis helped to design, the problem was not industrial monopoly but financial oligarchy. As a result, Wilson, on Brandeis's advice, championed a third approach that favored what Brandeis would call "the regulation of competition against the regulation of monopolies."[2] In other words, Brandeis argued that monopolies should be broken up or prevented from forming in the first place. He and Wilson determined to untangle the web of political and economic influence that allowed concentrated financial power to menace liberty and democracy.

Brandeis developed his views on the virtues of "regulated competition" in 1911, when he wrote to Alice, "I am dead against the Middle of the Road. No regulated private monopoly of the capitalists. Either competition or State Socialism. Regulate competition, not monopoly is my slogan."[3] He pressed these views on Woodrow Wilson at a lunch on August 28, 1912, declaring that "the system must be changed."[4] During their lunch and a long meeting afterward, Brandeis convinced Wilson that breaking up the trusts and establishing competition through strong antitrust laws was a better response to the power of the money trusts than powerful federal oversight bodies. The next day, Brandeis wrote to his brother Alfred, "Was very favorably impressed with Wilson. He is strong, simple, serious, open-minded, eager to learn and deliberate."[5]

Wilson was similarly impressed. After meeting with Brandeis, who endorsed him for president, Wilson launched the "New Freedom" in a Labor Day speech in which he distinguished himself from Roosevelt in Brandeisian terms. Denouncing the "unregulated competition" that created the monopolies, Wilson declared, "We can prevent these processes through remedial legislation, and so restructure the wrong use of competition that the right use of competition will destroy monopoly. Ours is a program of liberty; theirs is a program of regulation."[6] At the end of September, Brandeis set out to stump for Wilson and Wilson asked Brandeis to "set forth as explicitly as possible the actual measures by which competition can be effectively regulated."[7]

Brandeis complied with a series of articles and speeches that helped Wilson make opposition to monopolies a central issue in the campaign. ("America is never going to submit to monopoly," Wilson told supporters in Lincoln, Nebraska, a month before the election. "America is never going to choose thralldom instead of freedom.")[8] In a speech to the Economic Club, reprinted in the *New York Times* in November, Brandeis made explicit the connection between constitutional liberty and economic liberty. "We learned long ago that liberty could be preserved only by limiting in some way the freedom of action of individuals; that otherwise liberty would necessarily lead to absolutism and in the same way we have learned that unless there be regulation of competition, its excesses will lead to the destruction of competition, and monopoly will take its place."[9] Brandeis and Wilson were concerned, in other words, not only about the effect of monopoly on the economy but also about its effect on democracy; they focused on the way monopolists appropriated the businesses and property of independent citizens, and how this harmed democratic institutions at the local, state, and federal levels.

In discussing solutions to the problem of trusts, Brandeis rejected "wholly judicial" enforcement, preferring administrative commissions that prevented monopolies from forming in the first place. He did not share Theodore Roosevelt's Progressive faith in the power of an enlightened government to complete the centralization that J. P. Morgan had begun, and he opposed Roosevelt's efforts to oversee and plan the U.S. economy through a Bureau of Corporations. The Hamiltonian Herbert Croly published *The Promise of American Life* in 1909, criticizing Jefferson for failing to create a "set of efficient institutions" for the American economy. Brandeis, when he read this, responded that this was precisely the point because the framers preferred liberty to efficiency.[10] He was not persuaded by Croly's attempt to use Hamiltonian means to achieve Jeffersonian ends, or by his proposal to nationalize corporations and strengthen both unions and the federal government.

Brandeis helped to shape the reforms of the Wilson administration, which set out to break up some of the trusts rather than to manage them from the top down. (The Wilson administration did not, however, blindly target all big firms for breakup, recognizing that some networks—such as the electric utilities, telephone companies, and railroads, which the government directly controlled during World War I—should be left intact and regulated to ensure they served the public interests.) These Brandeisian reforms included the Clayton Antitrust Act of 1914, the Federal Trade Commission, and the Federal Reserve. In endorsing the Federal Trade Commission bill, introduced by Senator Robert La Follette,[11] Brandeis argued that it would strengthen enforcement of the Sherman Antitrust Act and perform an invaluable role in educating the public about facts that would prevent anticompetitive behavior. "In the complicated questions involved in dealing with 'Big Business' the first requisite is knowledge—comprehensive, accurate, and up-to-date—of the details of business operations," he wrote in *Harper's* days after Wilson won the election.[12]

Brandeis also believed that the fact-finding capacities of the Federal Trade Commission would help give small-business owners access to the tremendous capacity for data gathering that he considered the only legitimate efficiency of large corporations. "[T]he disadvantages of size outweigh in many respects the advantage of size; but there is one respect in which the great industry has an important advantage. That is in the collection, the getting of knowledge, the collection of data in regard to trade, that knowledge for which great concerns extend their bases of inquiry all over the world."[13] Brandeis insisted that the FTC could serve as a kind of administrative prototype of Google search, giving small owners the same access to facts and education about the state of the market in different parts of the country.[14] The result, he predicted, would make it "affirmatively the business of the Government to extend to the manufacturer throughout this country the opportunity of knowing about his particular line of manufacture the best that can be known."[15]

Wilson considered appointing Brandeis as attorney general, but changed his mind in the face of Wall Street opposition. (Instead, Wilson appointed the anti-Semitic James McReynolds.) In March 1913, after Wilson announced his cabinet selections, Brandeis wrote to his brother Alfred professing ambivalence about the appointment. "As you know I had great doubts as for [the cabinet's] being desirable for me; so I concluded to literally let nature take its course and to do nothing either to get called or to stop the talk." He claimed to be bemused by his opponents. "State Street, Wall Street and the local Democratic bosses did six months unremitting work; but seem not to have prevailed until the last moment. . . . It is almost, indeed quite, amusing how much they fear me, attributing to me power and influence which I in no respect possess."[16] Brandeis was being modest. Over the next two years, as an advisor to Wilson, Brandeis worked behind the scenes to ensure that most of the reforms he had championed during the campaign became law.

As an advisor to Woodrow Wilson, Brandeis was especially influential in brokering the compromise that led to the creation of the Federal Reserve in 1913. The banking industry was stung by the Panic of 1907, in which J. P. Morgan had singlehandedly mobilized the capital that bailed out the American financial system. Led by Senator Nelson Aldrich, the son-in-law of John D. Rockefeller Sr., the bankers supported the creation of a strong central bank, controlled by the bankers themselves, that would save the financial system with taxpayer money in the event of future crashes while minimizing government regulation and oversight that might prevent the banks from gambling with other people's money in the first place. But this alternative became politically infeasible after the creation of the Pujo Committee, a House Banking subcommittee in 1912 headed by Arsene Pujo of Louisiana. Convened to investigate the excesses of the "money trust," the Pujo Committee concluded that a small group of Wall Street bankers had abused the public's trust by consolidating their control over banks and industries, choking off credit and competition in the process. The Pujo Committee seemed to suggest that a secret cabal of big banks was running the country for its own benefit.

As a result of the findings of the Pujo Committee, and Brandeis's relentless publicizing of them in a series of articles for *Harper's*, Congress created the Federal Reserve as a decentralized coalition of not more than twenty private banks that could bail out the banking system by issuing short-term loans and lowering interest rates. The federal government would control the central bank through a Federal Reserve Board appointed by the president, but the Federal Reserve banks would remain technically private and would have the power to appoint two-thirds of their directors.[17] The decentralized Fed was a distinctively Brandeisian solution to the challenge of financial regulation: he feared the curse of bigness in government as well as business, and opposed a government-owned banking system supported by Democratic populists like William Jennings Bryan as well as the Wall Street proposal that would have allowed private banks to issue currency. (Today, some see the decentralization of the Fed as a cause of its ineffectiveness.)

Brandeis's legacy as an economic prophet rests on *Other People's Money and How the Bankers Use It*, the remarkable book that he published in 1914, based on the prescient articles he had written the previous year for *Harper's* to promote the findings of the Pujo Committee. "The American people have as little need of oligarchy in business as in politics,"[18] Brandeis declared. In the book, Brandeis set out to enumerate the ways that "our financial oligarchy" threatened not only the American economy but also American democracy. The villain of *Other People's Money* was not Roosevelt's nemesis, the industrial monopolist

John D. Rockefeller. It was Brandeis's nemesis, the financial oligarch J. P. Morgan. "And to think, he wasn't even a rich man,"[19] Rockefeller reportedly said when Morgan died in 1913 and his estate was reported to be worth $80 million, as compared to Rockefeller's worth of almost $1 billion. Rockefeller and Roosevelt missed the point that Brandeis grasped. Morgan's power came not from his own money but from the billions of dollars of what Brandeis unforgettably called "other people's money" that he controlled. By 1911, according to some estimates, Morgan controlled 40 percent of the capital raised in America.

How did Morgan and his fellow oligarchs leverage themselves into this kind of power? Brandeis accused investment bankers of using other people's money to take control of large companies, which they then used to promote their own interests rather than the public interest. *Other People's Money* begins by warning about the dangers of merging the functions of the commercial banker and the investment banker. "The dominant element in our financial oligarchy is the investment banker."[20] The key to the investment bankers' power, Brandeis wrote, was not ability or wealth but oligarchical consolidation that allowed them to become the directors of huge combinations of railroads, insurance companies, banks, and trust companies, all of which relied on them for funds. Brandeis then drew a connection between financial and political oligarchy: "The development of our financial oligarchy followed, in this respect, lines with which the history of political despotism has familiarized us:—usurpation, proceeding by gradual encroachment rather than by violent acts; subtle and often long-concealed concentration of distinct functions, which are beneficent when separately administered, and dangerous only when combined in the same persons. It was by processes such as these that Caesar Augustus became master of Rome. The makers of our own Constitution had in mind like dangers to our political liberty when they provided so carefully for the separation of governmental powers."[21]

The original—and proper—function of the investment banker, Brandeis wrote, was that of a dealer in stocks and bonds. People needed to invest their savings; investment bankers would advise them about which securities were the soundest investments. But then investment bankers such as J. P. Morgan began to form and to control massive trusts—such as the railroad trusts—and corrupted the system by becoming directors of the corporations they controlled. Brandeis described how the board of directors would make a decision to issue stock and the investment banker, sitting on the board, would issue the securities. "The investment banker, through his controlling influence on the Board of Directors, decides that the corporation shall issue and sell the securities, decides the price at which it shall sell them, and decides that it shall sell the securities to himself," Brandeis wrote. "Can there be real bargaining where the same man is on both sides of the trade?"[22]

Rather than putting his own capital at risk, Brandeis wrote, "it is the investment banker's access to other people's money in controlled banks and trust companies"[23] that allowed bankers such as Morgan to dominate and control credit for the entire country. The investment bankers "tak[e] the golden eggs laid by somebody else's goose" and bind the people in fetters "forged from the people's own gold."[24] (Brandeis's gift for the memorable aphorism is one of the many sources of his rhetorical power.) Brandeis distinguished his targets from industrialists like the Astors, whose "vast fortunes" were "regrettable," "unsocial," "inconsistent with democracy," and "unjust" but did not "endanger political or industrial liberty" because the industrialists' power was commensurate with their wealth.[25] By contrast, "the power and the growth of power of our financial oligarchs" was "dynamic" because it came from "wielding the savings and quick capital of others."[26] The assets of Morgan and his associates swelled exponentially because they had achieved "the supposedly impossible feat of having their cake and eating it too,"[27] buying the bonds and stocks of railroads they controlled, paying the purchase price and still not parting with their money "by the simple device of becoming the bank of deposit of the controlled corporations."[28] They further accumulated wealth and power by paying themselves huge and unreasonable underwriting commissions for their self-dealing services. And "the invasion of the investment banker into the banks' field of operation was followed by a counter invasion by the banks into the realm of the investment banker,"[29] as commercial banks realized that they could make much more through risky investments with other people's money than by their traditional function of making temporary loans to small businesses.

Brandeis showed how the growth of America's most productive industries—from railroads to steamships to telegraphs, cars, and electricity—was originally financed by risk-taking investors (we would call them venture capitalists) rather than investment bankers. (This pattern would be repeated during the high-tech revolution.) And once the investment bankers took control of industries, Brandeis argued, they threatened to run them into the ground through "financial recklessness," threatening the smaller investors whose assets they were supposed to protect.

The recklessness of investment banker-managers took the form of fraudulent accounting practices and a huge increase in short-term borrowing to buy stock in other companies, all in an effort to boost stock prices. This indebtedness, Brandeis charged, represented an "extraordinary lack of financial prudence":[30] when money became tight and the loans had to be repaid, the companies were forced to sell at depressed prices that left no money for dividends. In Brandeis's view, the failure of banker management was not accidental but structural: "It was the natural result of confusing the functions of banker and business man."[31]

The famous phrase "curse of bigness" is in the title of Brandeis's chapter denouncing "Bigness [as] an important factor in the rise of the Money Trust: Big railroad systems, Big industrial trusts, big public service companies; and as instrument of these Big Banks and Big trust companies."[32] Brandeis criticized leading bankers who floated "large securities issues" for the purpose of creating monopolies, or of "transfer[ring] the ownership of railroad stocks from one set of persons to another,"[33] rather than for industrial development. "Size, we are told, is not a crime," he wrote. "But size may, at least, become noxious by reason of the means through which it was attained or the uses to which it is put."[34] He then gave an example of the effect of stock acquisitions by the Union Pacific Railroad, which issued more than $365 million in securities to buy stock in other railroads. Quoting from an Interstate Commerce Commission report, he noted, "Mr. Harriman may journey by steamship from New York to New Orleans, thence by rail to San Francisco, across the Pacific Ocean to China, and, returning by another route to the United States, may go to Ogden [Utah] by any one of three rail lines, and thence to Kansas City or Omaha, without leaving the deck or platform of a carrier which he controls, and without duplicating any part of his journey."[35] Even though the Supreme Court found some of these acquisitions to be illegal, the result was "a banker's paradise" where investment bankers retained commissions for underwriting the securities for the illegal combinations.

Brandeis went on to denounce "interlocking directorates" in which financial oligarchs like George F. Baker, chairman of the board of the First National Bank, served as directors of twenty-two railroad and industrial corporations whose securities the First National Bank underwrote, guaranteed, or distributed. "The practice of interlocking directorates is the root of many evils," Brandeis wrote. "It offends laws human and divine. Applied to rival corporations, it tends to the suppression of competition and to violation of the Sherman law. Applied to corporations which deal with each other, it tends to disloyalty and to violations of the fundamental law that no man can serve two masters."[36]

In quoting the New Testament maxim "No man can serve two masters" from Matthew 6:24, Brandeis did not perceive any conflict with his own attempt to serve two masters as the "lawyer for the situation." (He viewed himself as a servant of the public interest.) Instead, the quotation was the basis for his argument that oligarchy is inefficient because of the limits of human understanding. "[B]anker-management contravenes the fundamental laws of human limitation: First, that no man can serve two masters; second, that a man cannot at the same time do many things well."[37] Returning to the roots of his German education, he quoted his favorite maxim from Goethe: "It is only . . . when working within limitations, that the master is disclosed."[38] Developing the connection between leisure—defined as the time necessary to accumulate facts—and good judgment, he objected that "[t]he banker, with his multiplicity of interests, cannot ordinarily give the time essential to proper supervision and to acquiring that knowledge of the facts necessary to the exercise of sound judgment."[39]

For Brandeis, size made responsible economic judgments impossible because bankers "start usually with ignorance of the particular business which they are supposed to direct."[40] Describing the creation of U.S. Steel, Brandeis wrote, "When the last paper was signed which created the Steel Trust, one of the lawyers (as Mr. Perkins frankly tells us) said: 'That signature is the last one necessary to put the Steel industry, on a large scale, into the hands of men who do not know anything about it.'"[41] As other examples of the failure of banker management, Brandeis focused on the decline of the New Haven Railroad and the fall of Mellen, which he had tried to avert with his work in Massachusetts. He insisted that the New Haven and Boston & Maine railroads were safe investments paying steady dividends to "many thousands of small investors throughout New England" until the banker-managers destroyed them with "financial recklessness"[42]—paying far more than they were worth with borrowed money. "These loans were incurred unnecessarily," he wrote, since they represented not improvements in the railroads but "money borrowed either to pay for stocks in other companies which these companies could not afford to buy, or to pay dividends which had not been earned."[43]

Lacking detachment and undivided loyalty, the banker-director of a railroad had conflicting interests that "necessarily prevent single-minded devotion to the corporation. When a banker-director of a railroad decides as railroad man that it shall issue securities, and then sells them to himself as banker, fixing the price at which they are to be taken, there is necessarily grave danger that the interests of the railroad may suffer."[44] As a result, investment bankers violated the trust of small investors, who couldn't themselves collect the facts on which to base a proper judgment of the soundness of securities. "Advice cannot be unbiased where the banker, as part of the corporation's management, has participated in the creation of the securities which are the subject of sale to the investor."[45]

Brandeis proposed a series of remedies for the evils he associated with financial oligarchy and the curse of bigness. He believed that disclosure of the excessive underwriting fees, commissions, and profits of the investment banks would lead to public protests against them. Developing the idea of sunlight as a disinfectant, which he had first shared with Alice in 1891, he noted that "publicity has already played an important part in the struggle against the Money Trust." The Pujo Committee, by disclosing the facts of financial concentration, had already

contributed to "attainment of The New Freedom. The battle-
field has been surveyed and charted. The hostile forces have
been located, counted and appraised."[46] But more publicity was
necessary. As a remedy for the excessive commissions charged by
investment bankers for promoting and underwriting securities—
commissions charged not for assuming risk but for "securing
others to sell the bonds and incur risks"[47]—Brandeis suggested
publicity about the banker's excessive commissions and profits
and how they watered down the value of stocks. "The investor's
servility is due partly . . . to his ignorance of the facts."[48] His
insistence on transparency and proper reporting anticipated
current debates about warning labels on food or on investment
products such as blended securities. "The archaic doctrine of
caveat emptor is vanishing. The law has begun to require publicity in aid of fair dealing. The Federal Pure Food Law does
not guarantee quality or prices; but it helps the buyer to judge
of quality by requiring disclosure of ingredients," he wrote.[49]
But just as warning labels on food needed to include a clearly
understandable list of ingredients, so financial disclosure had
to be publicly accessible. "To be effective, knowledge of the
facts must be actually brought home to the investor, and this
can best be done by requiring the facts to be stated in good,
large type in every notice, circular, letter and advertisement inviting the investor to purchase. Compliance with this requirement should also be obligatory, and not something the investor
could waive."[50]

Recommending a ban on interlocking directorates and all
"corporate contracts in which one of the management has a
private interest," Brandeis understood the constitutional limits
of Congress's power—he opposed bigness in government as
well as business. But he proposed a creative way of working
around those limits. Although Congress's constitutional authority to regulate interstate commerce did not allow it directly to
regulate state banks, insurance companies, and railroads, Bran-

deis argued, Congress could regulate "*indirectly* by virtue either of its control of the mail privilege or through the taxing power."[51] (This distinction between Congress's power to regulate interstate commerce and its power to tax anticipates one that Chief Justice John Roberts would make in his landmark vote to uphold the Affordable Care Act of 2010.) Brandeis urged Congress to use its power over the mail, telephone, and telegraph—which it was invoking at the time to control free speech about birth control under the Comstock Act—to rein in the money trust, restore "industrial liberty," and break the power of "our financial oligarchy." He endorsed "democratic rural banking," such as that found in German cooperative credit organizations, but gave them a Lincolnian twist. "People's savings banks," Brandeis wrote, should be founded with resources "of the people," management "by the people," and loans "for the people."[52] He called for stronger enforcement of the Sherman Antitrust Act through the creation of a "commission with administrative functions" as well as "complete separation of our industries from railroads and public utilities."[53] He expressed faith that industrial democracy would make better citizens, turning "tens of thousands" of ordinary Americans into business leaders. "Liberty is the greatest developer," Brandeis wrote, anticipating his opinions in free speech cases.[54] "When merchants and manufacturers learn this lesson, money kings will lose subjects, and swollen fortunes may shrink; but industries will flourish, because the faculties of men will be liberated and developed."[55] And he concluded *Other People's Money* with a quotation from President Wilson praising farmers, clerks, and workingmen: "Every country is renewed out of the ranks of the unknown, not out of the ranks of the already famous and powerful in control."[56]

Brandeis's attack on the House of Morgan has been criticized for its economic naiveté. Urofsky argues that Brandeis, with his romantic vision of Massachusetts railroads financed by

Massachusetts banks and controlled by Massachusetts directors, "seemed oblivious to the economic realities that led many people to support consolidation" of the railroads at a time when it no longer made sense to have multiple lines with parallel tracks in local markets.[57] The business historian Thomas McCraw has argued more generally that Brandeis's ideological opposition to bigness in all of its forms led him to ignore the distinction between large "center firms," such as Standard Oil, and smaller peripheral firms such as the family merchants, the Hechts and the Filenes, that he had represented as a lawyer in Boston. Brandeis was concerned about loose horizontal combinations of both peripheral and center firms, in which producers of the same item could agree to limit production or keep prices high. But McCraw argues that Brandeis failed to recognize the way vertical integration—the collection of different business functions under a single large roof—could bring economies of scale for the most successful center firms, lowering prices and ultimately helping consumers.[58]

McCraw and others criticize Brandeis for his focus on maximizing the numbers of small wholesalers and retailers. But his ultimate goal was to promote not efficiency but democracy; to secure not the lowest prices in the short term but the best citizens and communities in the long term. (The least modern—though perhaps most prescient—aspect of Brandeis's thought was his contempt for the consumer, whom he viewed as "servile, self-indulgent, indolent, ignorant,"[59] and easily manipulated by advertising—the very opposite of the engaged citizen.) For Brandeis, the real curse of bigness was not economic inefficiency but financial and political oligarchy.

Consumers, of course, are also citizens, and to the degree that Brandeisian policies lead to higher prices, they impose a tax on one group of citizens—consumers—for the benefit of a smaller group—producers. Moreover, avoiding oligarchy doesn't necessarily require a large number of small competitors; oligarchy could also be avoided if there are ten relatively large players rather than a hundred small players. If Brandeis's view of antitrust focused on the welfare of small producers, the dominant modern view focuses on maximizing the efficiency of production and, at least purportedly, the welfare of consumers. Arguably, both poles are wrong, but there's no question that Brandeis's view tolerated more inefficiencies than policy makers are willing to accept today.

Still, Brandeis's most important contribution as a political economist, like Jefferson, was to view economics in democratic and ultimately constitutional terms. As Norman Hapgood noted in his introduction to *Other People's Money*, when Brandeis said that every institution had a size or unit of greatest efficiency, he understood "efficiency" as a social rather than an economic term. Considered "as part of a social organism," Hapgood wrote, channeling Brandeis, a business or unit "is inefficient, socially considered, if it injures the whole. Even, therefore, if it makes for itself more money than a smaller unit, it may be a social liability where the smaller business or institution is a social asset. Frequently size gives power, and power that no business ought, for the general welfare to have."[60] Brandeis, like the framers of the Constitution, understood that a relentless focus on efficiency is the surest way to destroy liberty.[61] And like Madison and Jefferson, he wanted to maximize the number of independent citizens in society—citizens, that is, in control of their economic destiny.

Several of the reforms that Brandeis advocated in *Other People's Money* became law, including not only the Federal Trade Commission Act but also the Clayton Antitrust Act of 1914. Brandeis also supported the Sixteenth Amendment, ratified in 1913, which allows Congress to levy an unapportioned tax on income from property, such as interest, dividend, and rent income. Yet light federal regulation in the 1920s, combined with the cheap money made possible by the Fed's refusal to raise interest rates, created a speculative frenzy that culminated in the crash of 1929. As Norman Hapgood wrote, "[T]he fatalities following 1929 came to a large extent from the failure to act on the principles sharply drawn in *Other People's Money*."[62] Devices such as the "broker's loan" allowed banks to engage in increasingly risky behavior—lending investors funds to buy inflated stocks on margin—a dangerous practice because when stocks go down rather than up, borrowers have to repay the loan, quickly wiping out the leveraged investors who had to sell everything at fire-sale prices. Brandeis disapproved of new methods and instruments that allowed consumers to buy on credit, which he also viewed as dangerous speculation. "I wish to record my utter inability to understand why a lot of folks don't go broke," he observed in 1926, predicting "a breakdown within a year."[63]

The regulatory response to the crash and Great Depression that Brandeis predicted occurred in two phases. As Arthur Schlesinger notes, "The First New Deal breathed the spirit of the New Nationalism of Theodore Roosevelt and Herbert Croly; the Second New Deal, the spirit of the New Freedom of Woodrow Wilson and Louis D. Brandeis. First New Dealers saw economic concentration as inevitable and national planning as desirable; Second New Dealers wished to restore a competitive marketplace."[64] Still, the Brandeisian capstone of the First New Deal was the Banking Act of 1933, known as the Glass-Steagall Act, which separated commercial banks and investment banks by prohibiting commercial banks from selling stocks. In exchange for strict regulation, commercial banks would be protected from failure with federally insured deposits. (The regulation of investment banks, overseen by the Securities and Exchange Commission, focused on the Brandeisian goals of disclosure and preventing fraud—the goal was to protect investors rather than the bankers themselves.) The separation of commercial banking from investment banking forced the House of Morgan to divest its investment banking operations into Morgan Stanley. Morgan blamed its troubles on Brandeis and was convinced that the 1933 reissue of *Other People's Money* had been responsible for Glass-Steagall.[65]

For Brandeis, the separation of commercial banking and investment banking was not an adequate response to the curse of bigness. His boldest response to the Great Depression, outlined in letters to Felix Frankfurter in 1933, was a massive public works program to put people to work on projects ranging from irrigation and slum clearance to adult education. The program was to be financed initially by loans and then "by high estate & income taxes with [a] share to the States."[66] More broadly, Brandeis wrote to Frederick Howe that he would limit corporate size by levying "an annual excise tax rapidly progressing in the rate as the total capitalization of the Corporation rises."[67] He also proposed sharp increases on income taxes for corporations and rich individuals; a steep federal inheritance tax; unemployment insurance; and breaking up the banking system into commercial, savings, and investment units.[68]

The Second New Dealers, inspired by Brandeis and by Wilson's New Freedom, adopted many of the reforms that Brandeis advocated, including the Robinson-Patman Act of 1936, designed to protect "the weak from the strong" and "the independent merchant, the public who he serves and the manufacturer from whom he buys," from price discrimination, ensuring that "trade and industry [are] divided among as many different parties as possible."[69] (The driving forces behind the decentralization of the Second New Deal came from Congress, not the White House.) New Dealers also adopted an antitrust policy designed to break up large enterprises—the goal was not to lower prices but "competition for the sake of competition"; industrial ownership policies that empowered small investors; the Commodities Exchange Act, which allowed producers, not speculators, to set prices; and democratic banking that compartmentalized different banking activities in different institutions.[70]

The financial reforms of the 1930s that Brandeis inspired—particularly the Glass-Steagall Act—helped to ensure financial stability for the next half a century, which was marked by the lowest bank failure rate in American history. But in the 1990s those regulations were repealed, owing to the cozy relationship between Wall Street and Washington that confirmed Brandeis's fears about the political power of "our financial oligarchy." The Gramm-Leach-Bliley Act of 1999 delivered the coup de grâce to Glass-Steagall. Dismantling what was left of the wall between commercial banking and investment banking, it allowed both kinds of banks to consolidate with each other and with insurance companies, and to own subsidiaries that engaged in either commercial or investment banking. The demise of Glass-Steagall, which freed commercial banks such as Citibank to compete as investment bankers, allowed the concentration of financial assets in a way that surpassed even the concentrations that galvanized Brandeis during the Progressive Era. As a result of the repeal, the twenty largest financial institutions in the United States went from controlling 35 percent of America's financial assets to 70 percent,[71] and the six largest banks—Morgan Stanley, JPMorgan Chase, Citigroup, Bank of America, Goldman Sachs, and Wells Fargo—came to own assets equivalent to 60 percent of the gross national product—up from less than 20 percent in the 1990s.[72]

The power of our modern financial oligarchy expanded during the last days of the Clinton administration with the enactment of the benignly named Commodity Futures Modernization Act, which removed the ability of the federal government to regulate derivatives or complicated bundles of subprime mortgages and other financial instruments whose value derives from their expected future price rather than their actual value, which may be only dimly understood. The result was an explosion of the complicated and highly risky financial instruments that Brandeis most feared—such as credit default swaps that allowed the banks to insure their debt obligations against default and write off the tremendous associated risk. Fiercely competing with investment banks for customers after the repeal of Glass-Steagall, the commercial banks were rapaciously buying up credit swaps to loosen their capital in search of higher yields. (As Brandeis predicted, they were more concerned about bonuses and short-term profits than the long-term risks to their shareholders and to the economy.) The deregulation of derivatives allowed companies like the insurance giant AIG to sell investment banks billions of dollars in credit swaps without having any assets to back them up. Moreover, investors did not need to understand the risks associated with the underlying asset to purchase a credit swap; through AIG, investors could take bets on whether mortgagors and other debtors would default on their loans, creating a trillion-dollar market in unregulated gambling.

Although the crash of 2008 occurred in an economy vastly more complex than those in which the crashes of 1907 and 1929 took place, it vindicated all of Brandeis's fears about the curse of bigness and the dangers of financial oligarchy. Like their predecessors a hundred years ago, the huge investment banks of today made their money by capturing brokers' fees based on the volume of trades they placed rather than on the underlying soundness of the investments. ("[T]hese great bankers frequently get huge commissions without themselves distributing any of the bonds, or ever having taken any actual risk," Brandeis warned.)[73] The brokers had no interest in whether the subprime mortgages they were bundling and reselling for profit were in fact sound, since their soundness had been (falsely) certified by greedy ratings companies. (Brandeis on the element of time: "[H]ow can the leading bankers, necessarily engrossed in the problems of their own vast private business, get time to know and to correlate the facts concerning so many other complex businesses?")[74] They maximized their profits by borrowing as much of "other people's money" as possible (evading or diluting capital requirements) and leveraging themselves into recklessly risky positions. And Brandeis anticipated the crash of 2008 in two other ways: in our time, as in his, the financiers destabilized, and broke, vital systems on which millions of ordinary people depend. And the financiers concentrated immense political power, both over entire realms of human economic activity and within the political system itself.

The modern version of the legalized gambling that Brandeis abhorred was the ability of the megabanks to use their domination of the market to engage in proprietary trading—that is, to place risky and volatile bets for their own accounts, rather than earning commissions by trading for their customers' accounts. Proprietary trading desks, which often risked the most money for firms like Goldman Sachs and were responsible for the biggest profits and losses, are the equivalent of internal hedge funds. When the bets went bad in 2008, the biggest investment banks were rescued by the then unspoken guarantee that the government would step in if necessary to prevent a catastrophic failure of the system, as it had done in 1987 and 1998. That expectation did not save Lehman Brothers—or Barings Bank, which was brought down by traders who placed proprietary bets. But the idea that certain banks are "too big to fail" had virtually become government policy. As a result, the megabanks could take on even more risks than their competitors, since everyone knew the government would levy taxes from regular citizens to clean up after them.

The idea of "too big to fail" was the perverse culmination of Brandeis's dystopian view of high finance. His main concern was not, as his critics suggest, the economic inefficiency of large firms, but the oligarchic influence they wielded over the

American financial and political system that allowed them to shield themselves from accountability for their own greed and recklessness. In an irony that Brandeis would not have relished, the smaller banks that resisted the risky proprietary trading of the megabanks were allowed to fail, while the biggest banks, which caused the crisis by flooding the market with junk securities, were rescued.

What about regulatory responses to the crash of 2008? There was a vigorous debate between the heirs of Jefferson, Wilson, and Brandeis, who wanted to break up the big banks and prevent them from engaging in risky behavior, and the heirs of Hamilton, Theodore Roosevelt, and Herbert Croly, who preferred top-down government regulation. The Brandeisians were led by Paul Volcker, the former chairman of the Federal Reserve, who argued, like Brandeis, that the megabanks should be broken up into smaller units that are not too big to fail. Brandeis's suggestion was to tax size: he argued that every business unit above a certain size should be forced to pay a tax large enough to be a burden for an inefficient mammoth. The modern version of Brandeis's proposal to break up big banks came from a Senate bill that would have capped the size of the megabanks.

The bill would have limited the liabilities of any single bank to 2 percent of GDP and would have limited the total amount of insured deposits any bank could hold to 10 percent.[75] But the attempt to break up the banks was opposed by the Hamiltonians in the Obama administration, Lawrence Summers and Timothy Geithner, and it failed in the Senate.

In addition to proposing to limit the size of banks, the Brandeisians had another proposal to limit risky gambles by megabanks. Dubbed the "Volcker Rule" by President Obama, it bans the banks from engaging in proprietary trading for their own accounts. Although the Volcker Rule was adopted as part of the Dodd-Frank Wall Street Reform and Consumer Protection

Act, regulatory agencies delayed its implementation for years in the face of criticism by the banks as well as by consumer groups. Brandeis understood the likelihood that federal officials who are given broad discretion to regulate the financial industry will be successfully defanged by the lobbying power of our financial oligarchy, as the delayed implementation of the Volcker Rule confirmed.

The Dodd-Frank Act, which became law in 2010, represented the most sweeping overhaul of the financial system since the Great Depression. In its complexity and regulatory scope, it also represented a triumph of Roosevelt's vision of regulated monopoly over Brandeis's vision of regulated competition. The law sought to end the "too big to fail" phenomenon by creating a new "financial stability regulatory council" to identify "systemic risks," in the hope of preventing companies from becoming too big to fail. It authorized the Federal Reserve to supervise the largest and most complex megabanks and to require them to increase their reserves—that is, savings that can't be used for lending or business costs. The bill also empowered the federal government, in extreme cases, to liquidate troubled companies by seizing them, firing their management, and funding their operations until they can be broken up and sold off. It required the riskiest derivatives, such as credit swaps, to be traded in a public clearinghouse and empowered the Securities and Exchange Commission to regulate hedge funds.

Brandeis would have supported the capital requirements in the new financial regulations, which had the effect of doubling the capital ratios of the largest banks in the four years after the Dodd-Frank Act passed. He also would have supported the transparency requirements, which provide that complex derivatives must be traded through third parties instead of between customers and banks. But he would have questioned the New Nationalistic premise of the Dodd-Frank Act—that megabanks should be regulated by federal oversight bodies rather than broken up with caps on size. He would have been disappointed by all that wasn't done to protect competition and liberty in the face of the crash. (In this sense, his contemporary heirs include principled libertarians on the Tea Party right and the civil libertarian left who seek "freedom to fail.") Brandeis would have objected that neither transparency nor allowing federal regulators to wind up troubled banks addresses the central problem that he identified in *Other People's Money:* once the banks start to trade instruments that are too complicated for buyers and sellers to investigate and to understand, management by bankers is doomed to fail, according to "the fundamental laws of human limitations."[76] And if bankers cannot understand the risks posed by complicated derivatives, federal regulators, who suffer from the same human limitations, are not likely to do better. For these reasons, Brandeis would have insisted that unless the size of the banks is limited, the risky behavior will continue, leading to future crashes. He also would have assumed that the Hamiltonian regulations that Congress adopted would be a recipe for future conflicts of interests.

Brandeis would have been especially appalled by the wave of mergers that followed the crash of 2008, starting with the sick banks that the government deployed bailout funds to combine. He might have predicted the bailout of the auto industry, justified on the grounds that if one company failed, all the others would as well. As the CEO of Ford said in asking for government aid for his supposed competitors, GM and Chrysler, all the giant automakers were "uniquely interdependent" because they shared "more than 90 percent commonality among our suppliers."[77] This concentration means that ten nominal competitors in the auto industry relied on the structural monopoly of one or two giant suppliers to provide outsourced parts for all the cars produced in the United States. This represented the opposite of the resiliency Ford enjoyed throughout most of its history, when a vertically integrated company produced its own pistons and rings in house but divided the production among at least two factories. And it reflected the merger mania that began in the 1980s and accelerated in the 1990s, resulting in structural monopolies in industries ranging from semiconductors to mining, automobiles, agriculture, software, and media companies.[78]

In responding to monopolies, Brandeis was a passionate advocate of fair-trade laws that protected small, independent businesses against unfair competition by chain stores. He insisted that in preventing megastores from driving their smaller competitors out of business by undercutting them on pricing, the law allowed smaller, family-owned businesses to provide the best jobs and service to the community. In 1913, he wrote an article in *Harper's* called "Cutthroat Competition—The Competition That Kills" supporting retail price–fixing agreements by small producers rather than big retailers. In a series of articles that year, Brandeis set out to demonstrate how "price standardization helps competitive business; how it develops the individual man; how it preserves the small retailer as against the great chain stores and the great department stores."[79] His critics, he argued, "failed to draw the distinction between a manufacturer fixing the retail selling price of an article of his own creation and to which he has imparted his reputation, and the fixing of prices by a monopoly or by a combination tending to monopoly."[80]

In other words, Brandeis supported vertical price maintenance—which occurs when producers agree with distributors on the price at which goods will be resold. Brandeis's view is unfashionable today among economists on the right and the left who argue that allowing manufacturers, rather than a marketplace of competitive retailers, to set prices ultimately harms consumers. But Brandeis's view was consistent with the practice throughout most of the nineteenth and twentieth centuries, when producers, rather than the distributor, generally set the price of goods. That changed in 1911 when the Supreme Court held in the *Dr. Miles* case[81] that it is a violation of the Sherman Antitrust Act for distributors and manufacturers to agree on price.[82] (The Supreme Court eventually overturned the *Dr. Miles* decision in 2007.)

In reaction to the decision, nineteen states passed laws forbidding price-cutting and Congress debated the first national price maintenance bill, known as the Stevens bill. Introduced in Congress in 1914, the Stevens bill would have overturned the *Dr. Miles* decision and allowed vendors in nonmonopolized industries to set uniform resale prices. In Brandeis's detailed testimony before Congress the following year, he said the Stevens bill was necessary to restore Congress's policy of "preventing monopoly" by "preventing cutthroat competition," a policy embraced by the Democratic Party, a large part of the Republican Party, and some Progressives. "The public interest clearly demands that price standardization be permitted," Brandeis declared, to protect the interests of "[t]he small manufacturer, the small producer, and the small retailer. Ultimately also of the consumer."[83]

Brandeis's definition of the public interest is instructive and memorable. "The public interest is made up of a number of things," Brandeis explained. "It is made up in the first place, or in the last, whichever you put it, of the consumer, that he should get a good article at the lowest price that he reasonably can, consistently with the good quality and good business." But, Brandeis continued, "there is another interest that the public has, and that we should look out for, namely the interest of the rest of the public, the dealer and his clerks and the producer and his employees." Brandeis maintained, in other words, that the survival of a variety of competitive small businesses was necessary for the welfare of the entire community. As he concluded,

"We are all part of the public and we must find a rule of law that is consistent with the welfare of all the people."[84]

Despite the support of small businesses such as drugstores, groceries, and hardware stores, the Stevens bill was strongly opposed by mass retailers such as Macy's and Wanamaker's, and it ultimately failed to pass.[85] Nevertheless, the Supreme Court eventually took a more relaxed view of price fixing.[86] Brandeis, as a justice, joined the 1919 *Colgate* decision, which recognized the producer's right to set prices under some circumstances.[87] Moreover, Congress finally endorsed Brandeis's view during the New Deal. The Miller-Tydings Act of 1937 allowed manufacturers who sold goods in competitive industries to set prices as long as state laws allowed retail price maintenance. This helped empower small producers and distributors in America until 1975, when a neo-progressive Congress passed the Consumer Goods Pricing Act, which explicitly rejected Brandeis's view and made it illegal for manufacturers to fix the prices of products sold by retailers. The goal of this well-intentioned but ill-conceived law was to allow big retailers to put pressure on giant producers such as Procter & Gamble. Combined with the wave of mergers that began in the 1980s, however, the law set in motion a transformation of the American pricing system so that today, in a Brandeisian dystopia, it is giant distributors, not small producers, that set the prices of products. And although the 1975 act brought down the price of many consumer goods, the distributors today do not always use their power in ways that ultimately result in lower prices.

By 1916, some of the Progressive arguments that law should reflect the needs of social justice were beginning to take effect. On January 2, Brandeis delivered a speech called "The Living Law" to the Chicago Bar Association.[88] In this speech, he lamented the "new dangers to liberty" that had emerged during the Industrial Revolution of the past fifty years: notably "the introduction of the factory system" and the development of "large publicly owned corporations which replaced small privately owned concerns." As a result, "Individual personal relations between the proprietor and his help ceased." Brandeis noted that legislatures were responding to new demands for "democracy and social justice" by passing laws protecting the individual and collective rights of workers—including minimum wage and maximum hour laws—but that the activist courts had struck down many of these progressive laws by complacently applying "18th century conceptions of the liberty of the individual and of the sacredness of private property." It was hardly surprising, Brandeis said, that both workingmen and businessmen had responded by clamoring for "the recall of judges and of judicial decisions" as well as "amendment of the constitutions and even for their complete abolition." Brandeis said that "the assaults upon courts and constitutions culminated in 1912," and he singled out the *Lochner* case, in which the U.S. Supreme Court struck down New York's maximum hour laws for bakers.

Since 1912, Brandeis said, courts had become more attentive to "the movement, begun some years prior to 1912, which has more recently resulted in a better appreciation by the courts of existing social needs." The U.S. and Illinois supreme courts, he noted, had changed their minds about the constitutionality of maximum hour laws for women, and the New York Court of Appeals had changed its about the constitutionality of laws prohibiting night work for women. All these decisions, Brandeis said, reflected a "judicial awakening to the facts of life," a realization that "no law, written or unwritten, can be understood without a full knowledge of the facts out of which it arises and to which it is to be applied." But "the struggle for the living law has not been fully won"—as evidenced by the fact that the *Lochner* case had not been expressly overruled. For Brandeis, the remedy came, as always, in education. Lawyers and judges had to be trained in the facts of modern life by the "study of economics and sociology and politics which embody the facts and present the problems of today." Escaping from the specialization of corporate lawyers, Brandeis held up instead the model of "the All-Round Lawyer," trained in small communities, representing rich and poor, employers and employees, who "took some part in political life." Brandeis concluded "our greatest judges, Marshall, Kent, Story, Shaw," secured this training, as had Alexander Hamilton, whom Brandeis called "an apostle of the living law." (Brandeis, of course, might have been describing himself.) By praising Hamilton's flexibility, Brandeis was endorsing not his expansive vision of corporate power but his pragmatic notion that legislatures should have wide discretion to experiment with economic innovations without being second-guessed by courts. Still, Brandeis would become more self-consciously Jeffersonian in the following decade.

On January 28, 1916, less than a month after Brandeis delivered his "Living Law" talk, Woodrow Wilson nominated him to the U.S. Supreme Court. Responding to a congratulatory telegram from his brother Alfred, Brandeis wrote: "I am not entirely sure that I am to be congratulated, but I am glad the President wanted to make the appointment & I am convinced, all things considered, that I ought to accept."[89] The Senate battle that resulted was one of the longest and most hotly contested in American history, and Brandeis, having refused to fight to secure the nomination, fought hard to win confirmation. As he wrote to Alfred from Boston on February 12: "[T]he fight that has come up shows clearly that my instinct that I could not afford to decline was correct. It would have been, in effect, deserting the progressive forces. Now my feeling is rather—'Go it husband, go it Bear' with myself as 'interested spectator.' Nothing could demonstrate more clearly the concentrated power of the interests than some of the incidents, which I will tell you about when we meet."[90] In fact, Brandeis was much more than a spectator of his own confirmation battle. His partner Ned McClennen was in Washington, D.C.,

and whenever a new charge arose, McClennen would telegraph it to Brandeis, who, with the help of his secretary, would
consult his files and send a detailed response defending his
actions. Although Supreme Court nominees did not begin to
testify at their own confirmation hearings for another quarter
century, Brandeis was a pioneer in rapid response to a negative
campaign.

The interests arrayed against Brandeis were captured graph-
ically in a chart prepared by a lawyer in Brandeis's office showing the overlapping financial interests, social and business connections, and directorships of fifty-one prominent Bostonians
who had signed a petition opposing Brandeis's nomination.
There are five circles on the chart delineating the various hubs
of the Brahmin oligarchy: "the Somerset Club," "Banker," "State
Street," "Back Bay Resident," and "Large Corporation Connections." On one side, the chart connects each of the signers
of the petition, led by Harvard president A. Lawrence Lowell,
to each of the five hubs; on the other side, the signers are connected to each other. (The group had been coordinated by
George Wickersham, Taft's attorney general and Brandeis's
nemesis in the Pinchot-Ballinger hearings.)[91] Herbert Croly,
the founder and editor of the *New Republic,* sent the chart to
Willard Straight, the owner of the magazine, along with a draft
editorial called "The Motive of Class Consciousness." "I want
you to understand right away that this chart and article will not
be published without your consent," Croly assured Straight.

Neither the chart nor the article ultimately appeared in
the *New Republic.* Straight had worked for J. P. Morgan as the
Morgan Bank's representative in China, and he refused to associate the magazine with "ideological recriminations against his
friends and social acquaintances," according to an explanation
accompanying the chart. But despite this confirmation of the
social and political power of what Brandeis called "our financial oligarchy," the magazine strongly supported his nomina-

tion. During the confirmation fight, Croly, Walter Lippmann, and Felix Frankfurter wrote vigorous responses to the attacks on Brandeis, and Brandeis later joked to Learned Hand that the *New Republic* should bear at least some responsibility for his confirmation.[92]

The forces arrayed against Brandeis reflected the political calculations that had led Wilson to nominate him in the first place. Leading Progressives had championed his nomination, including the Progressive Republican Robert La Follette, with whom Wilson secretly consulted.[93] Wilson respected and liked Brandeis and had been urged to appoint him by his attorney general and treasury secretary.[94] But Wilson was also looking ahead to the election of 1916. Despite his large electoral victory in 1912 against a divided Republican Party, Wilson had won only 42 percent of the popular vote,[95] 1.3 million fewer votes than those received by Taft and Roosevelt combined. To win in 1916 against a united Republican Party, Wilson had to sway a significant number of the Progressive and independent voters who had supported Roosevelt four years earlier. In announcing the nomination, the *New York Sun* asserted that Wilson had nominated the first Jew to the Supreme Court in order to win over the Jewish vote in New York and other northeastern states with large Jewish populations.[96] Under the headline "He's First Jew Ever Picked for Bench: Long and Bitter Fight Expected in Senate over Confirmation," the *Sun* reported, "It is clearly apparent that if he were obliged to go before the Senate purely on his merits he would be defeated. There is, however, danger that the racial issue will become involved in the struggle, and that in that event it would be difficult to predict how members of the Senate would vote."[97]

In fact, Brandeis was not the first Jew considered for the court. In 1852, President Millard Fillmore offered a seat to Judah P. Benjamin, but he declined the nomination in order to take a seat in the Senate; he would go on to serve as Jefferson

Davis's most trusted advisor as the Confederate attorney general, secretary of war, and secretary of state. And although Brandeis's Judaism did indeed become an issue in his confirmation hearings, it cut in different directions. Jews were not closely linked to the Democratic Party at the time, in part because of the anti-Semitism of southern Democrats. This put Democrats like Senator Hoke Smith of Georgia in a difficult position. On the one hand, a vote against Brandeis, the Jewish outsider, might have been popular in Georgia. However, Smith was also something of a populist who hated Wall Street. In the end, he voted for Brandeis. But Republicans were in a similar bind. In the wake of the ratification of the Seventeenth Amendment, which allowed the people, rather than state legislatures, to choose senators, Henry Cabot Lodge faced his first popular election, and while he opposed Brandeis on economic grounds, he didn't want to offend the Jewish voters in Massachusetts. Lodge also feared that Brandeis, lionized as "the people's lawyer" in Massachusetts, might have run against him for the Senate. In the end, Lodge voted against Brandeis.

In the popular press, even the editorial boards that supported Brandeis did so with backhanded compliments that seem breezily anti-Semitic today. "Mr. Brandeis is a Jew and, up to now there has never been a Jew on the Supreme Court. Perhaps it's time we had one," *Life* editorialized on February 10, 1916, in a piece illustrated with a cartoon of Uncle Sam exhorting Americans, "Drop Your Hyphens Here!" to ensure "Safety First" as America prepared to enter World War I.[98] "Mr. Brandeis is an able and remarkable man with a reputation for altruism. We presume his forbears came from Germany." (They didn't.) The editors continued:

> He represents, therefore, Judea, Germany, Kentucky and Massachusetts, and if he has picked up what was coming to him from those derivations he has unusually varied international equipment.

Back of the Jewish mind are traditions, impulses, values, aspirations and feelings that are different from those of a man of another race, and actuate thoughts and feelings which often perplex and sometimes displease observers. The Jewish point of view is apt to be different from the Gentile, just as the Roman Catholic point of view is apt to be different from the Protestant, or the Irish from the Anglo-Saxon.

But that is not a reason for objecting to Mr. Brandeis as a member of the Supreme Court, but rather the contrary. It is better that the great questions that come before that court should be seen from all angles. . . .

Nine Brandeises in the Court would justify nervousness, but one Brandeis among nine is something like internment. Nothing terrifying in that.[99]

Wilson's support for his nominee was unwavering. In a letter to the chair of the Senate Judiciary Committee in May 1916, Wilson clearly explained why he appointed Brandeis to the Supreme Court:

I have known him. I tested him by seeking his advice upon some of the most difficult and perplexing public questions about which it was necessary for me to form a judgment. I have dealt with him in matters where nice questions of honor and fair play, as well as large questions of justice and the public benefit, were involved. In every matter in which I have made test of his judgment and point of view, I have received from him counsel singularly enlightening, singularly clear-sighted and judicial, and, above all, full of moral stimulation. . . . You will remember that in the opinion of the late Chief Justice Fuller he was the ablest man who ever appeared before the Supreme Court of the United States. "He is also," the Chief Justice added, "absolutely fearless in the discharge of his duties."[100]

With fifty-six Democrats and only forty Republicans in the Senate, any Democratic nominee should have sailed through.

Brandeis's support was complicated by the fact that he was re-
placing the recently deceased Justice Joseph Rucker Lamar of
Georgia for what was considered a southern seat. Although
Brandeis had been born and raised in Kentucky, and although
southerners wrote to support him, some southern Democrats
viewed him as a Bostonian and were peeved that Wilson had
not chosen someone more clearly identified with the South.
Also, Wilson had not vetted the nomination with southern senators, and Brandeis's home-state senators from Massachusetts,
conservative Republicans, both opposed him.

None of this would have mattered if Brandeis hadn't inspired such a powerful array of opponents. As the *New Republic*'s
unpublished chart suggests, the most determined opposition
focused on his social and economic views. Traditional lawyers,
bankers, industrial leaders, and conservative Republicans saw
him as a radical. Brandeis's law partner, George Nutter, wrote
in his diary: He "will be opposed because he is supposed to be
radical. But he is really not a radical."[101] But Brandeis's perceived radicalism was not the only reason for the opposition.
Arthur D. Hill, a State Street lawyer in Boston, wired his friend
Senator Lodge, "If it were not that Brandeis is a Jew, and German Jew, he would never have been appointed and he would
not have a baker's dozen of votes in the Senate."[102] Hill then
urged Lodge to block the nomination because of Brandeis's
"unprofessional" conduct and "unpopularity at the Bar." As
Hill put it, "[F]irst, . . . he has been always an active radical,
consistently attacking all sorts of established institutions, and
thereby inevitably inciting considerable enmity; and second,
[he has] a certain hard and unsympathetic quality which is
largely racial."[103]

The opposition to Brandeis on "racial" grounds took several forms. Brandeis's religion was mentioned only once in his
confirmation hearings, but the reference was revealing. Francis
Peabody, a Boston attorney, testified that Brandeis's "reputation

is that he is not always truthful, that he is untrustworthy, and that he sails under false colors." The example Peabody offered was that, when they first met, Peabody did not know he was a Jew.[104] Peabody's Freudian slip was uncharacteristic; most of the Brahmin opposition to Brandeis was expressed in the genteel codes of the day, focusing on his supposed lack of character. As Hill wrote to Lodge: "He has no power of feeling or understanding the position of an opponent, and none of that spirit of playing the game with courtesy and good-nature which is part of the standard of the Anglo-Saxon. He fights to win, and fights up the limit of his rights with a stern and even cruel exultation in the defeat of his adversary. It is not for nothing that in the Old Testament there isn't a word from beginning to end of admiration for a gallant enemy."[105]

The Brahmin elite used similar code words in attacking Brandeis. A. Lawrence Lowell, the president of Harvard who instituted Jewish quotas at the college, told the other Massachusetts senator, John W. Weeks, that Brandeis had a "reputation" for being "unscrupulous," but when asked for evidence, he had none to offer.[106] Former president William Howard Taft, whom Brandeis had embarrassed (and arguably unseated) after the Pinchot-Ballinger affair, yearned to be on the Supreme Court himself. Taft's supporters fantasized that Wilson would appoint him, although there was no realistic chance that Wilson would appoint his presidential rival, a conservative Republican.[107] Taft attacked Brandeis in words that may seem to have distinctly anti-Semitic overtones today: "He is a muckraker, an emotionalist for his own purposes, a socialist, prompted by jealousy, a hypocrite, a man who has certain high ideals in his imagination, but who is utterly unscrupulous, in method in reaching them, a man of infinite cunning . . . of great tenacity of purpose, and, in my judgment, of much power for evil."[108]

Still, Taft was no anti-Semite: in a noble speech to the

Anti-Defamation League in 1920, he declared: "There is not the slightest ground for Anti-Semitism among us. It is a vicious plant. It is a noxious weed that should be cut out. It has no place in free America."[109] Instead, Taft's opposition to Brandeis's nomination was both personal and philosophical, focusing on his own ambitions to be chief justice, the grudge he nursed about the Pinchot-Ballinger affair, and his belief that the courts should protect property rights rather than defer to Progressive regulations. After Taft was appointed chief justice in 1921, he graciously buried the hatchet, inviting Brandeis to serve with him on a committee to explore ways of increasing the efficiency and distributing the workload of district judges—a topic of interest to them both. The overture succeeded. "Brandeis and I are on most excellent terms," Taft soon reported enthusiastically, and Brandeis reciprocated his good feelings. All went "happily in the conference room with Taft," he reported. "When we differ we agree to differ without any ill feeling. It's all very friendly."[110]

Still indignant about the opposition to Brandeis's nomination at the justice's memorial service twenty-six years later, Senator George W. Norris declared that some of his ablest colleagues had been moved to make "a bitter, unreasonable, and unconscionable attack" on Brandeis for lacking "the necessary 'judicial temperament.'"[111] Norris recalled that "some of these men were moved into action because of Justice Brandeis' religion, but I have thought the great bulk of this opposition . . . came from a combination of financial interests which wanted to punish an able man who had often thwarted them in their evil ways."[112] And support for Brandeis came from unexpected corners. Despite the opposition of President Lowell, nine of the eleven members of the Harvard Law faculty—including Dean Roscoe Pound—supported his nomination, and only one, Edward H. Warren, opposed it. In the end, after two months of hearings in which forty-three people testified for and against Brandeis (the nominee himself was not called to testify), the Senate Judiciary Subcommittee voted 3–2 in Brandeis's favor.

Senator Thomas J. Walsh, a Democratic senator from Montana, offered a crisp summary[113] of the case against Brandeis in the course of explaining why he planned to vote in favor:

> The real crime of which this man is guilty is that he has exposed the iniquities of men in high places in our financial system. He has not stood in awe of the majesty of wealth. . . . He has been an iconoclast. He has written about and expressed views on "social justice," to which vague term are referred movements and measures to obtain greater security, greater comfort, and better health for the industrial workers signifying safety devices, factory inspection sanitary provision, reasonable hours, the abolition of child labor, all of which threaten a reduction of dividends. They all contemplate that a man's a man and not a machine. . . . The man who never represents the public or the impecunious citizen in any great forensic contest, but always the cause of corporate wealth, never has these troubles. It is always the other fellow whose professional character is a little below par.[114]

In the end, the vote was not close. On June 1, 1916, the Senate voted 56–28 to confirm Louis Brandeis to the Supreme Court, with five Republicans joining fifty-one Democrats in favor of the nomination.[115] Only one Democrat voted no—Francis Newlands of Nevada—and twelve senators (four Democrats and eight Republicans) abstained. It's clear that Wilson pressured some southern Democrats who might otherwise have opposed Brandeis to vote for him. One of the Republicans voting no was Senator George Sutherland of Utah, who would later serve with Brandeis on the Supreme Court as one of the four conservative justices—the press called them the "four horsemen"—who voted to strike down the New Deal. Brandeis— along with liberal justices Benjamin Cardozo and Harlan Fiske

Stone—became one of the "three musketeers" who generally voted to uphold it. On June 5, 1916, Wilson wrote to Henry Morgenthau, "I have never signed any commission with such satisfaction." And two days later, the president wrote exuberantly to another colleague, "I am going to see the new Justice today and tell him how happy it makes me to see him on the Great Court."[116]

3

Laboratories of Democracy

BRANDEIS'S REPUTATION could rest alone on the premoni-
tory brilliance of his analysis of corporate bigness. And this
he accomplished before he joined the Supreme Court. On the
bench, however, further distinction followed. He became the
most far-seeing progressive justice of the twentieth century,
the one whose judicial philosophy is most relevant for the court
today as it confronts questions involving regulation in a time
of economic crisis and the preservation of constitutional liberty
in a time of technological change. The judicial philosophy of
Justice Brandeis rested on three pillars: a commitment to judicial deference to legislative experimentation and states' rights;
a crusading opposition to the effects of big corporations and
big government on American democracy; and a determination
to translate the text of the Constitution and the values of the
framers into concepts and rulings that were demanded by an
era of social and technological change, to interpret the docu-

ment not just in light of its original understanding but also as a synthesis of the history of the United States.

On the Supreme Court, Brandeis was part of the progressive tradition that advocated judicial restraint, although he never went so far as to embrace the most radical progressive proposals to limit the courts, such as the popular recall of judicial decisions. Instead, Brandeis insisted that judges should hesitate to strike down state and federal laws unless they clearly violated rights and limitations enumerated in the text of the Constitution, and he insisted that decisions should be written as narrowly as possible to avoid broad constitutional rulings. "The most important thing we do is not doing," Brandeis once remarked to Felix Frankfurter. In *Ashwander v. Tennessee Valley Authority* (1936),[1] Brandeis articulated the doctrine of constitutional avoidance, which holds that because of the limitations of human reason, judges were more likely to achieve consensus on narrow technical questions involving procedure and jurisdiction than on broad constitutional questions involving a clash of values, and therefore the court should not "formulate a rule of constitutional law broader than is required by the precise facts to which it is to be applied."[2]

Brandeis was a quick study and a team player: in December 1916, just months after the beginning of his first term, he handed down five opinions, which he wrote for a unanimous court.[3] Overall, in his twenty-three years on the court, Brandeis wrote 455 majority opinions and 65 dissents.[4] Still, some of Brandeis's most memorable opinions are his dissents, in which he defended the constitutionality of the progressive labor laws he had championed as an advocate—laws that his activist colleagues were striking down with impunity.

Consider one of Brandeis's earliest dissents, in *Adams v. Tanner* (1917).[5] The voters of Washington State had passed an initiative forbidding employment agencies from collecting fees from prospective employees. The court's majority opinion was written by Brandeis's nemesis, Justice James C. McReynolds, appointed first as attorney general and then to the Supreme Court by Woodrow Wilson because of his trust-busting populism. (The virulently anti-Semitic McReynolds, who refused to sit next to Brandeis or to shake his hand, often left the conference room when Brandeis spoke; in declining Chief Justice Taft's invitation to a ceremony in Philadelphia with all the members of the court, McReynolds replied, "I am not always to be found when there is a Hebrew abroad.")[6] In a conclusory opinion, McReynolds struck down the law as "arbitrary and oppressive," on the grounds that "it unduly restricts the liberty of appellants, guaranteed by the 14th Amendment, to engage in a useful business."[7]

With meticulous attention to facts, Brandeis systematically demolished each of McReynolds's arguments. Using a rhetorical structure that recurred in his briefs and opinions, he began by describing the "evils" that the people of Washington State intended to correct when they passed a particular pro-labor law. He then asked what the experience of other states and countries had been in adopting similar remedies. After having exhaustively demonstrated that the people of Washington State were amply justified in adopting the reforms they did, he went on to stress that the reforms must be upheld even if they were not amply justified, as long as the state's decision wasn't clearly arbitrary or unreasonable.

As for what he called the "evils," Brandeis quoted from congressional reports noting that employee agencies were committing fraud by colluding with employers who fired workers after a few days and that the consequence was irregularity of employment—one of Brandeis's obsessions as an advocate. As for remedies, Brandeis noted that in the fifteen years before 1914, forty-three states and the federal government had passed direct or indirect regulations of private employment agencies, but these experiments had proved unsatisfactory. After this review of the political history of the laws in question, Brandeis pulled back his lens from the narrow question at hand to identify the underlying "fundamental problem" that confronted the people of Washington: "It was the chronic problem of unemployment,—perhaps the gravest and most difficult problem of modern industry,—the problem which, owing to business depression, was the most acute in America during the years 1913 to 1915."[8] In the spirit of his "Living Law" speech, he concluded by quoting an opinion emphasizing that, since the Magna Carta, "the law has been forced to adapt itself to new conditions of society, and particularly to the new relations between employers and employees as they arise."[9] By the end of his dissent, the reader has the sense that far from acting in an arbitrary and oppressive fashion, the people of Washington had no other choice but to pass the law that the Supreme Court cavalierly invalidated.

Brandeis continued to emphasize the need for courts to defer to state legislatures in his dissent in *Truax v. Corrigan* (1921).[10] The court, in a 5–4 opinion, written this time by Chief Justice William Howard Taft, struck down an Arizona law allowing courts to issue injunctions in labor disputes only against acts of violence. After a strike in 1916 to protest a restaurant the union felt was unfair to organized labor, the restaurant wanted to enjoin the strike and claimed that the law was unconstitutional. Chief Justice Taft agreed, holding that business was a property right and that the epithets of the strikers deprived the restaurant of liberty and property, despite the absence of violence. In his dissenting opinion, Brandeis characteristically stressed the importance of facts and of deferring to decisions reached by democratic deliberation. "Whether a law enacted in the exercise of the police power is justly subject to the charge of being unreasonable or arbitrary can ordinarily be determined only by a consideration of the contemporary conditions, social, industrial, and political, of the community to be affected thereby," he wrote. "Since government is not an exact science, prevailing public opinion concerning the evils and the remedy is among the important facts deserving consideration, particularly when the public conviction is both deep-seated and widespread and has been reached after deliberation."[11]

Brandeis's convictions about the need to strengthen unions as a counterweight to strong corporations are also clear in his dissent in the *Duplex Printing* case (1921).[12] The New York local branch of the International Association of Machinists organized a countrywide boycott of Duplex's products to induce the company to hire only union workers and to adopt an eight-hour day. In a 6–3 opinion for the court, Justice Mahlon Pitney agreed with Duplex that the boycott constituted a violation of the Sherman Antitrust Act, which prohibits unreasonable restraints of trade. He rejected the claim that Congress had legalized these boycotts in the Clayton Antitrust Act, whose progressive purposes Brandeis understood. The court had repeatedly held that legislative history was not a reliable guide to Congress's motives, Pitney wrote, and in any event the legislative history was unclear.

Brandeis disagreed, reviewing the judicial and legislative debates over the past two decades, which he had helped to shape. "When centralization in the control of business brought its corresponding centralization in the organization of workingmen, new facts had to be appraised," Brandeis wrote in his dissent.[13] "A better realization of the facts of industrial life" had led judges to recognize that, in a centralized economy, a refusal of an employer in one state to hire union workers threatened the interests of union workers across the country.[14] And Congress had codified this new understanding in the Clayton Act, which Brandeis described as "the fruit of unceasing agitation, which extended over more than 20 years and was designed to equalize before the law the position of workingmen and employer as industrial combatants."[15] Although Brandeis left no doubt that he agreed with Congress and the lower courts about the importance of allowing secondary boycotts, he concluded, once again, by emphasizing the importance of deferring to a legislature's decision about when new economic conditions require new economic interventions.

In early dissents, Brandeis defended the original understanding not only of the progressive laws he helped to shape but also the progressive agencies he helped to design. In *Federal Trade Commission v. Gratz* (1920),[16] a majority of the court, led again by McReynolds, overturned an order of the newly created Federal Trade Commission. The commission concluded that the Gratz firm of St. Louis engaged in unfair competition when it required purchasers of the steel ties used for binding cotton bales to buy a similar amount of cotton bagging. "Nothing is alleged which would justify the conclusion that the public suffered injury or that competitors had reasonable ground for complaint," McReynolds declared, without analysis.[17] Brandeis demolished the conclusion on factual grounds, emphasizing that steel ties and jute bagging are essential to baling cotton, and that two companies—the Carnegie Steel Company and the American Manufacturing Company—dominated the production, and could effectively fix the prices, of both products in the United States. Because the Gratz firm was the sole western agent for both Carnegie Steel and the American Manufacturing Company, it could force would-be purchasers of one company's ties also to buy the other company's bagging.

Brandeis went on to discuss Congress's purpose in creating the Federal Trade Commission in 1914, with which he was intimately familiar. (McReynolds, who had been attorney general when Brandeis helped to write the Federal Trade Commission Act, was similarly familiar with Congress's purposes but chose in his opinion to ignore them.) Brandeis emphasized that, as a remedy for monopoly power, Congress and the American people had chosen to embrace Wilson's policy of regulated competition rather than Roosevelt's policy of regulated monopoly. In 1914, he recalled, "[m]any believed that concentration (called by its opponents monopoly) was inevitable and desirable; and these desired that concentration should be recognized by law and be regulated. Others believed that concentration was a source of evil; that existing combinations could be disintegrated, if only the judicial machinery were perfected; and that further concentration could be averted by providing additional remedies, and particularly through regulating competition. The latter view prevailed in the Sixty-Third Congress," which passed the Clayton Act and created the Federal Trade Commission.[18] Brandeis concluded that the task of the Federal Trade Commission was prophylactic: "Its purpose in respect to restraints of trade was prevention of diseased business conditions, not cure."[19] In other words, the American people had embraced Brandeis's conclusions about the need to ban uncompetitive practices before they became rampant, and he insisted that the Supreme Court should have deferred to the people's considered judgment, which happened to coincide with his own.

In the 1920s, under President Warren Harding, the Justice Department repudiated Brandeis's theory of regulated competition and persuaded the Supreme Court to repudiate it as well. Harding's attorney general, Harry M. Daugherty, who was later forced to resign by President Coolidge for failing to intervene in the Teapot Dome scandal, began his campaign against small firms by challenging the American Hardwood Manufacturers Association's "Open Competition Plan," whereby four hundred members, representing one-third of domestic hardwood producers, exchanged information about prices, production, sales, costs, and inventories.[20] The brief filed by Daugherty's Justice Department openly assaulted Brandeis's economic legacy, arguing that the idea of "regulated competition" was an oxymoron and that between "monopoly" and "competition," there was no Brandesian third way.[21]

In *American Column Co. v. United States* (1921), the court—this time in an opinion by Justice Clarke, who had previously joined Brandeis in progressive dissents—agreed with Daughtery and struck down the Open Competition Plan.[22] After quoting from confidential communications in business meetings in which the hardwood manufacturers had called for the Sherman Antitrust Act to be repealed, Clarke concluded that the plan violated the Sherman Act, despite the absence of an explicit price-fixing agreement.

Brandeis dissented, insisting that the plan by small businesses to restrict production did not amount to illegal coercion, and that the small businesses needed to pool information to counteract the data-gathering advantages of their large competitors. "The cooperation which is incident to this plan does not suppress competition," he wrote. "On the contrary, it tends to promote all in competition which is desirable. By substituting knowledge for ignorance, rumor, guess, and suspicion, it tends also to substitute research and reasoning for gambling and piracy, without closing the door to adventure, or lessening the value of prophetic wisdom."[23] Thus the apostle of facts acknowledged the distinction between information and knowledge. Brandeis emphasized that information sharing by small producers promoted equality rather than monopoly. "In making such knowledge available to the smallest concern, it creates among producers equality of opportunity," he continued. "In making it available, also, to purchasers and the general public, it does all that can actually be done to protect the community from extortion."[24] The purpose of the Open Competition Plan, Brandeis declared, was "to make rational competition possible, by supplying data not otherwise available, and without which most of those engaged in the trade would be unable to trade intelligently."[25]

Developing an idea that would flower in his free speech opinions, Brandeis stressed the importance of untrammeled access to facts in order to form intelligent opinions. "Intelligent conduct of business implies not only knowledge of trade facts, but an understanding of them," he noted. "Opinions expressed may be unsound; predictions may be unfounded; but there is nothing in the Sherman Law which should limit freedom of discussion, even among traders."[26] And he concluded that the aim of the Sherman Act was not the lowest prices for consumers but the welfare of the community in general. "May not these hardwood lumber concerns, frustrated in their efforts to rationalize competition, be led to enter the inviting field of consolidation?" Brandeis warned. "And, if they do, may not another huge trust, with highly centralized control over vast resources, natural, manufacturing, and financial, become so powerful as to dominate competitors, wholesalers, retailers, consumers, employees, and, in large measure, the community?"[27]

Although Brandeis initially failed to persuade his colleagues, his approach to regulated competition was soon resurrected by the Supreme Court. After firing Attorney General Daugherty, President Coolidge replaced him in 1924 with Harlan Fiske Stone, an Amherst classmate and a progressive Republican who had served as dean of Columbia Law School. Stone, who was more sympathetic to information pooling by small firms, instructed his antitrust division to bring a Supreme Court case to test his more flexible approach. In 1925, soon after his reelection, Coolidge appointed Stone to the Supreme Court, where he promptly wrote the court's majority in *Maple Flooring Manufacturers' Association* (1925), holding that information pooling for the benefit of individual firms promoted competition while pooling for collective purposes promoted monopoly.[28] Brandeis joined Stone's majority opinion; three conservative justices—Taft, Sanford, and McReynolds—dissented. Brandeis, in other words, was amenable to light forms of cartel as a way of avoiding corporate concentration.

Brandeis's most memorable defense of judicial deference to state experimentation came in *New State Ice v. Liebmann* (1932), in which he dissented from the court's decision to strike down an Oklahoma law requiring ice manufacturers to get a license from a state commission before opening a new business. Although Brandeis may have questioned the intrusiveness of the government planning, he believed that local responses to economic challenges had to be encouraged. As Brandeis put it:

> To stay experimentation in things social and economic is a grave responsibility. Denial of the right to experiment may be fraught with serious consequences to the Nation. It is one of the happy incidents of the federal system that a single courageous State may, if its citizens choose, serve as a laboratory, and try novel social and economic experiments without risk to the rest of the country. This Court has the power to prevent an experiment. We may strike down the statute which embodies it on the ground that, in our opinion, the measure is arbitrary, capricious or unreasonable. . . . But in the exercise of this high power, we must be ever on our guard, lest we erect our prejudices into legal principles. If we would guide by the light of reason, we must let our minds be bold.[29]

Two strains of Brandeis's judicial philosophy—his judicial restraint and his crusading anticorporate progressivism—are on display in one of his most memorable and yet quixotic dissenting opinions, in *Liggett Co. v. Lee* (1933), a case striking down a Florida anti–chain store law that aimed to protect small, independently owned businesses in competition with out-of-state chain stores by taxing the chain stores with a license fee.[30] Brandeis read his dissent from the bench on March 13, 1933, just days after the newly inaugurated President Roosevelt had declared a bank holiday to quell the financial panic. Brandeis fervently defended what he saw as the social and historical realities that justified the Florida legislature's protectionist action, and the economic reality of the Depression suffuses his entire dissent. "There is a widespread belief," Brandeis wrote,

> that the existing unemployment is the result, in large part, of the gross inequality in the distribution of wealth and income which giant corporations have fostered; that, by the control which the few have exerted through giant corporations, individual initiative and effort are being paralyzed, creative power impaired and human happiness lessened; that the true prosperity of our past came not from big business, but through the courage, the energy and the resourcefulness of small men; that only by releasing from corporate control the faculties of the unknown many, only by reopening to them the opportunities for leadership, can confidence in our future be restored and the existing misery be overcome, and that only through participation by the many in the responsibilities and determinations of business can Americans secure the moral and intellectual development which is essential to the maintenance of liberty.[31]

This passage is characteristic of Brandeis's greatest opinions, which begin with close technical analysis and end with passionate generalizations about the political and economic beliefs of the American people.

Brandeis was outraged that the Supreme Court had prevented states such as Florida from trying to protect local businesses from out-of-state rivals. In his view, the decision failed to defer to the superior fact-finding abilities of the legislature and offended principles of federalism and judicial restraint. But in addition to these abstract concerns, Brandeis made an affirmative case for the protectionist law as a principled response to the curse of bigness and as a way of translating time-honored American values into the twentieth century. Brandeis had long been looking for a case that allowed him to set out his views on the dangers of big corporations. *Liggett* offered him an ideal chance to develop the ideas at the center of his economic thought, including his affinity for democratically accountable small businesses with clear ties to the community; his distrust of large business combinations, in which ownership and control were separated and managerial decisions were made far away from the actual economic activity they affected; and his broad view of government's ability to use its tax and regulatory power to make corporations accountable to the general welfare.

Instead of resting his opinion solely on his own progressive beliefs, Brandeis in *Liggett* offered nothing less than a history of the corporation over the entire range of American history. He showed how state governments had initially been reluctant to grant the privilege of incorporation, because they were wary of the potential for abuses arising from the creation of an immortal and artificial corporate entity, accountable only to a dispersed and changing set of owners and to the fickle whims of the market. Accordingly, the statutes that made incorporation possible carefully limited the size, the scope, and the capitalization of corporate enterprises.

Brandeis argued that the states' rush to discard safeguards against corporate power resulted in the creation of institutions powerful enough to challenge and to dominate the states themselves. Pointedly, he noted that the new megainstitutions created through the advent of easy incorporation were controlled by only a few men—a state of affairs inimical to democracy. Worst of all, these few men refused to risk their own fortunes in promoting the goals of the enterprise: limited liability made corporate directors even less accountable, for when the enterprise went bankrupt, as so many did in the first years of the Depression, its creditors had no individual pockets to open.

To Brandeis, vast and unaccountable corporations threatened the autonomy and the fulfillment of workers, citizens, and communities. With so much at stake, states such as Florida were not just to be tolerated but actively encouraged in reassuming

their historical role as checks against the concentration of corporate power. This was enough to convince Brandeis that the
tax law under consideration in *Liggett* served a "broader and
deeper" purpose than merely protecting a handful of small
businesses from out-of-state competition.[32] Indeed, the tax was
meant to protect the very viability of "American ideals," such
as equal opportunity, economic self-sufficiency, and personal
liberty.[33]

Despite his professed devotion to facts, Brandeis was ultimately more interested in using his opinions to articulate and
defend American ideals. But many observers joined the *Liggett*
majority in viewing the Florida statute in the prosaic terms
of economic protectionism. Brandeis's former law clerk Henry
Friendly was in Tallahassee at the time the Florida anti–chain
store statute had been adopted, and he observed the Florida
legislature's deliberations as the drugstore industry lobbied for
the anti–chain store law. "I was watching the Florida Legislature," Friendly told Brandeis, "and I don't think they had any
of those social benefits in mind that you discussed. I think they
were influenced by the drug lobby." According to Friendly,
Brandeis did not smile or respond and simply changed the
subject.[34]

In drafting his *Liggett* dissent, Brandeis drew on notes for
another dissenting opinion, ultimately unpublished, that joins
Liggett and *New State Ice* as expressing Brandeis's most memorable judicial reflections on the curse of bigness. In *Stratton
v. St. Louis Southwestern Railway*, argued in January 1930, the
question was whether states could require foreign corporations
—that is, those incorporated in another state—to pay a tax determined in part by the corporation's size as measured by its
out-of-state holdings. In his draft opinion for the court, Justice
Sutherland struck down the tax on the grounds that it was too
large, noting that "the power to tax is the power to destroy." As
Alexander M. Bickel discovered in his study of Brandeis's un-

published opinions, Brandeis, in preparing his dissent, studied Gerard C. Henderson's *The Position of Foreign Corporations in American Constitutional Law* (1918), which was dedicated to Brandeis. On eleven handwritten pages, Brandeis copied passages from the book, including a reference to Jefferson's identification of "incorporation with monopoly" and another reference to the Jeffersonian view condemning corporations "as encroachments on the citizen's natural right to freely exercise his faculties in trade and commerce."[35] He distilled this history into a powerful passage about the history of state efforts to curb corporate power that he later transposed into his *Liggett* dissent:

> [T]hroughout the greater part of our history, the States guarded jealously their control over grants of the corporate privilege and they have made it a source of revenue. Severe restrictions on corporate size and activity long prevailed. These restrictions originated in fear. First, there was the fear of monopoly. Then, the fear of domination more general. Fear of encroachment upon the liberties and opportunities of the individual. Fear of the subjection of labor to capital. Fear that the absorption of capital by corporations and their perpetual life, might bring evils similar to those which attended mortmain [the hated medieval laws granting churches and corporations perpetual title in real estate]. There was a sense of some insidious menace inherent in large aggregations of capital. Incorporation for business purposes was long denied after it had been freely granted for religious, educational and charitable purposes. And when finally granted for business purposes, fees graduated according to the capital stock were commonly exacted as compensation for the privilege.[36]

Brandeis's dissents in *New State Ice*, *Liggett*, and *Stratton* express the core of his faith that "[m]an is weak and his judgment is at best fallible," as he put it in *New State Ice*. But Brandeis also held, in Bickel's words: "that man's judgment, properly informed, has an immense potential, and that it should enable him to command circumstances and to shape the conditions of his life to a rational and satisfactory pattern. Man's single fatal limitation was his reluctance to understand his own limitations and to pace himself and his efforts accordingly. But this reluctance could be, and it had to be, overcome. The paradox of limited man and his practically limitless potential was thus at the core of Brandeis' faith, and it gave him his unique combination of passion and patience."[37]

Brandeis was a defender of judicial deference but not judicial abstinence: he opposed bigness in government as well as business, and after voting to uphold federal child labor laws in 1918, he voted to strike them down in 1922. (His decision to join Chief Justice Taft's 8–1 opinion in the 1922 *Bailey* case arguably ignored founding-era principles establishing a broad congressional power to tax and Reconstruction-era principles condemning unfree labor practices.) As he wrote to his daughter Susan after the second decision, "If we may hope to carry out our ideals in America, it will be by development through the State and local Governments. Centralization will kill—only decentralization of social functions can help."[38] Accordingly, he was alarmed by the growing centralization of the federal government under Franklin D. Roosevelt. Brandeis had supported Roosevelt's election and he worked with his protégée, the Harvard Law professor Felix Frankfurter, to persuade Roosevelt and his advisors (many of them handpicked by Frankfurter) of the benefits of taxing big corporations out of existence rather than expanding the scope of the federal government. This behind-the-scenes lobbying of the White House by a Supreme Court justice, which was questionable at the time and would never be tolerated in Washington today, was not new for Brandeis: in June 1921, months after Woodrow Wilson left the White House, Brandeis and Wilson secretly drafted a Progressive manifesto, known as "the Document," that Wilson hoped would guarantee a Democratic victory in 1924. (Brandeis may have thought he was writing a document to rally Progressive reformers disheartened by the 1920 elections.) Wilson seems to have written the part of the Document calling for "the immediate resumption of our international obligations and leadership," Brandeis the section calling for laws allowing retail price agreements.[39] Throughout the 1920s, Brandeis continued to use Frankfurter to publicize his views—writing letters to his protégée about issues ranging from the dangers of "big money" in politics to the condition of farmers that Frankfurter redrafted and published as unsigned editorials in the *New Republic*.[40] After the crash of '29 vindicated Brandeis's warnings about the curse of bigness, Brandeis was delighted by the revival of interest in *Other People's Money*. "The present depression, the debunking of the great financial kings, and the losses of those who followed them have made men think, and i.a. realize that 'Other People's Money' should have been heeded," he wrote to his nephew Louis Brandeis Wehle in January 1932, adding, "Find out, if you can, what the sales have been."[41] (He donated all royalties to the Savings Bank Insurance League.)

Brandeis was also pleased when Franklin Roosevelt, on September 15, 1933, told Frankfurter that he wanted to consult with Brandeis before the court convened. (Brandeis wanted to discuss "irregularity of employment.")[42] Frankfurter had already arranged a first meeting between the justice and the new president at the Mayflower Hotel in Washington, D.C., in November 1932, soon after Roosevelt's election. Brandeis was enthusiastic about Roosevelt, concluding that "a new era" had arrived and emphasizing that he was "ready to help in any way."[43] Through Frankfurter, Brandeis tried to press on FDR's advisors his ambitious economic recovery program, including proposals for massive government spending on agrarian public works, such as flood control, irrigation, and the creation of ponds and lakes, to be financed, in part, by massive tax increases on the wealthiest individuals and corporations.[44] As he wrote to his daughter Elizabeth on November 19, 1933: "Curb of bigness is indispensable to true Democracy & Liberty. It is the very foundation also of wisdom in things human." Unless Progressives could see this truth, Brandeis warned, "we are apt to get Fascist manifestations. . . . If the Lord had intended things to be big, he would have made man bigger—in brains and character." In this remarkable letter, Brandeis went on to endorse a program of "extensive public works" to overcome the Depression, including, "for every state, (1) afforestation; (2) running water control; (3) adult education; (4) appropriate provision for dealing with defectives and delinquents." (The casual reference to "defectives," with its distasteful scent of eugenics, reminds us that Brandeis joined Justice Oliver Wendell Holmes's 8–1 opinion upholding mandatory sterilization laws in *Buck v. Bell.*) The core of his Jeffersonian program was control of "all running waters, by reservoirs, etc." to prevent floods and soil erosion, to irrigate all land, and for recreation that would ensure that "every state should have its lakes and ponds galore."[45]

But the Roosevelt administration never adopted the kind of confiscatory taxation that Brandeis thought was necessary to limit corporate size. Instead, the First New Deal included aggressive assertions of executive and congressional power that, in Brandeis's view, transferred the loathed curse of bigness from business to the federal government. The architects of Roosevelt's First New Deal—the Columbia Law professors Rexford Tugwell, Raymond Moley, and Adolf Berle, known as the "Brains Trust"—were devotees of central planning and consolidation who disdained Brandeis's concerns about bigness as outdated and inefficient.[46] In the 1932 preface to *The Modern Corporation and Private Property*, Berle declared that "the translation of perhaps two-thirds of the industrial wealth of the country from individual ownership to ownership by the large, publicly financed corporations" was essentially unstoppable.

"Mr. Brandeis struggled to turn the clock backward in 1915," Berle wrote dismissively. "To us there is much to indicate that the process will go a great deal further than it has now gone."[47] Scorning Brandeis's proposed public works economic recovery program as "frivolous to the point of absurdity," Moley and his colleagues created massive federal bureaucracies in 1933, such as the National Recovery Administration (NRA), which allowed the president to regulate industry in an attempt to raise prices, and the Agricultural Adjustment Administration (AAA), which paid farmers not to plant crops. Brandeis detested both of these new agencies because of their bigness: the NRA, he believed, violated antitrust laws, and the AAA was driving small farmers off the land by promoting corporate farming. In April 1934, he wrote to his daughter Elizabeth: "As you may have imagined, I see little to be joyous about in the New Deal measures most talked about. N.R.A. and A.A.A. seem to be going from bad to worse."[48]

Brandeis made his displeasure clear, warning Berle and Tugwell that he would vote to strike down the New Deal unless the big business trend were reversed.[49] And he made good on his threat. In January 1935, Brandeis joined an 8–1 opinion in the *Panama Refining Co.* case, striking down the "hot oil" clause of the National Industrial Recovery Act, which permitted the president to ban interstate shipments of oil that exceeded state production limits.[50] In the view of Brandeis and his colleagues, Congress had delegated lawmaking power to the president without providing sufficient guidelines to constrain executive discretion. (The same argument would be raised decades later against President Bush's and President Obama's Troubled Asset Relief Program.)

On Black Monday—May 27, 1935—the court handed down three opinions striking down elements of the First New Deal on the grounds that they created unchecked centralized federal power. Brandeis wrote or joined these opinions—in fact, all three were unanimous. (These were the opinions that stunned FDR when he learned that "Old Isaiah" had joined.) In his opinion for the court in *Louisville Joint Stock Land Bank v. Radford*, Brandeis struck down a 1934 bankruptcy law that, in his view, unconstitutionally seized private property without just compensation by transferring property from creditors to debtors.[51] In a Jeffersonian twist, the case involved a Louisville bank that had foreclosed on a bankrupt farmer and challenged the New Deal law that allowed him to make payments to a court, rather than to the bank. Brandeis held that Congress could change the bankruptcy laws to apply to future bankruptcies but that its attempt to redefine the property rights of the Louisville bank, which now owned the farm, violated the Fifth Amendment, which says that "private property" shall not be "taken for public use, without just compensation."

In *Humphrey's Executor v. United States*, the court held that Roosevelt could not fire a conservative federal trade commissioner who had been less than enthusiastic about the New Deal.[52] Independent agencies such as the Federal Trade Commission (which Brandeis had helped to found in 1914) were constitutional, the court held, because they exercised "quasi-legislative" powers, and therefore the president lacked the power to dismiss commissioners for purely political reasons. The *Humphrey's Executor* case assumed that independent agencies were permissible attempts by Congress to check executive overreach. The Hamiltonian justice Antonin Scalia, by contrast, has questioned the constitutionality of independent agencies that Brandeis helped to establish, such as the FTC, and suggested that he would overturn the *Humphrey's Executor* case because of his devotion to "unitary" executive power.[53]

Humphrey's Executive distinguished the *Myers* case, in which Brandeis had filed a dissent nearly a decade earlier. In *Myers*, Chief Justice Taft held for the court that Congress could not limit the president's unitary authority to fire executive branch officials he appointed. "The doctrine of the separation of powers was adopted by the Convention of 1787 not to promote efficiency, but to preclude the exercise of arbitrary power,"[54] Brandeis objected in his dissent. "The purpose was not to avoid friction but, by means of the inevitable friction incident to the distribution of the governmental powers among three departments, to save the people from autocracy."[55] Brandeis in *Myers* said the framers had focused on the "protection of the individual, even if he be an official, from the arbitrary or capricious exercise of power."[56] As Brandeis put it, "The separation of the powers of government did not make each branch completely autonomous."[57] (Madison had proposed a failed constitutional amendment that would have required this autonomy.) Instead, Brandeis stressed, the framers had given Congress oversight power over the president in an effort to secure liberty. (Today, however, Brandeis's vote to uphold a legislative veto of the president's power to fire cabinet officers has been rejected by liberal and conservative justices and scholars alike.)

Finally, in *Schechter Poultry Corp. v. United States*, known to law students ever since as the "Sick Chickens" case, because the government claimed the Schechter company sold ailing poultry, the court struck down the National Industrial Recovery Act (NIRA), which created the NRA, as a "sweeping delegation" of lawmaking power to private parties.[58] The NIRA authorized the president to endorse "codes of fair competition" for the chicken industry; the court held that the centerpiece of FDR's New Deal aspired to regulate an industry that had only indirect effects on interstate commerce. Also, Congress could not delegate legislative power to an executive agency without clearer standards about how to define "fair competition."[59] Convinced that "our Court did much good for the country," Brandeis asked a friend to deliver his prophesy to Felix Frankfurter and FDR: "They must understand that these three decisions change everything."[60]

When Brandeis voted against aspects of the New Deal, he did so not because he believed in an unregulated market, but because he believed that corporations should be broken up by taxation so they were small enough to be effectively regulated by the states. (Whether the states are powerful enough to perform this task in a post–New Deal era is open to question.) He also believed, as he wrote in the *Myers* case, that each of the three branches had to check the others in order to prevent "the exercise of arbitrary power."[61] This led him to focus on limiting the size and scope of the judiciary along with the other branches. He supported proposals to limit the jurisdiction of the lower federal courts, writing to Felix Frankfurter, "[I]n no case practically should the appellate federal courts have to pass on the construction of state statutes."[62] And in the landmark *Erie v. Tompkins* case (1938), Brandeis held for the court that federal judges had no power to create a "general federal common law" that could displace decisions by state court judges.[63] *Erie* was consistent with Brandeis's pragmatic devotion to judicial restraint and states' rights. The fact that Brandeis was requiring federal judges to defer to more populist state court judges, whose decisions (at least in his time) were less likely to be sympathetic to big corporations, must have been, for Brandeis, icing on the cake.[64]

In addition to combining judicial restraint with a commitment to checking centralized power in business or government, Brandeis's opinions exemplify a third aspect of his judicial philosophy: his commitment to interpreting the text of the Constitution and the ideals of the founders in light of the entire range of constitutional history. In this sense, Brandeis provides a model for citizens today who are searching for an alternative to the rigid originalism championed by some Roberts Court conservatives, and also for an alternative to the untethered "living constitutionalism" of some Warren Court liberals. Brandeis combines elements of originalism and living constitutionalism into a kind of living originalism.

Brandeis believed that the values of the founders were immutable, but had to be translated into a very different world in light of dramatic changes in society, technology, and economics. He believed in constitutional change—in his talk "The Living Law," he charged that the law had "not kept pace with the rapid development of our political, economic, and social ideals" and said that "the challenge of legal justice [was] to conform to our contemporary conceptions of social justice."[65] But Brandeis insisted that efforts to render constitutional values into a contemporary vocabulary always had to be rooted in the text and in the broad, unchanging natural law ideals of the framers. By interpreting the values of the framers in light of Jeffersonian principles and progressive movements across the range of American history, Brandeis believed they could be preserved in a way that served the needs of citizens in the here and now.

In the age of the Internet, then, Brandeis is the most relevant figure, the prophet, not only of privacy but also of free speech. His concurring opinion in *Whitney v. California* (1927) is the most far-seeing essay on the purposes and boundaries of free speech in American history[66]—more so than the free speech opinions of Holmes, which are quoted more often but are less substantively appealing. Brandeis's opinion in *Whitney* completed the evolution that he and Holmes began in March 1919, when both justices wrote four opinions for the court upholding the convictions, under the federal Espionage Act, of Socialists, including Charles Schenck and Eugene V. Debs, for their criticisms of World War I. (While in prison, Debs went on to win nearly a million votes as the Socialist Party's candidate for president.) "The most stringent protection of free speech would protect a man in falsely shouting fire in a theater and causing a panic," Holmes famously wrote for the court in *Schenck v. United States.* "The question in every case is whether the words used are used in such circumstances and are of such nature as to create a clear and present danger that they will bring about the substantive evils that Congress has a right to prevent."[67]

With the guidance of Zechariah Chafee of Harvard Law School, Holmes converted his "clear and present danger" test from an invitation to suppress free speech into a shield for its protection. In the *Abrams* case, decided in November 1919, the court upheld the conviction of Russian immigrants for distributing leaflets protesting the deployment of U.S. troops to Russia.[68] Holmes wrote a memorable dissent, joined by Brandeis, which represents his best vision of the First Amendment. "The ultimate good desired is better reached by free trade in ideas," Holmes declared. "The best test of truth is the power of the thought to get itself accepted in the competition of the market."[69] Holmes's libertarian defense of free speech as the currency of the marketplace of ideas was consistent with his nihilistic vision of American democracy, which he developed out of his experience in the Civil War. Holmes believed that majorities had to be given virtually unlimited power to crush minorities through law, or else their disagreements would break out into actual violence. The only exceptions for Holmes were laws restricting the competition of ideas itself.

Brandeis and Holmes were not alone in changing their minds about the value of free speech in wartime; many Progressives (Holmes, of course, was not a Progressive) experienced a similar evolution. They had supported Woodrow Wilson and World War I but came to lament the repression of free speech that followed in their wake. In a series of essays for the *New Republic* in 1917, for example, John Dewey had criticized pacifists who opposed the war for their failure to grasp the war's potential to make the world safe for democracy. After the war ended in disappointment and red-baiting, he and other Progressives came to appreciate the social value of free speech in educating citizens for full participation in American democracy.[70] And although Brandeis joined Holmes's dissents, he provided in *Whitney* a much more idealistic and positive vision for why courts should protect free expression in democracy. Brandeis stipulated that speech could be restricted only if it threatened to result in harms both imminent and serious and only if there was no time for informed deliberation to defuse the danger. (The court would embrace these conditions more than forty years later.) Brandeis's opinion in *Whitney* represents the most important defense of freedom of thought and opinion since Jefferson's First Inaugural, on which it relies. Its genesis can be seen in Brandeis dissents from 1920, in which he developed his views with increasing confidence and creativity.

Some of these cases, like *Schenck*, involved convictions under the Espionage Act of 1917. Others involved convictions under state laws passed to suppress the speech of the Industrial Workers of the World, or the Wobblies, a militant union organization of farmers, construction workers, and other laborers who viewed America's entry into World War I as a sacrifice of the lives of workingmen to the business interests of J. P. Morgan.[71] Although Brandeis denounced Morgan and exalted the workingman, he was no socialist and viewed with alarm the Wobblies' call for One Big Union that would embrace all industries, just as he viewed with alarm Morgan's attempt to monopolize banking. In other words, he deplored Big Unions as well as Big Business. As a counterweight to the Wobblies, Brandeis had helped to organize the National Civic Federation before the war in an effort to create "some conservative substitute for radical measures."[72] At the same time, he had protested the repression of the Wobblies' "civil rights" during a strike in Massachusetts in 1912 and objected that the rampant use of injunctions and police officers to break strikes would threaten free speech.[73] Philippa Strum has speculated that Brandeis may have had some sympathy for the revolutionaries of his era because his parents expressed sympathy for the revolutionaries of 1848.[74]

Nevertheless, the most direct influence on Brandeis and Holmes was Zechariah Chafee, whose 1919 article in the *New Republic*, expanded into a book the following year called *Freedom of Speech in War Time*, emphasized the value of what he called "public discussion of all public questions." As Chafee put it in a passage he considered crucial: "One of the most important purposes of society and government is the discovery and spread of truth on subjects of general concern. This is possible only through absolutely unlimited discussion, for . . . once force is thrown into the argument, it becomes a matter of chance whether it is thrown on the false side or the true, and truth loses all its natural advantage in the contest."[75] By the end of 1919, Brandeis, too, had changed his mind about the Red Scare and the wisdom of Espionage Act convictions. "I have been daily renewing my apologies to Signor Torquemada for all the evil impressions I had harbored. He was doubtless a thorough patriot," Brandeis wrote archly to his daughter Susan on December 7, 1919. "The intensity of the frenzy is the most helpful feature of this disgraceful exhibition:—of hysterical, unintelligent fear—which is quite foreign to the generous American nature. It will pass like the Knownothing days, but the sense of shame and of sin should endure."[76]

In the *Schaefer* case (1920), Brandeis cited Chafee in his dissent from an opinion upholding convictions under the Espionage Act of editors and journalists for the Philadelphia German newspaper *Tageblatt* who were charged with publishing "false reports" by translating—and in some cases mistranslating— articles from German newspapers critical of America's war effort.[77] By reviewing the original German newspaper items (his Dresden schooldays proved to be useful) and quoting them in full rather than out of context, Brandeis discovered they had not, in some cases, been mistranslated, as the government claimed.

And in any event, Brandeis concluded, minor mistranslations of German opinion pieces could hardly constitute a "false report," because the state had no power to criminalize thoughts and opinions, rather than actions, and no power "to condemn men, not merely for disloyal acts, but for a disloyal heart."[78] This attempt to resurrect the thought crime of "constructive treason," Brandeis predicted, would discourage criticism of the government after the emergency of war had passed. "In peace, too, men may differ widely as to what loyalty to our country demands; and an intolerant majority, swayed by passion or by fear, may be prone in the future, as it has often been in the past to stamp as disloyal opinions with which it disagrees," he concluded. "Convictions such as these, besides abridging freedom of speech, threaten freedom of thought and of belief."[79]

Brandeis further developed his ideas about the importance of freedom of thought and belief in his dissent in *Pierce v. United States* (1920).[80] The court upheld the Espionage Act conviction of four men for distributing a leaflet published by the Socialist Party. Brandeis insisted that the distribution of a leaflet could not create a clear and present danger of inducing violence. The leaflet charged that our financial oligopoly exerted a sinister influence over the government; Brandeis noted that President Wilson himself had made a similar charge in the New Freedom, where he declared, "The masters of the government of the United States are the combined capitalists and manufacturers of the United States." (Brandeis himself had made the same charge, of course, in *Other People's Money*.) Brandeis then explained why statements of opinion should never be declared to be falsifiable statements of fact; to hold otherwise, he warned, "would practically deny members of small political parties freedom of criticism and of discussion in times when feelings run high and the questions involved are deemed fundamental."[81] He noted once again that the leaflet had been read out of context: "[F]ar from counseling disobedience to law, [it] points to the hopelessness of protest, under the existing system, pictures the irresistible power of the military arm of the government, and indicates that acquiescence is a necessity."[82] Brandeis concluded by stressing the value of dissent in a free society; only dissent could preserve what he called "the fundamental right of free men to strive for better conditions through new legislation and new institutions."[83] And, at least in private, he freely acknowledged the evolution in his thought. As he told Felix Frankfurter in 1921, "I have never been quite happy about my concurrence in [the] Debs and Schenck cases. I had not then thought the issues of freedom of speech out—I thought at the subject, not through it. Not until I came to write the Pierce and Schafer [dissents] did I understand it."[84]

Throughout the 1920s, Brandeis continued to develop his ideas about the connections between freedom of thought and opinion and the ability of citizens to develop their faculties as full participants in American democracy. And those ideas culminated in his magnificent opinion in the *Whitney* case, issued in May 1927. In fact, Brandeis had first expressed his mature reflections on free speech in an unpublished dissenting opinion earlier that year. (The plaintiff was Charles Ruthenberg, executive secretary of the Communist Party, a man known as "the most arrested red in America"; the case became moot when Ruthenberg unexpectedly died.)[85] As a result, Brandeis cut and pasted the most important sections of his unpublished dissent into a concurring opinion in a case involving Anita Whitney. The niece of Justice Stephen Field, who distinguished himself on the Supreme Court as the nineteenth century's most enthusiastic libertarian defender of freedom of contract,[86] Whitney espoused politics very different from her celebrated uncle's. A Wellesley graduate, women's suffrage advocate, and member of the Socialist Party, she was arrested after giving a speech called "The Negro Question" to the Women's Civics League of Oakland in which she protested race riots and lynching.[87] She was then convicted—in a verdict that sparked national protests and a write-in campaign for clemency in the *New Republic*—for violating California's "criminal syndicalism" law when she presented the report of the Credentials and Resolutions Committee of the California branch of the Communist Labor Party. Although she herself never advocated terrorism, she was convicted of "assist[ing] in organizing an association to advocate" terrorism.

Rather than dissenting from the court's decision to uphold Whitney's conviction, Brandeis concurred, for technical reasons that are not, in hindsight, entirely clear or convincing.[88] But he refined Holmes's "clear and present danger test" in crucial ways. "Fear of serious injury cannot alone justify suppression of free speech and assembly. Men feared witches and burnt women," he wrote. "It is the function of speech to free men from the bondage of irrational fears."[89] As a result, Brandeis concluded, "To justify suppression of free speech, there must be reasonable ground to fear that serious evil will result if free speech is practiced. There must be reasonable ground to believe that the danger apprehended is imminent. There must be reasonable ground to believe that the evil to be prevented is a serious one."[90]

Brandeis's insight that speech could be restricted only if it threatened to cause harms that were both "imminent" and "serious" finally came to define the parameters of free speech in America when the Supreme Court overturned *Whitney* more than forty years later in the *Brandenburg* case of 1969.[91] Today, it is the principal barrier in America against the prosecution of hate speech and other offenses against dignity that European courts have come to take for granted.

But Brandeis's opinion in *Whitney* did not merely refine Holmes's legal test for protecting free speech; it offered an entirely different philosophical justification for doing so, and in the process achieved a kind of constitutional poetry. Here, once again, are his memorable words:

> Those who won our independence believed that the final end of the state was to make men free to develop their faculties, and that in its government the deliberative forces should prevail over the arbitrary. They valued liberty both as an end and as a means. They believed liberty to be the secret of happiness and courage to be the secret of liberty. They believed that freedom to think as you will and to speak as you think are means indispensable to the discovery and spread of political truth; that without free speech and assembly discussion would be futile; that with them, discussion affords ordinarily adequate protection against the dissemination of noxious doctrine; that the greatest menace to freedom is an inert people; that public discussion is a political duty; and that this should be a fundamental principle of the American government.[92]

Brandeis's footnote at the end of this remarkable passage quotes Jefferson's 1801 letter to the future U.S. senator Elijah Boardman, cited by Charles Beard the year before in the *Nation:* "We have nothing to fear from the demoralizing reasonings of some, if others are left free to demonstrate their errors and especially when the law stands ready to punish the first criminal act produced by the false reasonings; these are safer corrections than the conscience of the judge." Brandeis also quotes Jefferson's First Inaugural Address: "If there be any among us who would wish to dissolve this union or change its republican form, let them stand undisturbed as monuments of the safety with which error of opinion may be tolerated where reason is left free to combat it."[93] Both citations to Jefferson are apt and timely. Recall that Brandeis had read Jefferson's letters in 1926 and Nock's biography of Jefferson in 1927, immediately before and after he was preparing his pathbreaking free speech opinions in the *Whitney* and *Ruthenberg* cases.

Whitney confirms Brandeis's status as Jefferson's philosophical successor. Jefferson had questioned the constitutionality of the draconian Alien and Sedition Acts of 1798 and pardoned critics of the Adams administration convicted of sedition once he became president. (After the Sedition Act expired on his succession, however, Jefferson quietly supported state prosecutions of his opponents.) In his letter to Boardman, Jefferson had criticized a Connecticut pastor who insisted that the utterance of "an opinion with the wanton view to excite broils and cause needless dissentions, or to influence others to do evil" should be banned. And in his First Inaugural, in addition to declaring that "every difference of opinion is not a difference of principle" ("We are all Republicans, we are all Federalists"), Jefferson went on to articulate a faith in the power of education to allow citizens in American democracy to develop their faculties of reason and self-government that anticipated Brandeis's own.[94] As Jefferson wrote of his fellow citizens "entertaining a due sense of our equal right to the use of our own faculties," Brandeis wrote that "[t]hose who won our independence believed that the final end of the state was to make men free to develop their faculties."[95]

Like Brandeis, Jefferson held a view of psychology that was inseparable from his view of political economy. Jefferson believed that human nature was divided into separate "faculties"— from passions at the bottom to reason at the top—and that the purpose of the state was to free men to pursue the happiness that they could obtain only by developing their faculties of reason. This was why he supported both the protection of the natural rights of religious liberty and the public provision of education to all citizens of Virginia.[96] It is also why he opposed, at least in theory, the suppression of differences of opinion and favored the protection of political dissent. In the First Inaugural, he declared "that though the will of the majority is in all cases to prevail, that will to be rightful must be reasonable; that the minority possess their equal rights, which equal law must protect, and to violate would be oppression."[97] Brandeis compressed this insistence on reasoned deliberation into the statement that "those who won our revolution" believed "that in its government the deliberative forces should prevail over the arbitrary."[98]

Jefferson's First Inaugural warned of the dangers of both "religious intolerance" and "political intolerance" and emphasized the importance of protecting constitutional rights, including "freedom of religion; freedom of the press, and freedom of person under the protection of the habeas corpus, and trial by juries impartially selected."[99] Brandeis, too, connects the protection of rights with the importance of reasoned deliberation as he completes his remarkable paragraph in *Whitney*. "Those who won our independence," he wrote,

> recognized the risks to which all human institutions are subject. But they knew that order cannot be secured merely through fear of punishment for its infraction; that it is hazardous to discourage thought, hope and imagination; that fear breeds repression; that repression breeds hate; that hate menaces stable government; that the path of safety lies in the opportunity to discuss freely supposed grievances and proposed remedies; and that the fitting remedy for evil counsels is good ones. Believing in the power of reason as applied through public discussion, they eschewed silence coerced by law—the argument of force in its worst form. Recognizing the occasional tyrannies of governing majorities, they amended the Constitution so that free speech and assembly should be guaranteed.[100]

In his final evocation of Jefferson, Brandeis explicitly connects the importance of reasoned discussion and counter-speech with the value of public education. And because he is examining the circumstances under which advocacy of revolution can be made a crime, he refers explicitly to Jefferson and his fellow icons of the American Revolution not as founders but as revolutionaries:

> Those who won our independence by revolution were not cowards. They did not fear political change. They did not exalt order at the cost of liberty. To courageous, self-reliant men, with confidence in the power of free and fearless reasoning applied through the processes of popular government, no danger flowing from speech can be deemed clear and present unless the incidence of the evil apprehended is so imminent that it may befall before there is opportunity for full discussion. If there be time to expose through discussion the falsehood and fallacies, to avert the evil by the processes of education, the remedy to be applied is more speech, not enforced silence. Only an emergency can justify repression. Such must be the rule if authority is to be reconciled with freedom. Such, in my opinion, is the command of the Constitution. It is therefore always open to Americans to challenge a law abridging free speech and assembly by showing that there was no emergency justifying it.[101]

In other words, Brandeis's faith in deliberation was based on his conviction that if people were given time and opportunity to engage in "public discussion," then "the power of reason" would prevail. Like Jefferson, he stressed the importance of combating errors of opinion with courage, reason, and deliberation, rather than fear. In his *Whitney* concurrence, Brandeis argues that free speech is necessary both for "the discovery and spread of political truth" and for men to "develop their faculties." There is no greater statement of faith in America of the value of counter-speech as the best response to hate speech or subversive speech ("more speech, not enforced silence"), the ability of "the processes of education" to expose falsehoods, as long as there is time for "full discussion," and the power of "courageous, self-reliant" citizens to govern themselves and develop their faculties by applying "free and fearless reasoning . . . through the processes of popular government."[102] It is the perfect expression of Brandeis's Jeffersonian creed.

Jefferson was a significant influence in *Whitney*, but not Brandeis's only influence. He asked his law clerk James Landis to examine the calls by abolitionists for resistance to the fugitive slave laws.[103] And Brandeis's argument "that the greatest menace to freedom is an inert people; that public discussion is a political duty"[104] offers a defense of free speech rooted in the classical republicanism of the ancient Greeks, a defense that rests on the idea that people are capable of collective virtue and that the goal of political deliberation is the common good.

Brandeis's law clerk Paul Freund noted that one sentence in Brandeis's peroration about the framers' views of free speech— "they believed liberty to be the secret of happiness and courage to be the secret of liberty"—comes almost directly from Pericles' funeral oration.[105] (Pericles to the Athenians, in Alfred Zimmern's translation, which was Brandeis's bible: "For you now it remains to rival what they have done and, knowing the secret of happiness to be freedom and the secret of freedom a brave heart, not idly to stand aside from the enemy's onset.")[106] Philippa Strum also notes that Brandeis's favorite verses, the ones he quoted most frequently, were from Euripides' *The Bacchae*.[107] His law partner Samuel Warren had sent him the lines in 1890, the year the two men published their famous article on the right to privacy, and Brandeis felt they expressed his views of public service and the duties of citizenship better than any other:

> Thou has heard men scorn the city, call her wild
> Of counsel, mad; thou has seen the fire of morn
> Flash from her eyes in answer to their scorn!
> Come toil on toil, 'tis this that makes her grand.

Peril on peril! And common states that stand
In caution, twilight cities, dimly wise—
Ye know them; for no light is in their eyes!
Go forth, my son, and help.[108]

Brandeis's opinion had immediate reverberations. A month after the decision came down, the governor of California pardoned Anita Whitney on the grounds that it would be unthinkable to punish her for her political activities. He called free speech "the indispensable birthright of every American," quoting at length from Brandeis's most memorable paragraphs.[109] And Brandeis's core ideas—that no idea or opinion is too evil to be expressed in public debate, and that speech on public affairs cannot be regulated because it is intemperate or unfair—were embraced by the Supreme Court in cases like *New York Times v. Sullivan* (1964).[110] Brandeis's other central arguments—that citizens have a duty to participate in public affairs and to listen to one another's opinions; that opinions have to be absolutely protected under law because judges are ill equipped to distinguish between opinions and facts; that counter-speech by citizens, not censorship by courts, is the best remedy for false opinions and ideas; and that free speech produces better democratic citizens—all were eventually embraced by the Supreme Court as well.[111]

When Brandeis issued his *Whitney* opinion in May 1927, both his personal and professional accomplishments were abundant. The previous November, he had celebrated his seventieth birthday, responding to warm greetings from friends, including Holmes and Edward Filene, as well as the birth of his first grandchild, Louis Brandeis Gilbert, whom Brandeis called "the Crown Prince." Susan Brandeis Gilbert, who argued a case before the Supreme Court in 1925, gave Brandeis two more grandchildren, Alice, born in 1928, and Frank, born in 1930. Her sister, Elizabeth, had one son, Walter Brandeis Raushenbush, who was born in 1928 and raised as a Christian by his father, Paul

Raushenbush, whose own father had been a pastor of social justice. (Walter Raushenbush's son, Paul Brandeis Raushenbush, also became a Christian minister, executive editor of Global Spirituality and Religion at the *Huffington Post*, and author of an essay about his interfaith upbringing called "Why Don't You Just Convert?")[112] In 1965, Walter Raushenbush recalled summers with his grandparents on Cape Cod, rejecting criticisms of A. L. Todd's recently published book on Brandeis's confirmation battle, *Justice on Trial*, for depicting Brandeis as a saint. "My grandmother, several years younger, was a lovely but quite human lady, very able to become irritated with a doubtless impertinent boy, and also very able to irritate him in turn," Raushenbush recalled. (In particular, he was irked by the small portions of chicken that his grandmother meted out to her grandchildren because she thought they were the right size for her husband, who had tried but failed to carve the chicken properly himself.) "By contrast, I have no recollection of ever being angry at LDB, or of even seeing him show anger."[113] Raushenbush remembered Brandeis's generosity with his time during the August vacations. Brandeis's other grandchildren and great nephews had similarly warm members of summers with their doting grandfather, and his extraordinary ability to focus on small details in their lives, such as the name of a favorite horse.

When Brandeis returned to the court in October 1927, therefore, he had plenty of reasons for satisfaction. But the First Amendment vision that he offered in *Whitney* created a dilemma for Brandeis: as Neil Richards has noted, it is the source of the strongest argument for why the right to privacy that Brandeis and Samuel Warren had proposed as young men violates the Constitution.[114] That right allowed celebrities to sue newspapers for the emotional injury produced by the publication of truthful but embarrassing information; the opinion held that the avoidance of hurt feelings can never trump the public's interest in uninhibited public debate. The right to privacy Brandeis proposed in 1890 required judges to decide what speech was in the public interest and what speech was not; the *Whitney* opinion insisted that the decision about what speech was fit for public discussion should be made by speakers rather than by courts. As a result, Richards concludes, Brandeis changed his mind about the dignitary right he had proposed as a young man and came to embrace a different conception of privacy—rooted in the importance of freedom of thought and opinion—that supports the First Amendment rather than clashing with it.

Although Brandeis had second thoughts about his youthful article soon after he wrote it, his evolution toward the view that courts should not be able to restrain the publication of true but embarrassing facts and opinion, even when they violated privacy and dignity, was evident soon after he joined the Supreme Court in the *International News Service v. Associated Press* case from 1918.[115] The Associated Press had sued the International News Service for copying breaking news items that had originally been gathered by the AP and published in its member newspapers. The Supreme Court, in an opinion by Justice Pitney, held that although facts can't be privately owned, news reports "must be regarded as *quasi* property" whose value depended on their freshness.[116]

Justice Brandeis dissented, arguing that "the fact that a product of the mind has cost its producer money and labor, and has a value for which others are willing to pay, is not sufficient to ensure to it this legal attribute of property."[117] Here again, he was channeling Jefferson, who had expressed skepticism about using private property as the basis for copyright protections, because he feared that state-granted monopolies over the way ideas were expressed could lead to the suppression of the ideas themselves. Albert Jay Nock reports that Jefferson never patented any of his inventions, "never having thought of monopolizing by patent any useful idea which happens to offer itself to me."[118] Instead, Jefferson published descriptions of his inventions because of his abhorrence for money made from monopoly of any kind. As Jefferson wrote, "If nature has made any one thing less susceptible than all others of exclusive property, it is the action of a thinking property called an idea, which an individual may exclusively possess as long as he keeps it to himself, but the moment it is divulged, it forces itself into the possession of everyone and the receiver cannot dispose himself of it."[119] Jefferson insisted that ideas had no natural scarcity and their value did not diminish when they were shared. "Its peculiar character, too, is that no one possesses the less, because every other possesses the whole of it. He who receives an idea from me, receives instruction himself without lessening mine; as he who lights his taper at mine, receives light without darkening me."[120] That is why Jefferson—who, one scholar says, would have applauded the file-sharing service Napster—proposed to amend the copyright and patent protections in the Constitution to allow monopolies only "to persons for their own productions in literature, and their own invention in the arts," and only for a limited term.[121] To allow monopolies for any other purpose, Jefferson feared, could lead to centralization and the suppression of thought and opinion.

For Brandeis, the Supreme Court's recognition of a quasi-property right in news gathering vindicated Jefferson's fears. He wrote in his dissent in *International News Service* that that the extension of property rights in ideas could lead to a corresponding curtailment of the free use of knowledge and of ideas. As Brandeis put it, "The general rule of law is, that the noblest of human productions—knowledge, truths ascertained, conceptions, and ideas—became, after voluntary communication to others, free as the air to common use. Upon these incorporeal productions the attribute of property is continued after such communication only in certain classes of cases where public policy has seemed to demand it."[122] In particular, Brandeis feared that the four hundred newspapers that were members of the International Service might operate in countries where news gathering was forbidden during World War I; without the ability to republish items from the AP, their members would be denied access to crucial facts of public importance. And Brandeis questioned the ability of courts to distinguish between the private interests of a media company and the public's interest in receiving news. "[W]ith the increasing complexity of society, the public interest tends to become omnipresent; and the problems presented by new demands for justice cease to be simple."[123] This conclusion undermined the central claim in Brandeis's original article on the right to privacy: that courts could and should try to balance free speech against other values, such as privacy and dignity, by deciding which truthful publications served the public interests and which did not.[124]

Brandeis continued to develop his new understanding of the balance between free speech and privacy in *Gilbert v. Minnesota* (1920), in which the court, with Holmes concurring, upheld the conviction under a state law of a man who made a speech at the Nonpartisan League critical of the war effort.[125] In his dissent, Brandeis, for the first time, emphasized the connection between the privacy of the home, protected by the Fourth Amendment, and the various rights in the First Amendment, including freedom of speech, freedom of assembly, freedom of religious conscience, and freedom of thought and opinion. He objected to the fact that the law forbade "a single person" from speaking out against enlistment "in any place . . . no matter what the relation of the parties may be. Thus the statute invades the privacy and freedom of the home. Father and mother may not follow the promptings of religious belief, of conscience or of conviction, and teach son or daughter the doctrine of pacifism. If they do, any police officer may summarily arrest them."[126]

Brandeis also worried that other citizens might criticize

the war before groups who had gathered for other private meetings, and they, too, could be arrested for their beliefs rather than their acts. "The prohibition is made to apply whatever the motive, the intention, or the purpose of him who teaches," he objected. "It applies alike to the preacher in the pulpit, the professor at the university, the speaker at a political meeting, the lecturer at a society or club gathering. Whatever the nature of the meeting and whether it be public or private, the prohibition is absolute. . . . For the statute aims to prevent not acts, but beliefs."[127] In *Gilbert*, Brandeis went on to suggest that privacy of thought and opinion, far from threatening free speech and democracy, could in fact reinforce them. "The right of a citizen of the United States to take part, for his own or the country's benefit, in the making of federal laws and in the conduct of the government, necessarily includes the right to speak or write about them; to endeavor to make his own opinion concerning laws existing or contemplated prevail; and, to this end, to teach the truth as he sees it," Brandeis wrote.[128] Anticipating his conclusion in *Whitney* that engaging in political speech was both a right and a duty, he wrote that "full and free exercise" of the rights of speech and assembly by the citizen "is ordinarily also his duty; for its exercise is more important to the nation than it is to himself. Like the course of the heavenly bodies, harmony in national life is a resultant of the struggle between contending forces. In frank expression of conflicting opinion lies the greatest promise of wisdom in governmental action; and in suppression lies ordinarily the greatest peril."[129]

Brandeis's mature understanding of the importance of privacy from government surveillance as a precondition for freedom of thought and political dissent appears in his most memorable attempt to adapt constitutional values to changes in technology. Just a year after *Whitney*, in the 1928 case *Olmstead v. United States*, the Supreme Court first encountered the problem of the constitutionality of electronic searches.[130] When the federal government began to tap phones in an effort to enforce Prohibition, it indicted a Seattle policeman turned successful bootlegger named Olmstead, whose business importing illegal booze from England by way of Vancouver led to revenue of more than $2 million a year. Olmstead protested that the wiretaps violated the Fourth Amendment, which protects the right of the people to be secure in their "persons, houses, papers, and effects."[131] In fact, wiretapping was illegal under Washington state law, and both Attorney General Stone and FBI director J. Edgar Hoover had officially repudiated it. Nevertheless, federal agents, frustrated in their other attempts to enforce the Prohibition laws, tapped Olmstead's phone for five months, producing 775 pages of typewritten notes on his conversations with suppliers and clients, which led to more than ninety indictments.[132] In a literal-minded majority opinion, Chief Justice William Howard Taft disagreed with Olmstead's argument. The Fourth Amendment, he said, was originally understood to forbid only searches or seizures accompanied by physical trespass. The agents had not trespassed on Olmsted's property when they placed wiretaps on the phone lines in the streets near his house, Taft held, and conversations were not tangible "effects" that could be searched or seized.

Brandeis was acutely interested in the question of technological espionage: he asked Herbert Croly, the editor of the *New Republic*, to investigate examples of employers hiring spies to get information about workers who were union activists, and he wanted Felix Frankfurter to assign a student to investigate the founders' views about secret political operatives.[133] In his visionary dissenting opinion in *Olmstead*, Brandeis grappled with the challenge of translating the founders' late eighteenth-century views about privacy into a twentieth-century world. As private life had begun to be conducted over the wires in the age of radio, he observed, telephone conversations contained even more intimate information than sealed letters, which the

Supreme Court had held in the nineteenth century could not be opened without a warrant. To protect the same amount of privacy that the framers of the Fourth and Fifth amendments intended to protect, Brandeis concluded, it had become necessary to translate those amendments into the new problematics, extending them to prohibit warrantless searches and seizures of conversations over the wires, even if the invasions occurred without physical invasions. It took the Supreme Court—and Congress—decades to answer Brandeis's challenge.

At the time of the framing of the Constitution, Brandeis noted, the government had to break into homes to seize private papers, but changes in technology had now made it possible to invade privacy without trespassing on private property. At this point, Brandeis wanted to cite a new device called television, recently developed by General Electric, but he misunderstood it as a two-way video technology. (He anticipated Skype!) "And now, with the advent of television, it will be possible to peer into the innermost recesses of the home," he wrote in an early draft. A skeptical law clerk—Henry Friendly again—persuaded him to remove the reference after looking into the matter at the Library of Congress and concluding that "you can't just beam a television set out of somebody's home and see what they're doing."[134]

Today, of course, you can. And in a remarkably prescient passage, Brandeis seemed to look forward to the age of web cams and cyberspace, predicting that technologies of surveillance were likely to progress far beyond wiretapping.[135] Unless the Constitution could address the new technologies, it would protect less privacy and freedom in the twentieth (and twenty-first) century than the framers of the Constitution expected of the eighteenth century. Here are Brandeis's prophetic reflections about how electronic surveillance could threaten the privacy of communication far more than the general warrants and writs of assistance of the eighteenth century issued by King

George's henchmen and denounced in 1761 by the Massachusetts patriot James Otis for allowing massive fishing expeditions
into private papers:

> Discovery and invention have made it possible for the gov-
> ernment, by means far more effective than stretching upon
> the rack, to obtain disclosure in court of what is whispered in
> the closet. Moreover, "in the application of a Constitution,
> our contemplation cannot be only of what has been, but of
> what may be." The progress of science in furnishing the gov-
> ernment with means of espionage is not likely to stop with
> wire tapping. Ways may some day be developed by which the
> Government, without removing papers from secret drawers,
> can reproduce them in court, and by which it will be enabled
> to expose to a jury the most intimate occurrences of the
> home. Advances in the psychic and related sciences may
> bring means of exploring unexpressed beliefs, thoughts and
> emotions. "That places the liberty of every man in the hands
> of every petty officer" was said by James Otis of much lesser
> intrusions than these. To Lord Camden a far slighter intru-
> sion seemed "subversive of all the comforts of society." Can
> it be that the Constitution affords no protection against such
> invasions of individual security?[136]

This extraordinary passage anticipates the development of
functional magnetic resonance imaging, or fMRI, technologies, such as brain scans, which can indeed, with increasing
precision, reveal "unexpressed beliefs, thoughts and emotions,"
such as whether someone is thinking of faces or places. Here
Brandeis connects the privacy of the mind, or cognitive liberty,
with the importance of protecting the political dissent that
sparked the American Revolution. To make the connection explicit, Brandeis invokes *Boyd v. United States* (1886), which he
called a "case that will be remembered as long as civil liberty
lives in the United States."[137] After reviewing the history behind the Fourth and Fifth amendments, and citing scholarship

by Justice Horace Gray[138] (for whom Brandeis had clerked) on James Otis and the writs of assistance, the *Boyd* court, too, had quoted Lord Camden's judgment in the trial of John Wilkes. Even without a physical trespass, the *Boyd* court had stressed, "any forcible and compulsory extortion of a man's own testimony or of his private papers to be used as evidence of a crime or to forfeit his goods" violates the Constitution. "In this regard the Fourth and Fifth Amendments run almost into each other."[139]

Brandeis then implicitly invoked Jefferson, connecting the cognitive liberty protected by the Fourth and Fifth amendments with the natural right to pursue happiness invoked in the Declaration of Independence and protected by the First Amendment as well as the Fourth and Fifth.

> The makers of our Constitution undertook to secure conditions favorable to the pursuit of happiness. They recognized the significance of man's spiritual nature, of his feelings, and of his intellect. They knew that only a part of the pain, pleasure and satisfactions of life are to be found in material things. They sought to protect Americans in their beliefs, their thoughts, their emotions and their sensations. They conferred, as against the government, the right to be let alone—the most comprehensive of rights and the right most valued by civilized men. To protect that right, every unjustifiable intrusion by the Government upon the privacy of the individual, whatever the means employed, must be deemed a violation of the Fourth Amendment. And the use, as evidence in a criminal proceeding, of facts ascertained by such intrusion must be deemed a violation of the Fifth.[140]

In this passage, Brandeis has reconceived the right to privacy, which he called as early as 1890 "the right to be let alone," from a right that threatens free speech by allowing celebrities to sue the press for hurt feelings to one that supports free speech by allowing citizens to sue the government when it surveils their "beliefs, their thoughts, their emotions and their sensations." Brandeis recognized that surveillance could inhibit not only the political dissent of citizens but also their "spiritual nature," their "feelings," and their "intellect" in ways that could undermine their "pursuit of happiness." Brandeis also had come to realize the importance of anonymity and freedom of thought as preconditions for self-governance. The scholar Neil Richards synthesizes Brandeis's new conception of the right to be let alone into a theory of what he calls "intellectual privacy," which he defines as "protection from surveillance or interference when we are engaged in the processes of generating ideas."[141] In other words, Brandeis came to believe that we don't need to choose between privacy and free speech because, far from clashing with the democratic values of public debate, intellectual privacy is essential to it.[142]

Brandeis's opinion may have helped Roy Olmstead, just as his earlier opinion had helped Anita Whitney. After serving the four years of his sentence, Olmstead received a full pardon from President Franklin D. Roosevelt—recognition, perhaps, of the popular distaste for mass wiretapping sparked by the failed experiment of Prohibition.[143] And later in the twentieth century, the Supreme Court came to endorse Brandeis's view that the Fourth Amendment protects people, not places, from state surveillance. But it has yet to embrace Brandeis's conviction that ubiquitous surveillance is unconstitutional, whether or not it is authorized by a valid warrant. Brandeis stressed that "writs of assistance and general warrants are but puny instruments of tyranny and oppression when compared with wiretapping," and that dragnet searches could not be justified even if neutral magistrates blessed them.[144] The Supreme Court, by contrast, has suggested that ubiquitous surveillance with a valid warrant satisfies the Fourth Amendment. In the process, the court has failed to heed Brandeis's caution against an "unduly literal" construction of the constitutional text. Instead, Brandeis insisted, "Clauses guaranteeing to the individual protection against specific abuses of power must have a similar capacity of adaptation to a changing world."[145]

Brandeis's opinion in *Olmstead* contains one final note that shows his moralism at its most steely and galvanizing. In addition to his constitutional objections, Brandeis insisted that the evidence obtained by wiretapping should have been suppressed because it violated Washington state law and was not authorized by Congress or the Department of Justice. Government officials, he emphasized in one of his most memorable passages, should not be allowed to benefit from their "unclean hands": "Experience should teach us to be most on our guard to protect liberty when the government's purposes are beneficent. Men born to freedom are naturally alert to repel invasion of their liberty by evil-minded rulers. The greatest dangers to liberty lurk in insidious encroachment by men of zeal, well-meaning but without understanding."[146]

In full prophetic mode, Brandeis concluded with a stern warning about the dangers of allowing the state to profit by its own ethical violations:

> Decency, security, and liberty alike demand that government officials shall be subjected to the same rules of conduct that are commands to the citizen. In a government of laws, existence of the government will be imperiled if it fails to observe the law scrupulously. Our Government is the potent, the omnipresent teacher. For good or for ill, it teaches the whole people by its example. Crime is contagious. If the Government becomes a lawbreaker, it breeds contempt for law; it invites every man to become a law unto himself; it invites anarchy. To declare that in the administration of the criminal law the end justifies the means—to declare that the Government may commit crimes in order to secure the con-

viction of a private criminal—would bring terrible retribution. Against that pernicious doctrine this court should resolutely set its face.[147]

Here, Brandeis was not exactly restrained: the court has not generally excluded evidence illegally obtained in a search of suspect A that is later used against suspect B, allowing the government to profit from its own wrongdoing. But he was, once again, prescient. Contemporary experience, rooted in the protests against police violence in minority communities, confirms that people are most likely to obey the law when they trust the legitimacy of the government officials administering it.[148] The government is indeed "the omnipresent teacher," and teaching by example, it can inspire respect or contempt for democratic government. The search for a government that could embody these Jeffersonian ideals of ethics, respect for human flourishing, and democratic participation on a small scale led Brandeis, late in life, to turn his prophetic gaze toward the Holy Land and Zionism.

4

◆│◆│◆

The Perfect Citizen in the Perfect State

BRANDEIS'S JEFFERSONIAN IDEALS about democratic participation and small-scale self-government eventually came to focus on a distant place where he dared to believe that they could be achieved. That place was Palestine. Raised as an unobservant and nonpracticing Jew, Brandeis experienced a remarkable personal and intellectual transformation in his fifties. He became the head of the Zionist movement in America.

How did he become a Zionist? Although he never denied his Judaism, Brandeis had identified only marginally with Jews since his childhood in Louisville, in keeping with the secular tradition of his ancestors. This changed in 1910. "Throughout long years which represent my own life, I have been to a great extent separated from the Jews," Brandeis declared in 1914 during his remarks at an emergency meeting of American Zionists at the Hotel Marseilles in New York, which he agreed to chair at the request of the young Zionist and cultural critic Horace

Kallen. "I am very ignorant in things Jewish."[1] But he went on to say that "recent experiences, public and professional, have taught me this: I find Jews possessed of those very qualities which we of the twentieth century seek to develop in our struggle for justice and democracy; a deep moral feeling which makes them capable of noble acts; a deep sense of the brotherhood of man; and a high intelligence, the fruit of three thousand years of civilization." All of these experiences convinced Brandeis "that the Jewish People should be preserved."[2]

What were the "public and professional" experiences that transformed Brandeis's outlook from indifference about Judaism to crusading Zionism? By his own account, he had come to Zionism through Americanism. Before 1910, Brandeis, like many upper-class American Jews of central European heritage, was skeptical of Zionism because of his concerns about "dual loyalties" and his support for melting-pot assimilationism. His first public comments about Judaism can be found in 1905, in a speech commemorating the 250th anniversary of Jewish settlement in America at the New Century Club in New York. In the speech, "What Loyalty Demands," Brandeis echoed Theodore Roosevelt and Woodrow Wilson in warning of the dangers of separatism. "In a country whose constitution prohibits discrimination on account of race or creed, there is no place for what President Roosevelt has called hyphenated Americans," Brandeis declared. "Habits of living or of thought which tend to keep alive difference of origin or to classify men according to their religious beliefs are inconsistent with the American ideal of brotherhood, and are disloyal."[3]

In the fall of 1910, Brandeis first met Jacob de Haas, the editor of the *Jewish Advocate* in Boston, who had been summoned with other local reporters by the public relations agent of the Savings Bank Insurance campaign. De Haas was the American secretary of Theodor Herzl, whose 1896 book *Der Judenstaat* had proclaimed the Jewish people's need for a state of their own.[4] He had come to America as Herzl's representative to convene the First Zionist Congress in Chicago the following year; after immigrating to America in 1902, he eventually moved to Boston. De Haas was initially ambivalent about the press roundup for Savings Bank Insurance—"the theme seemed both dry and remote,"[5] as he put it later in his biography of Brandeis—but the interview was a success. After his interview with de Haas, Brandeis made his first recorded statement on Zionism: "I have a great deal of sympathy for the movement and am deeply interested in the outcome of the propaganda," Brandeis declared in the *Advocate*. "I believe that the Jews can be just as much of a priest people today as they ever were in prophetic days."[6]

Brandeis was especially receptive to Zionism in 1910, having been moved by his experience working with eastern European Jews on both sides of a cloak makers' strike in New York earlier that year. During the negotiations, both the Jewish garment workers and their Jewish employers impressed him—with their intellectualism, idealism, and commitment to industrial democracy as well as their accounts of the anti-Semitism that had led them to emigrate from eastern Europe. The dispute was over the "closed shop"—whether nonunion workers could apply for jobs—and Brandeis brought the two sides together around the idea of the "preferential union shop," whereby union members would be favored but nonmembers could apply. The strike was Brandeis's first real contact with eastern European Jews, and he was deeply impressed by their ethical attitude and capacity for idealism and empathy. "What struck me most was that each side had a great capacity for placing themselves in the other fellows' shoes," Brandeis told de Haas. "They argued, but they were willing to listen to argument. That set these people apart in my experience in labor disputes."[7] Identifying with the earnest garment workers, Brandeis relaxed after an arduous day of negotiations by indulging in a glass of beer with them and telling them war stories about the Pinchot-Ballinger affair.[8] For the first time, at the age of fifty-four, he had gained faith in the Jewish immigrant masses and become conscious of his own Jewishness. Still, Felix Frankfurter noted, Brandeis would require "long brooding" before he could commit himself to Zionism.[9]

A second meeting with Jacob de Haas in August 1912 accelerated Brandeis's embrace of the Zionist cause. De Haas visited Brandeis in South Yarmouth at his summer house. (Brandeis always left the city for the month of August, writing, "I soon learned that I could do twelve months' work in eleven months, but not in twelve.")[10] De Haas had come to talk about fundraising for Woodrow Wilson, but on the way to the train station after the interview, he asked whether Brandeis was related to Lewis Dembitz. When Brandeis said yes—he had changed his middle name to Dembitz to honor his revered uncle—de Haas replied twice that "Lewis N. Dembitz was a noble Jew,"[11] because he had been one of the first American supporters of Theodor Herzl's plans to establish a Jewish homeland. Brandeis was pleased and intrigued by this tribute and promptly invited de Haas back to his cottage for lunch. There he learned that Dembitz, whom Brandeis had known as an abolitionist, a delegate to the Republican convention of 1860, and the only observant Jew in his extended family, was a committed Zionist. He urged de Haas to educate him about Theodor Herzl and the Zionist movement[12] and began a rigorous program of self-study. As de Haas put it, "[F]rom that first interview he began an earnest quest for knowledge. . . . He studied the footnotes as well as the printed page of Jewish history and made the Zionist idea his own."[13] Brandeis later told Felix Frankfurter that de Haas had kindled his interest in Zionism and declared de Haas to be "the maker of American Zionism."[14]

In fact, Brandeis became the maker of American Zionism. But he assumed that role only after meeting another Zionist and reading several life-changing books. The Zionist was Aaron Aaronsohn, the head of the Jewish Agricultural Experiment Station in Palestine, known as "the pioneer of scientific agriculture" for his discovery of "wild wheat."[15] Brandeis met Aaronsohn after hearing him lecture on agriculture in Chicago in 1912. The lecture hit its mark, as did the conversation afterward. In a speech called "To Be a Jew" delivered the following year, Brandeis, who was not known to gush, described Aaronsohn as "one of the most interesting, brilliant and remarkable men I have ever met . . . [who] made what is considered one of the most remarkable and useful discoveries in recent years, and possibly of all times."[16] Brandeis's Jeffersonian agrarianism was drawn to Aaronsohn's discovery of "wild wheat," which Brandeis thought could "immeasurably increase" the quantity of food available across the globe because wheat could now be cultivated in soil previously considered too arid. His sense of the Jews as a uniquely ethical people was kindled by Aaronsohn's report that "not a single crime was known to have been committed by one of our people" in Palestine during the past thirty years. When Brandeis asked him why, he replied: "Every member of those communities is brought up to realize his obligation to his people. He is told of the great difficulties it passed through, and of the long years of martyrdom it experienced. All that is best in Jewish history is made to live in him, and by this means he is imbued with a high sense of honor and responsibility for the whole people."[17]

Although Aaronsohn was strongly opposed to socialism, Brandeis was thrilled to learn from him that Jews were applying the principles he valued most—scientific agriculture and self-governing, small-scale democracy—in Palestine. As David Riesman wrote to me years later, "Brandeis was . . . a Zionist, in contrast to the assimilated German Jews (He belonged to a sect even more assimilationist than Americanized German Jews in general). This is because he saw Palestine as rural, made up of cooperatives rooted in the land, which he interpreted as not very different from the feeling of dedicated Southerners toward the land."[18] After hearing Aaronsohn's talk, Brandeis gave his first speech supporting Zionism to the Young Men's Hebrew Association in Chelsea. "We should all support the Zionist movement, although you or I do not think of settling in Palestine, for there has developed and can develop in that land to a higher degree, the spirit of which Mr. Aaronsohn speaks."[19] Brandeis's idea—that American Jews had a duty to support Palestine but no obligation to move to Palestine—was, for the Zionist movement, an intellectual breakthrough.

Fired up by the example of de Haas and Aaronsohn, Brandeis began a program of systematic reading on Zionism, starting with the work of Horace Kallen, the leading American theorist of cultural pluralism, who was also one of the first American Zionists. Brandeis had first met Kallen when the younger man was a Harvard undergraduate at the turn of the century, a time when teachers such as William James were convincing Kallen of the influence of the Hebrew Bible on the Puritan mind and the American founding fathers.[20] These Yankee intellectuals led Kallen from Cotton Mather to Jefferson to Zionism; he concluded that Zionism would extend the Jeffersonian values of liberty and equality to all members of a self-governing Jewish state.[21] Far from being inconsistent with American ideals, he concluded, American support for Zionism could help to spread them across the globe. In 1913, Kallen sent Brandeis an essay he had written, "Judaism, Hebraism, Zionism."[22] In this essay, Kallen introduced an idea that Brandeis would later develop: that preserving a distinct Jewish identity in Palestine was the best way to preserve a unique Hebraic culture that could enrich both America and the world. As Kallen recalled of Brandeis much later, in a 1972 interview, "The important thing for him was that the proclaimed antagonism between Americanism and Zionist was a false claim—it didn't have to be. . . . Because to begin with he believed that he could not be an American and a Zionist completely. Then he came to believe that he could, and that he would, and he did."[23]

Kallen rejected the assimilationist ideology in "Democracy versus the Melting Pot," a 1915 essay in the *Nation* that he later incorporated into his book *Cultural Pluralism*. He wrote that members of immigrant groups could not, and should not, try to shed their unique cultures and values, since by retaining their hyphenated identities and personalities they could better contribute to the diversity of the American whole. Kallen concluded that preserving group differences was the best way of achieving the Jeffersonian equality promised in the Declaration of Independence. "As in an orchestra," he wrote, "every type of instrument has its specific timbre and tonality. . . . [A]s every type has its appropriate theme and melody in the whole symphony, so in society, each ethnic group is the natural instrument . . . and the harmony and dissonances and discords of them all may make the symphony of civilization."[24] Kallen also insisted that Jewish immigrants, as they became free Americans, tended to become more Jewish, not less. "The most eagerly American of the immigrant groups are also the most autonomous and self-conscious in spirit and culture."[25] This insight helped Brandeis to reconcile two ideals—Zionism and Americanism—that he had previously found to be in conflict. For American Jews to support a Jewish homeland, he now concluded, would create better Americans and better Jews at the same time.

In addition to helping Brandeis to solve the problem of dual loyalty, Kallen also helped to connect Brandeis to yet another intellectual influence who proved to be decisive in his thinking about Zionism: Alfred Zimmern.[26] An Oxford classicist and active Zionist, Zimmern had recently published *The Greek Commonwealth* (1912), which Brandeis read during the winter of 1913–14. Brandeis later recalled it was his only recreation during the New Haven Railroad investigation and that it pleased him more than anything he had read, except for Gilbert Murray's translation of *The Bacchae*.[27] The book helped Brandeis unite his interests in ancient Greece, Jeffersonian democracy, and Zionism, and he recommended it to everyone he encountered—from law clerks to family and friends—for the rest of his life.[28] Like Zimmern, Brandeis came to see the Jewish return to Palestine as a fulfillment of the democratic ideals he admired in fifth-century Athens.

The similarities between Brandeis's and Zimmern's vision of the possibility of democracy in Palestine and Greece are striking. As Philippa Strum has noted, Zimmern believed that geography and economic conditions were a central determinant of culture, and that Palestine's geography, like that of Athens, made it ripe for a democratic society. By juxtaposing Jewish sources—from the Old Testament, the prophets, and Jewish history—alongside Greek sources, Zimmern suggested that classical civilizations of both cultures shared many of the same values.[29] With Zimmern's guidance, Brandeis came to view Palestine as a society that could achieve the kind of small-scale Jeffersonian agrarian democracy that had reached its fullest expression in fifth-century Athens and that allowed men and women to develop their faculties of reason and self-government on a human scale.

Reading *The Greek Commonwealth* today, one can imagine Brandeis nodding with appreciation and intellectual excitement as he found his ideas about the importance of geography and economics for democratic self-government illustrated and confirmed on page after page. Zimmern's discussion "Politics and the Development of Citizenship" begins with this epigraph: "They spend their bodies, as mere external tools, in the City's service, and count their minds as most truly their own when employed on her behalf."[30] Brandeis embraced, as we saw in the introduction, Zimmern's definition of leisure as time spent away from work on creative and intellectual pursuits that made personal and political self-government possible. And Brandeis found in Zimmern's account of Periclean Athens other axioms that reinforced his Jeffersonian belief that self-government on a human scale could be realized in Palestine.

Zimmern's chapter "Self-Government, or the Rule of the People," for example, stressed the duty of political participation and small-scale deliberation: "Democracy is meaningless unless it involves the serious and steady co-operation of large numbers of citizens in the actual work of government."[31] Compare Brandeis on banker management: "[N]o man can serve two masters" and "[A] man cannot at the same time do many things well."[32]

In his chapter "Happiness, or the Rule of Love," Zimmern notes that "the extraordinary resemblance between Lincoln's speech at Gettysburg and Pericles's has often been noticed."[33] He then translates the funeral oration in words that clearly moved Brandeis in composing his *Whitney* concurrence, emphasizing that only by avoiding gossip and focusing on matters of public concern can citizens be fully engaged in public deliberation: "Our constitution is named a democracy, because it is in the hands not of the few but of the many. But our laws secure equal justice for all in their private disputes, and our public opinion welcomes and honors talent in every branch of achievement, not for any sectional reason but on grounds of excellence alone. And as we give free play to all in our public life, so we carry the same spirit into our daily relations with one another. We have no black looks or angry words for our neighbor if he enjoys himself in his own way."[34]

Up until this point, Brandeis could, and did, translate Zimmern's vision of Periclean Athens into his own vision of Jeffersonian America. "What are the American ideals?" Brandeis asked in "True Americanism." "They are the development of the individual for his own and the common good; the development of the individual through liberty, and the attainment of the common good through democracy and social justice."[35] But there were aspects of Jefferson's agrarian America that could never be recovered in Wilson's industrial America. Brandeis was especially struck, therefore, by Zimmern's discussion of Greek geography, craftsmanship, and cooperative ownership, which he yearned to re-create in the wilderness of rural Palestine.

In Periclean Athens, the craftsman "lived in close touch with the public for whom he performed services, not separated, like the modern workman, by a host of distributors and inter-mediaries. It was on the direct appreciation of the citizens that he depended for a livelihood."[36] Brandeis would later attribute the spirit of the craftsman to "the educated Jew," quoting Car-lyle for the proposition that the two most honored men were "the toil-worn craftsman who conquers the earth and him who is seen toiling for the spiritually indispensable."[37] And Brandeis arranged his own personal and professional life to fulfill the ideal of the craftsman that the Athenians perfected.

Zimmern concludes *The Greek Commonwealth* in the first years of the Peloponnesian War, as Pericles is deposed as gen-eral and then dies in disappointment because he has forgotten his own warnings about the curse of bigness and the dangers of imperial overreach. "Thus it was that, by one of Fate's cruelest ironies, Pericles, the cautious and clear-sighted, the champion of the Free Sea and Free Intercourse, who had been warning Athens for a whole generation against the dangers of aggran-dizement, was the first to preach to her the fatal doctrine of Universal Sea-power."[38] And Zimmern ends with a romantic paean to the ideal civilization that has been lost: "For a whole wonderful half-century, the richest and happiest period in the recorded history of any single community, Politics and Moral-ity, the deepest and strongest forces of national and of individ-ual life, had moved forward hand in hand towards a common ideal, the perfect citizen in the perfect state."[39]

Brandeis resolved to re-create "the perfect citizen in the perfect state" in Palestine. And having made up his mind, he acted swiftly and dramatically. With the outbreak of World War I in Europe, the World Zionist Organization (WZO), headquartered in Berlin, was paralyzed due to its isolation. In response to this need, a group of American Zionists called an emergency meeting at the Hotel Marseilles in New York City on August 30, 1914.[40] As the conference approached, de Haas wrote to Brandeis and asked him "to take charge of practically the whole Zionist Movement." Acknowledging that he was asking a lot, de Haas added, "I think the Jews of America will accept your leadership in this crisis. . . . It is not too much to say that everything depends on American Jewry and that Jewry has to be led right."[41] Brandeis agreed to be nominated, and on the overnight boat trip from Boston to New York, he and Horace Kallen discussed Kallen's ideas of how Zionism and Americanism could reinforce rather than threaten each other. At the meeting, Brandeis was unanimously elected chair of the dauntingly named Provisional Executive Committee for General Zionist Affairs. His response in accepting the chairmanship of the American Zionist movement was appropriately modest, and it distilled the evolution in his thinking over the past four years about the unique qualities of the Jewish people. "Recent experiences," he said, "have made me feel that the Jewish people have something which should be saved for the world; that the Jewish people should be preserved, and that it is our duty to pursue that method of saving which most promises success."[42]

After this experience, Brandeis resolved to master Zionism with the same intensity that he focused on every other cause of his life, from Savings Bank Insurance to gas regulation. He wrote a torrent of letters to Zionist organizers and committees demanding regular reports, data, communications, and, as he called it, "propaganda." "Organize, Organize, Organize, until every Jew in America must stand up and be counted, counted with us, or prove himself, wittingly or unwittingly, of the few who are against their own people," he exhorted.[43] He devoted part of every day between 1914 and his appointment to the Supreme Court two years later to Zionist affairs, installing a time clock in the Zionist offices and irking volunteers as well as staff of the Provisional Executive Committee with his quiet but relentless demands for facts, efficiency, and results.[44] With a high faith in the intelligence of the Jewish people, his goal was to create a democratic movement that would appeal to masses of Jews by reason rather than demagoguery.[45] And the results of his organizing were striking. When Brandeis took over the Zionist movement in August 1914, the Federation of American Zionists had 12,000 members. Five years later, in September 1919, the number had swelled to more than 176,000.[46] The dramatic rise of Zionism in the United States and across the world reflected the fact that the British had conquered Palestine and published the Balfour Declaration; in the United States, however, Brandeis's organizational abilities, honed by his work as a reformer, helped him to rationalize the finances of the American Zionist movement and to transform it into a powerful influence in American Jewish life and politics. Brandeis was also a prodigious fund-raiser: during the same five-year period, the budget of the movement increased from a few thousand dollars to nearly two million.[47] His motto: "Members, Money, Discipline!"[48]

To mobilize recruits and raise money, Brandeis had to create an intellectual argument for Zionism that overcame the claim that the movement encouraged a divided loyalty for American Jews. This was especially important at a time when Jews were divided over the wisdom of Zionism. Anti-Zionists, led by Reform Jews in the 1890s, opposed the establishment of a Jewish state. "Non-Zionists," represented by the American Jewish Committee and led by central European émigrés such as Louis Marshall, raised money for European Zionist groups to aid the victims of European anti-Semitism but were ambivalent about a Jewish homeland because of their concerns about hyphenated Americanism. Zionists, led by Reform Jews such as Stephen Wise and including Orthodox immigrants from eastern Europe, were often Progressives, supporters of Woodrow Wilson, and backers of a Jewish homeland in Palestine.[49]

The ambivalence of the non-Zionists and anti-Zionists also reflected fears that the U.S. Congress would limit immigration for disfavored groups. By 1915, there were strong laws and movements to limit immigration from eastern and southern Europe, Asia, and the Middle East. Charges of dual loyalty could have led to a backlash against Jewish immigrants. Brandeis, who was especially drawn to the idea of loyalty,[50] neatly solved the problem of dual loyalty by concluding that American Jews could support Palestine without moving there, acting as loyal Zionists and loyal Americans at the same time.

As early as the fall of 1914, Brandeis saw the consonance of Zionism and Americanism and approached President Wilson, who said he fully sympathized with Brandeis's Zionist views.[51] For the next several months, Brandeis traveled across America giving speeches to mobilize American Jews and convince them of their wartime responsibilities. In all these speeches, he described his own conversion to the Zionist cause, explaining, "My approach to Zionism was through Americanism." As he put it, "In time, practical experience and observation convinced me that Jews were by reason of their traditions and their character peculiarly fitted for the attainment of American ideals."[52] He endorsed Ben Yehudah's crusade to resurrect Hebrew as the national language of the new Jewish state, emphasizing "that it is through the national language, expressing the people's soul, that the national spirit is aroused, and the national power restored."[53] He praised the forty "self-governing colonies" of Palestine for their small scale—"from a few families to

some 2,000"—as communities where "the Jews have pure democracy" that gave "women equal rights with men."[54]

Brandeis issued a series of statements in 1915 exploring the
connection between Judaism and Americanism. Along with Felix
Frankfurter, Julian Mack, Stephen Wise, and his friend Henri-
etta Szold, the founder of Hadassah, Brandeis joined the editorial board of the *Menorah Journal*, founded by the Intercollegiate Menorah Association as an "unqualifiedly non-partisan
forum for the discussion of Jewish problems." In his introduction to the first issue, published in January 1915, Brandeis
offered the following reflections on the connections between
Jewish and American law and history, which he said shared a
commitment to reason and social justice:

> To America the contribution of the Jews can be peculiarly
> large. America's fundamental law seeks to make real the
> brotherhood of man. That brotherhood became the Jews'
> fundamental law more than twenty-five hundred years ago.
> America's twentieth century demand is for social justice that
> has been the Jews' striving ages-long. Their religion and their
> afflictions have prepared them for effective democracy. Per-
> secution made the Jews' law of brotherhood self-enforcing.
> It taught them the seriousness of life; it broadened their sym-
> pathies; it deepened the passion for righteousness; it trained
> them in patient endurance, in persistence, in self-control,
> and in self-sacrifice. Furthermore, the widespread study of
> Jewish law developed the intellect, and made them less sub-
> ject to preconceptions and more open to reason.[55]

Brandeis also included in the issue "A Call to the Educated
Jew," which he later delivered as a speech at a conference of the
Intercollegiate Menorah Association. Referring to scandals of
the day such as the revelation of Jewish prostitution and the
1912 murder of Herman Rosenthal, a casino operator, by Jewish
gangsters, Brandeis stressed that Jews should consider themselves "our brothers' keepers, exacting even from the lowliest

the avoidance of things dishonorable," because of the inevitable public prejudice stoked by Jewish lawbreakers. But he then went further and stressed that the Jewish inheritance of "ideals of democracy and of social justice" imposed duties on all Jews to lead individual lives worthy of their great inheritance while also respecting the rights of others. Brandeis emphasized the singular "Jewish qualities . . . developed by three thousand years of civilization, and nearly two thousand years of persecution." They included "intellectual capacity," "an appreciation of the value of education," "indomitable will," and "capacity for hard work." They also included qualities that Brandeis called "essential to successful democracy: First: an all-pervading sense of duty in the citizen" (similar to that cultivated among New England Puritans, who were "trained in implicit obedience to stern duty by constant duty of the Prophets"); "Second: Relatively high intellectual attainments"; "Third: Submission to leadership as distinguished from authority"; and "Fourth: A developed community sense."[56] As World War I raged in Europe, Brandeis called on Jews at Columbia University in May 1915 to "make common cause with the small nations of the world," supporting every people trying to express its national instinct.[57]

The previous month, Brandeis had delivered his most comprehensive statement on Zionism in "The Jewish Problem—How to Solve It," a speech to the Conference of Eastern Council of Reform Rabbis in New York. He defined "the Jewish Problem" as posing two questions: "How can we secure for Jews, wherever they may live, the same rights and opportunities enjoyed by non-Jews? How can we secure for the world the full contribution which Jews can make, if unhampered by artificial limitations" imposed by anti-Semitism?[58] He argued passionately that hyphenated group identity was important for the development not only of American ideals but also of individual self-fulfillment. "This right of development on the part of the

group is essential to the full enjoyment of rights by the individual," he declared. "For the individual is dependent for his
development (and his happiness) in large part upon the development of the group of which he forms a part."[59] All this was
distinctly in the spirit of Zimmern, and anticipated his *Whitney*
concurrence. "We recognize," he continued, "that with each
child the aim of education should be to develop his own individuality, not to make him an imitator, not to assimilate him
to others. Shall we fail to recognize this truth when applied to
whole peoples? And what people in the world has shown greater
individuality than the Jews?" "Of all the peoples in the world,"
said Brandeis, "the Greeks and the Jews" are "preeminent as
contributors to our present civilization."[60]

Drawing on Kallen's ideas of cultural pluralism, Brandeis
distinguished between a "nation" and a "nationality." He declared, "[T]he difference between a nation and a nationality is
clear; but it is not always observed. Likeness between members
is the essence of nationality; but the members of a nation may
be very different. A nation may be composed of many nationalities, as some of the most successful nations are."[61] The Jews,
like the Greeks and the Irish, for example, shared "a community of sentiments, experiences and qualities" that made them a
nationality, whether the Jews admitted it or not.[62] Denouncing
the ancient notion that the development of one people involved
domination over another, Brandeis rejected the "false doctrine
that nation and nationality must be made co-extensive."[63] This
had led to tragedies caused by "Panistic movements," used by
Germany and Russia, as a "cloak for their territorial ambitions";[64] it also had led to the rise of anti-Semitism in Germany.
Instead, Brandeis proposed "recognition of the equal rights of
each nationality," and he insisted that the Jews deserved the
same right as every other nationality, or "distinct people," in
the world: "To live at their option either in the land of their
fathers or in some other country; a right which members of

small nations as well as of large, which Irish, Greek, Bulgarian, Serbian, or Belgian, may now exercise as fully as Germans or English."[65]

In his call for "recognition of the equal rights of each nationality,"[66] Brandeis found in Zionism his own best answer to "the Jewish Problem." He wrote that "Zionism seeks to establish in Palestine, for such Jews as choose to go and remain there, and for their descendants, a legally secured home, where they may live together and lead a Jewish life, where they may expect ultimately to constitute a majority of the population, and may look forward to what we should call home rule."[67] And he envisioned mutual benefits for Palestine and for America, as Zionism warded off assimilationist tendencies among American Jews who decided to support the Jewish homeland but not settle there, preserving the individuality of the American Jewish community. By "securing for those Jews who wish to settle there the opportunity to do so, not only those Jews, but all other Jews will be benefited, and . . . the long perplexing Jewish Problem will, at last, find solution."[68]

Now convinced of the value of group differences for preserving American ideals, Brandeis responded to what was his own previous antihyphenation position: "Let no American imagine that Zionism is inconsistent with Patriotism. Multiple loyalties are objectionable only if they are inconsistent. A man is a better citizen of the United States for being also a loyal citizen of his state, and of his city; for being loyal to his family, and to his profession or trade; for being loyal to his college or his lodge. Every Irish American who contributed towards advancing home rule was a better man and a better American for the sacrifice he made. Every American Jew who aids in advancing the Jewish settlement in Palestine, though he feels that neither he nor his descendants will ever live there, will likewise be a better man and a better American for doing so."[69]

Far from causing a clash of identities, he concluded memorably, "there is no inconsistency between loyalty to America and loyalty to Jewry" because both American and Jewish fundamental law seek social justice and the brotherhood of man. On the contrary, "loyalty to America demands rather that each American Jew become a Zionist."[70]

Brandeis argued, in short, that the Zionist ideals of democracy, individual liberty, freedom of religion, and progressive social values were entirely American and that, in fact, our "Jewish Pilgrim Fathers" would export Jeffersonian values to Palestine. He envisioned Palestine as a secular, liberal democracy ruled by ethical values of equality and social justice, and not by Jewish law. Although Jews would constitute a majority, in his vision, they would respect the equal political and civil rights of all inhabitants, including Arabs.

Brandeis continued his crusade for Zionist education throughout 1916, helping to found the American Jewish Congress to counterbalance the exclusivity of the American Jewish Committee. Four days before his Supreme Court nomination, he addressed a mass rally in Carnegie Hall, supporting the call for a national Jewish congress, composed of representatives from across America, that would discuss the fate of Jews overseas and the Zionist homeland. Brandeis rested his case on the demand by American Jews for democracy and self-determination: a public congress open to all Jews, he said, would educate and mobilize intelligent public opinion rather than leaving the movement dependent on the support of "the few generous, philanthropic millionaires."[71] "The Jews are a people of thinkers; and they have a passion for freedom," he declared from the stage of Carnegie Hall. "[T]he Congress itself will create needed public opinion in support of the measures which it determines upon."[72] Brandeis's call for a democratic, self-governing national congress was resisted by the philanthropic millionaires who led the American Jewish Committee, including Louis Marshall and other members of the German Jewish establishment. They preferred a closed conference to which only the heads of their organizations would be invited.[73]

During the six months of his confirmation battle, Brandeis was publicly silent about Zionism but remained active behind the scenes: on the day in June he was confirmed to the Supreme Court, he was with Jacob de Haas discussing the causes of Jewish poverty and misery in Galicia.[74] He then agreed to attend a conference called by the American Jewish Committee at the Astor Hotel in New York on July 16, 1916. Brandeis arrived at the Astor prepared for deference—he had just been confirmed to the Supreme Court, after all—but found to his surprise that members of the audience yelled at him, shook their fingers, and warned that the Jewish people would spurn his democratic vision. "The dove of peace is not likely to light on the Jewish factions and the association with the 'respectability' for 3 hours this afternoon is not to [be] counted among the summer's joys," Brandeis wrote to Alice that evening.[75] After the meeting, the *New York Times*, owned by Adolph Ochs, one of the German Jewish burghers who opposed Zionism, editorialized that the incident had embarrassed the court and called on Brandeis to resign from leadership of the Zionist movement.[76]

Brandeis responded by resigning his public offices on July 21, 1916, but did not diminish his behind-the-scenes activities. He continued to attend meetings of the Provisional Executive Committee and continued to be treated as the "silent leader" of the American Zionist movement, in de Haas's memorable phrase.[77] In April 1917, weeks after President Wilson had asked Congress to declare war against Germany, Wilson held a White House reception for Lord Balfour, the British foreign secretary. Balfour asked to speak privately to Brandeis and, after their meeting, declared, "I am a Zionist."[78] (Balfour had a lifelong interest in Jewish history, originating in his Scottish upbringing, which included rigorous Old Testament training from his mother.)[79] On May 6, Brandeis reported to de Haas and Felix

Frankfurter that he had had a forty-five-minute talk with Wilson in which the president assured the sitting justice "that he was entirely sympathetic to the aims of the Zionist movement, and that he believed that the Zionist formula to establish a publicly assured, legally secured homeland for the Jewish people in Palestine, would meet the situation: that from the point of view of national problems generally, he approved and would support the recognition of the nationality." Wilson added that he would make his views public at the proper time "and that his utterances under that head would be drafted by Mr. Brandeis."[80] Brandeis gave the administration a draft copy of the Balfour Declaration on Palestine in June 1917—it came to the State Department from Brandeis, not from the British Foreign Office— and Brandeis was instrumental in persuading Wilson to endorse the declaration after wavering about whether the time was ripe.[81] When Wilson received a final draft of the declaration, he passed it along to Brandeis for review, and the justice, after checking in with Stephen Wise, suggested a minor tweak in the language. Wilson then approved the Balfour Declaration, and the British Foreign Office issued it on November 2, 1917: "His Majesty's Government views with favour the establishment in Palestine of a national home for the Jewish people, and will use their best endeavours to facilitate the achievement of this object, it being clearly understood that nothing shall be done which may prejudice the civil and religious rights of existing non-Jewish communities in Palestine, or the rights and political status enjoyed by Jews in any other country."[82]

"If it had not been for [Brandeis's] influence on Wilson, who in turn influenced the British government, the Balfour Declaration would probably never have been issued," wrote Nahum Goldmann, president of the World Zionist Organization.[83] (This may be an overstatement: while Brandeis sold the idea of a Jewish political entity in Palestine to Wilson, it was Chaim Weizmann who sold it to the British.)[84] The Balfour

Declaration was a promise to the Jewish people of a homeland in Palestine, and it became the basis for the establishment of the state of Israel. Until the end of the Wilson administration, Brandeis successfully persuaded Wilson to maintain his support for the declaration, over the vigorous objections of the State Department. Brandeis was gratified by the success of his Zionist efforts: in December 1917, after the British army captured Jerusalem without much bloodshed, Brandeis wrote to his mother-in-law: "It was sweet of you to send me congratulations on the Liberation of Jerusalem. The work for Zionism has seemed to me, on the whole, the most worthwhile of all I have attempted; and it is a great satisfaction to see the world gradually acquiescing in its realization."[85]

Brandeis wrote to Chaim Weizmann that he hoped Palestine's development would be agricultural rather than industrial.[86] And by 1918, Brandeis's Zionist leadership was so globally acclaimed that his portrait hung reverently in the homes of eastern European Jews; indeed, Jews made pilgrimages from across the world to his Washington office.[87] Brandeis's support for the establishment of a Jewish homeland was part of his support for self-determination for all the oppressed people who had been colonized before World War I: as he wrote to Alice after reading the history of Czech oppression by Hapsburg-German wrongdoing: "Me for the small nations."[88] In the end, however, Brandeis's idealistic leadership of the Zionist movement became contested because European Zionist leaders resented his emphasis on fiscal responsibility and practical agricultural projects such as draining swamps to end malaria, preferring to maintain a loosely regulated political structure that would solicit funds for donations and investments.

In January 1918, Brandeis began to set out his vision of what Palestine could become by drafting a charter for the Jewish homeland. His initial draft is Jeffersonian in its agrarianism and Periclean in its endorsement of cooperative ownership:

"The utmost vigilance should be exercised to prevent the acquisition by private persons of land, water rights or other natural resources or any concessions for public utilities. These must all be secured for the whole Jewish people. In other ways, as well as this, the possibility of capitalistic exploitation must be guarded against. . . . And the encouragement of all kinds of cooperative enterprise will be indispensable. Our pursuit must be primarily of agriculture in all its branches. The industries and commerce must be incidental merely—and such as may be required to ensure independence and natural development."[89]

Brandeis and Horace Kallen expanded this manifesto into a terse code of social justice—known as the Pittsburgh Program because it was adopted at the Zionist Pittsburgh Convention of June 1918. De Haas calls their joint achievement "the apogee of Americanism Zionism."[90] At the convention, a delegate spotted the silent justice sitting alone in the gallery, and as a wave of recognition swept through the crowd, all five hundred delegates began cheering, singing, and calling out Brandeis's name. "It was as though a hurricane, elemental in its might, had swept through them," recalled an observer.[91] The convention, at Brandeis's urging, eliminated the loose coalition of Zionist organizations known as the Federation of American Zionists and created a central body, the Zionist Organization of America (ZOA), that would focus on the economic development of Palestine rather than on cultural or religious issues. The new ZOA adopted the Pittsburgh Program, which Kallen drafted and Brandeis refined. It encapsulates their vision of a Jeffersonian homeland for Jews that would promote education, social justice, and democracy, and would protect the equal civil rights of all inhabitants, men and women, Jews and Arabs alike. According to one scholar, the Pittsburgh Program "responded not to the realities of the Middle East, but to the decline of Jeffersonian liberalism and to the problems of an economically changing America. What the Pittsburgh Program sought to bring about in Zion was . . . what its authors also hoped in time to bring about in America."[92] Here is Brandeis and Kallen's vision:

FIRST: We declare for political and civil equality irrespective of race, sex, or faith of all the inhabitants of the land.

SECOND: To insure in the Jewish National Home in Palestine equality of opportunity we favor a policy which, with due regard to existing rights, shall tend to establish the ownership and control by the whole people of the land, of all natural resources and of all public utilities.

THIRD: All land, owned or controlled by the whole people, should be leased on such conditions as will insure the fullest opportunity for development and continuity of possession.

FOURTH: The cooperative principle should be applied so far as feasible in the organization of all agricultural, industrial, commercial, and financial undertakings.

FIFTH: The system of free public instruction which is to be established should embrace all grades and departments of education.[93]

In January 1919, de Haas, Felix Frankfurter, and other Brandeis acolytes sailed to Paris to attend the Versailles Peace Conference, where they presented the Pittsburgh Program to European Zionists. Unfortunately, the combination of de Haas's abrasive personality and the idealism, secularism, rationalism, and lack of mysticism of Brandeis's terms led the European Zionists repeatedly to reject them. De Haas later wrote that "had the Pittsburgh Program been accepted and enforced, many of the problems that have vexed Zionists in the actual upbuilding of Palestine would never have arisen."[94] Still, Frankfurter managed at the Paris peace conference to secure letters from Prince Faisal and President Wilson supporting a Jewish settlement in Palestine.[95] Wilson declared that the establishment of a Jewish homeland would be one of the two permanent achievements to emerge from the war.[96] As for the young and glamorous prince, he attended the Versailles conference in native robes, always attended by T. E. Lawrence of Arabia. (The prince would declare himself king of Syria and Palestine the following year; after being deposed by the French, he was then installed by the British as king of Iraq.)

As the State Department pressured Wilson to abandon his support for the Balfour Declaration, Frankfurter urged Brandeis to come to Paris and Palestine to shore up support for the Jewish state. The justice set sail for London on the RMS *Mauretania* with his daughter Susan and Jacob de Haas, who had just come back from Europe, only to turn around for a return trip. (Alice's health, as usual, precluded her from travel.) During the crossing, Brandeis read Paul Goodman's *History of the Jews* and the book of Daniel; and on arrival in London, he met with Chaim Weizmann, the new leader of European Zionists. The two men had a relatively positive first impression of each other: Weizmann detected "something Messianic"[97] in the justice's bearing, while Brandeis wrote that Weizmann impressed him with his "ability, resourcefulness & Mephistophelian quality."[98] (It must have been quite a meeting.) Nevertheless, they would soon have a falling-out that would divide European and American Zionists for a decade. Brandeis enthused to Alice that unlike "our American cities," which were "business machines," "London is civilization" and "London is living. All the horrors of bigness are absent."[99] They then stopped in Paris, where Lord Balfour assured Brandeis that the British would fulfill their promise to the Jewish people. They were joined by Alfred Zimmern, whom Brandeis, understandably, considered the ideal traveling companion for his first visit to the Periclean Holy Land.

Brandeis, Zimmern, and de Haas set off for Palestine by way of Marseilles, where they boarded a ship to Port Said. They brought with them what de Haas called "a satchel of reports," which Brandeis read on board, and "a small compact library," including a Bible, a Hebrew phrase book, George Adam Smith's *Historical Geography of the Holy Land*, Ellsworth Huntington's *Palestine and Its Transformation*, and John Kelman's *The Holy Land*.[100] (The Jeffersonian focus on geography was ever present.) After stopping in Cairo—where he was greeted by a twenty-three-piece band of Zionist Boy Scouts, proudly bearing the blue and white flag, who serenaded him with "Hatikva" —Brandeis detected a luxury in Egypt that explained for him "why the Jews had to leave it." The ascetic Brandeis believed that luxury sapped "the vigor on which effective idealism could be developed"; to counteract it, he concluded, "Moses led his people through a desert into stony fastness."[101] His romantic spirit was impressed, however, by the "beauty and joyousness" of Egypt: "Why should western *women* have made such a lamentable failure in utilizing the colors and the flowing gowns with which *man* here makes every moment interesting and every scene a picture?"[102] he wrote to Alice.

The party arrived in Jerusalem on July 8, and Brandeis immediately fell in love with the land itself. Standing by Rachel's tomb on Bethlehem Road, he told de Haas, "I know now why all the world wanted this land and why all peoples loved it."[103] His letter to Alice after two days in Palestine idealizes Jerusalem as an agrarian paradise. "It is a wonderful country, a wonderful city," he wrote. "It is a miniature California, but a California endowed with all the interest which the history of man can contribute and the deepest emotions which can stir a people. The ages-long longing, the love is all explicable now. It has also the great advantage over California of being small."[104] His conclusion—"it is indeed a Holy Land"[105]—seemed to emphasize "land" rather than "holy," reflecting agrarian rather than religious stirrings. He was thrilled that the scale and barrenness of the land would allow the Jewish people to display to the world their capacity to "create something out of nothing," as de Haas recalled, and he dreamed of restoring the Roman irrigation systems whose remains were still visible. He also dreamed of eliminating malaria, which he remembered from his Kentucky boyhood, when there were always quinine pills on the family table.[106]

Brandeis returned from Palestine more convinced than ever that the Jewish settlers were the twentieth-century equivalent of New England Puritans. "The land is an inspiration to effort" and "[w]e are trying to build a new land," he declared in a speech to the Palestine Land Development Council, founded to promote the economic development of Palestine.[107] "When Americans think of building a new land, at least those of us who have lived in New England, they are apt to think of the Pilgrim Fathers. . . . The Pilgrims had faith, we should have it."[108] Significantly, however, the Pilgrim faith of which Brandeis spoke was not religious but secular; it was faith in the ability of Jews to achieve economic and personal freedom in Palestine by cultivating the land.

Although Brandeis was transformed by his trip to Palestine, his quixotic, Jeffersonian fixation on agrarian economic development and eliminating malaria in the Hula valley failed to inspire the mass mobilization he expected. While the Europeans derided Brandeis's demand for the eradication of malaria, Brandeis understood that the Galilee could never be settled without draining the swamps. So he funneled his own money through Hadassah—which remained loyal to him and to his ideas—and in fact did drain the swamps, eradicate malaria, and create a habitable Palestine. In the end, Brandeis's idealistic vision was based not on real conditions on the ground but on his ideology, based on the experience of the American founding fathers.

In April 1920, Palestine and Iraq became a British mandate (the French got Syria), and in June, Brandeis returned to London for the World Zionist Conference. The World Zionist Organization wanted to make Brandeis its leader because he was the most prestigious Jew in the world. But his opening speech to the conference, "Efficiency in Public Service," left many of the European Jewish members of the organization cold. It was an entirely Brandeisian talk about money, accounting, and swamps. Channeling Taylorism and scientific management, he proposed reducing the size of the World Zionist Organization payroll, focusing on economic development and, above all, hard work. Here is a characteristic excerpt: "[N]ot only must we get the fittest men, but we must do with the least possible number. We must abolish every unnecessary office. We must make every man do every bit of work that it is possible for him to do. We must make men understand that every penny which they waste in any way, either by an unnecessary office or by a salary of more than is necessary, that just to that extent they are obstructing the work which lies before us. What we can do in Palestine depends wholly upon the amount of money we can raise and what men we can get to administer it."[109]

Brandeis also made clear that his support for cooperative ownership of the land did not include support for a socialist safety net for those who refused to become self-sufficient through individual effort:

> The highest work that can be done for Palestine is to earn a living in Palestine; to put the Jewish mind and Jewish determination and Zionist idealism and enthusiasm into the problem of earning a living in Palestine; thus setting an example for others to earn a living. That is real patriotism. A young woman who was in Palestine some time ago said that to make a good soup in Palestine was a contribution to the cause. I agree with her. But it is not a contribution to have someone else make a soup for you. It is not a contribution to get paid for making plans for a good soup. What we have to do is to make it possible for men to earn a living in Palestine. That is a very difficult thing. It cannot be done by subsidizing people. It can be done only by the individual efforts of men actuated by the proper motives, guided in the proper ways.[110]

With typical attention to administrative detail, Brandeis also proposed to change the organizational structure of the World Zionist Organization, which he was convinced had wasted money on salaries and luxuries. (He must have seen the WZO as a Zionist version of the junketeering he deplored at the New Haven Railroad.) In response, Brandeis proposed to separate donations to the organization as a whole from donations for specific projects. This, he believed, would conserve funds for the economic development of Palestine rather than allowing them to be squandered on unrelated political and cultural initiatives. Brandeis also proposed that an executive committee that included British businessmen who shared his vision of developing Palestine on agricultural lines would administer the restructured organization. Chaim Weizmann's colleagues balked, however, at the idea of having non-Zionists run the organization, and when Weizmann sided with them and endorsed the idea of keeping all the funds in one pot, Brandeis reacted with fury to the betrayal of his Taylorite organizational principles. He rejected calls by American Zionists that he resign from the Supreme Court to run the World Zionist Organization and instead pledged to have nothing more to do with the organization.

The debate about whether the Zionist movement should establish a global funding agency continued for the next year. When the Zionist Organization of America convened in Cleveland in June 1921, Brandeis challenged the convention to adopt his program of focusing all financial contributions on the economic redevelopment of Palestine. When the American convention, too, rejected Brandeis's proposals to put safeguards on the distribution of funds, Julian Mack, the president of the ZOA, promptly resigned, along with thirty-six other Brandeis allies, including Felix Frankfurter and Horace Kallen. Before walking out of the convention, Mack read to the stunned and silent delegates a letter he had received from Brandeis before the vote: "If their decision is adverse, you will, I assume, resign, and in that event present also my resignation as Honorary President. Our place will then be as humble soldiers in the ranks to hasten by our struggle the coming of the day when principles and policies in which we believe will be recognized as the only ones through which our great ends may be achieved."[111]

For nearly a decade, Brandeis kept a low public profile on Zionist matters, issuing a few public messages about the importance of supporting Palestinian economic development as "the only promising road toward the solution of the Jewish Problem."[112] On August 23, 1929, however, incited by their virulently anti-Semitic grand mufti, Arabs began to attack Jews in the Old City of Jerusalem. The violence spread to Hebron, site of the Tomb of the Patriarchs, where sixty-seven Jews were massacred, and then to Safed in the north. After eight days of riotous violence, 133 Jews and 110 Arabs were dead and six colonies destroyed. Brandeis, like other Zionist leaders, had romanticized Arabs as a group and failed to appreciate the force of Palestinian nationalism. (Brandeis's romanticism was both his strength and his weakness.) "Jews must not, after the present emergency is over, be denied the opportunity of defending themselves," he wrote to Felix Frankfurter in September. "As against the Bedouins, our pioneers are in a position not unlike the American settlers against the Indians."[113] Brandeis repeated his jarring analogy in a speech to a Palestine economic conference in November: "The situation reminds me of that in America, when the settlers who founded the Massachusetts Bay Colony had to protect themselves against the Indians."[114] One Brandeis critic, noting that this passage was excised from the ZOA's collection of Brandeis's speeches, charges that it shows Brandeis's "imperial mind-set," revealing the extent to which he and other American liberals "viewed the conflict through a mind-set developed over the prior two centuries to justify the conquest of one people by another."[115]

The charge of imperialism is overstated: in the same speech,

Brandeis repeated his long-standing demand for equal civil and political rights for Arabs, Christians, and Jews in Palestine. As he put it: "We should so conduct our affairs in Palestine that what we do shall inure to the interest of all the inhabitants of Palestine, Moslem and Christian as well as Jew."[116] He also renewed his call for "opening the co-operatives to the Arabs, of opening our labor unions to Arabs, of inviting Arabs to participate in our industrial enterprises and thus become more closely allied to them."[117] He stressed that Jews should learn the Arab language "so that we might familiarly visit them in their homes, as some Jews have been doing," and predicted that "through our medical organization, through the elimination of malaria and other diseases we have done for the amelioration of the condition of the Arabs an extraordinary amount, considering the shortness of time."[118] (In donating to the Hadassah malaria clinics, Brandeis suggested that the clinics put up signs saying that the services were "provided by Jews for the benefit of Arabs as well as of Jews.")[119]

Still, there is no question that Brandeis, with his romantic abstraction of the Arabs, failed to understand the power of both Arab and Jewish nationalism. Despite the riots, "the danger of the Arabs is grossly exaggerated," he declared.[120] "Arabs, unlike some other peoples, have no inherent dislike of the Jew, certainly they did not have it," he continued. "The recent difficulties are, in my opinion, due largely to persons who own land in Palestine but live elsewhere and who object to the emancipation of the previously subservient fellaheen and the improvement in their condition resulting from Jewish settlement."[121] Brandeis's notion that the riots were caused by absentee Arab landowners and implemented under "the cover of religious fanaticism" by "a very large number of Bedouins constantly coming into Palestine who are not Palestinians"[122] was uncharacteristically inattentive to the facts on the ground.

In response to the mounting clashes between Arabs and

Jews, the British backed away from the Balfour Declaration's commitments to a Jewish homeland. A British commission headed by Sir Walter Shaw issued a report in March 1930 that dismayed Brandeis and the Zionists and pleased the Arabs by recommending a reduction in Jewish immigration and the cutting of ties between the government in Palestine and the Zionist movement.[123] Two other reports that year—the Hope-Simpson Report and the Passfield White Paper—concluded (based on interviews with Arab but not Jewish groups) that the arable land in Palestine could not support a larger population and recommended that immigration be suspended entirely.[124] Brandeis, continuing his questionable practice of lobbying sitting presidents on political issues, met with President Hoover at the end of October 1930, and reviewed the entire history of his involvement with the British, beginning with his talks with Balfour in June 1919, and ending with the "rude shock" caused by the Shaw and Passfield reports, with their "pernicious enmity" in recommending "the suspension of immigration." In describing the meeting to Felix Frankfurter, Brandeis recalled, "I had been telling him of Jewish achievements in Palestine, of the benefits accruing to the Arabs generally; of the small body of Arab leaders responsible for stirring up the enmity . . . [and] the rapid increase of Arab population, through betterment of Arab conditions & seepage in from Syria & Transjordania."[125] Hoover mentioned "Transjordan possibilities for Arabs"; Brandeis added "also for Jews" and told the president of his complaint that "Transjordan had been excluded from Palestine territory; spoke of its fertility & possibilities."[126]

Brandeis's efforts throughout the 1930s to maintain the British commitment to a Jewish Palestine—one that he hoped would include Transjordan—were accelerated as anti-Semitism swept across Europe and the Nazi menace grew. As Hitler took power in 1933, Brandeis advised Stephen Wise, the head of the American Jewish Congress, to organize a mass protest against

German anti-Semitism that drew more than twenty thousand people to Madison Square Garden. "The Jews must leave Germany!" Brandeis told Wise. "The day must come when Germany shall be Judenfrei and Germany shall see for itself how to live without its Jewish population."[127] Alas, too many of them stayed where they were. Brandeis died in 1941, and so he never learned the worst.

Between 1933 and 1939, three hundred thousand Jews emigrated from Germany. Sixty-two thousand went to the United States and fifty-five thousand to Palestine.[128] (Brandeis's second cousins from Vienna were among those émigrés who escaped the Holocaust.) But the British continued to limit immigration to Palestine at the same time that the grand mufti of Jerusalem, Haj Amin al-Husseini, whom the British had appointed in 1921, was engineering the bloody riots of 1929 and 1936, calling on Arabs to attack the Jews. (The grand mufti eventually fled to Germany in 1941, where he met with Hitler in the Reich Chancellery and called on him to exterminate Jews throughout the Middle East. A photograph of the meeting suggests that Hitler welcomed the suggestion.)[129] Brandeis was appalled by the riots of 1936 and by the British reaction. As his law clerk David Riesman wrote to me years later: "An unforgettable occasion, giving a sense of Brandeis's fierceness, was when Harold Laski came to see him, an old friend. All this was in the 1935–36 term of the court. Brandeis said to Laski that he hoped that the British and the Germans would fight and destroy one another! Laski was horrified. Brandeis had not only the Nazis in mind, but also his antagonism to the British control of Palestine and the widely shared view of Americans about Britain as a colonial power."[130]

The British responded to the riots of 1936 with the Peel report of 1937, which recommended the restriction of any further Jewish immigration and the partition of Palestine into Arab and Jewish states, with Jerusalem and Bethlehem as neutral

zones under British supervision.[131] The Arabs immediately convened a summit and condemned the proposal, but Chaim Weizmann and David Ben-Gurion both supported partition as the
only viable solution. Brandeis, however, strongly opposed partition on the agrarian grounds that economic development in
Palestine would be impossible unless the Jews had sufficient
arable land. Instructing his acolytes to "stand firm against partition" as a "stupid, ignoble action,"[132] Brandeis summoned
Ben-Gurion to his summer house in Chatham, on Cape Cod,
to denounce the proposal. Although the World Zionist Congress voted to explore the possibility of partition, the British
abandoned the idea at the end of 1938 in the face of Arab opposition.[133]

In October 1938, Brandeis went to the White House to discuss the Palestinian question with President Roosevelt. During
the meeting, he advocated the immigration of the Arab population in Palestine to Transjordan or Iraq. (This position was
based on his belief that there was an influx of Arabs into Palestine, including Bedouins, who could be returned to their lands
of origin.)[134] As Brandeis wrote to Frankfurter, "F.D. went very
far, in our talk, in his appreciation of the significance of Palestine, the need of keeping it whole and of making it Jewish. He
was tremendously interested, and wholly surprised, on learning
of the great increase in Arab population since the war, and on
hearing of the plenitude of land for Arabs in Arab countries,
about which he made specific enquiries."[135] Roosevelt floated
the proposal to the British but later wrote to Brandeis that British officials didn't agree that "there is a difference between the
Arab population which was in Palestine prior to 1920 and the
new Arab population."[136] As an American who lived in an age
of immigration—in his lifetime, millions of Italians, Jews, and
Poles came to the United States—Brandeis welcomed the idea
of transnational migration. With progressive logic, he believed

that since the Arab nationalities had many homelands, the Jewish nationality needed at least one.

What is the pertinence to our contemporary vexations of Brandeis's vision of Zionism and hyphenated identity? In his idealization of small-scale agrarian democracy in Palestine as the culmination of Jeffersonian shires and the Athenian polis, Brandeis was, of course, something of an idealist. He envisioned a Jewish state that was democratic, secular, and cooperatively owned, a country whose economic success would be shared and embraced by the Arab minorities whose equal civil and political rights it would scrupulously respect. In this sense, he resembled Ben-Gurion and Golda Meir and the first two generations of idealistic Zionists after the creation of the state of Israel in 1948. (Brandeis greatly admired Ben-Gurion, whom he considered the representative of the new generation of Zionist leaders, and when Ben-Gurion said that Jews had to be able to defend themselves, Brandeis gave money—laundered through Stephen Wise and Robert Szold—that allowed the Yishuv—the Jewish residents of Palestine—to buy arms.) But the Jewish state did not develop in a communalist direction; it thrived economically as a bastion of democratic capitalism. With his single-minded focus on economic development fired by individual effort and the economic self-sufficiency of small enterprises, however, Brandeis would surely have approved of Israel's economic miracle as a "start-up nation": thanks to the technology that has been responsible for 95 percent of Israel's economic productivity, the country has produced more start-up companies than the United Kingdom, Japan, India, Korea, and Canada.[137] His favorite Palestinian enterprise in the 1930s was a loan bank that the Palestine Economic Corporation used for small loans to small businesses, including farmers and artisans; he viewed it as a model for "small loans" legislation in the U.S. Congress and state legislatures.[138]

Brandeis's idealistic vision never appealed to those immigrant Jews who were far more religiously and culturally Jewish than Brandeis and wanted a movement and a Jewish state that would be sectarian, ideological, and nationalistic rather than progressive, secular, and democratic. This charged division about the definition of the Jewish state continues to this day. As a progressive and a rationalist, Brandeis believed that once religious Jews were exposed to economic facts, they, too, would become progressive and rationalist. He did not anticipate, and would not have understood, the rise of Jewish fundamentalism that threatens Israel's secular identity. And Brandeis's other blind spot was his failure to anticipate or to understand Arab nationalism. His purely economic analysis of Jewish migration to Palestine assumed that a rising tide would lift all boats: through communal effort, swamps would be drained, the previously arid land would flow with milk and honey, and malaria would be eliminated for Jews and Arabs alike. In fact, Palestine's early economic success did indeed attract Arab migration as Brandeis had hoped: between 1922, the beginning of the British mandate, and 1948, the Arab population doubled from over six hundred thousand Muslim and Christian Arabs to over 1.2 million, and the Jewish population grew to over six hundred thousand.[139] (These numbers reflected the draconian immigration quotas for Jews imposed by the British in the 1930s.) The standard of living for both Arabs and Jews grew more rapidly than in neighboring lands. But Brandeis failed to anticipate the anti-Semitic eliminationism of the grand mufti—which is why he was surprised by the massacre of 1929 and tried to blame it on absentee landlords and Bedouins.

Brandeis supported "a legally secured home" for the Jews in Palestine, and he envisioned a secular, majority Jewish democracy that would respect the equal rights of all citizens, Jews and Arabs alike. But his Zionism was not so much about politics as about identity. Brandeis offers little guidance about wars and conflicts in the Middle East. Moreover, his identification of Zionism with Americanism was not, like the identification of *Deutschtum* with *Judentum*—of Germanness with Jewishness—made by many German Jews of the time, an assertion of exclusiveness. By rejecting the equation of nationhood and nationality, Brandeis's Zionism was in fact a doctrine of inclusiveness, welcoming similar expressions of group loyalty by other groups or "nationalities": it was, in this sense, a distinctly American sort of Zionism. And those German Jews who conflated their Germanness with their Judaism were often anti-Zionist, especially those who immigrated to America and sought to distinguish themselves from poorer and less assimilated eastern European Jewish immigrants. They aspired to a universality that worried about difference, whereas Brandeis chose to celebrate difference.

American Jews today, of course, often disagree about the success of the Israeli government in achieving the ideals that Brandeis attributed to both Zionism and Americanism: "the development of the individual for his own and the common good; the development of the individual through liberty, and the attainment of the common good through democracy and social justice."[140] But regardless of Israel's successes and failures, Brandeis's argument for the integrity of the Zionist commitment remains powerful. Israel's claim upon the support of American Jewry is based on not only the latter's Jewish identity but also its American identity. This was not "dual loyalty," in Brandeis's view; it was based upon a single philosophy: "[T]o be good Americans, we must be better Jews, and to be better Jews, we must become Zionists."[141] This may be a little tidy; but nothing in it contradicts the great American dispensation of pluralism, or the belief in the blessings of diversity that goes back even further to the founding era. In Brandeis's construction of Zionism, we are restored to one of the fundamental principles of modernity: the cultivation of the individual and the group, and the confidence that this cultivation is a universal good.

Brandeis was an individualist *and* a communalist. He believed that American Jews could not develop an individual identity without also cultivating and participating in a group identity, because individual happiness and development are dependent on the groups that define each of us. Given the options of embracing a Jewish identity on the one hand or declaring themselves "against their own people" by denying Israel's right to exist on the other, Brandeis thought the choice for American Jews was clear. And his vision of cultural pluralism is more urgent than ever in a globalized age. It provides a balanced alternative to the separatist tendencies of multiculturalism, which exalts group identity without insisting on universal values, and to the homogenizing assimilationist pressures of Internet culture, which, by destroying the boundaries between our public and private selves, is making it harder to maintain genuinely individual identities.

Brandeis reminds us that globalized Internet culture is just as destructive of individuality as huge corporate culture, and that true individuality has to be cultivated by active engagement in smaller groups, bounded by genuine shared values. This was how his reflections on Zionism transformed his thinking about American citizenship and led him back to Jefferson. As he put it in "True Americanism":

> Democracy rests upon two pillars: one, the principle that all men are equally entitled to life, liberty and the pursuit of happiness; and the other, the conviction that such equal opportunity will most advance civilization. . . . America has believed that we must not only give to the immigrant the best that we have, but must preserve for America the good that is in the immigrant and develop in him the best of which he is capable. . . . The new nationalism adopted by America proclaims that each race or people, like each individual, has the

right and duty to develop, and that only through such differentiated development will high civilization be attained.[142]

Kallen amplified Brandeis's vision and, by calling it "cultural pluralism," illuminated its relevance for our own multicultural society. "It is the variety and range of his participation which does in fact distinguish a civilized man from an uncivilized, a man of faith and reason from an unreasoning fanatic, a democrat from a totalitarian, a man of culture from a barbarian," Kallen wrote. "Such a man obviously orchestrates a growing pluralism of associations into the wholeness of his individuality."[143] After Brandeis's death, Kallen described the interaction between Jews and non-Jews as a source of mutual enrichment, noting that "the social orchestration which this intercultural exchange consummates actualizes the American idea and gives the culture of the American people the qualities that Whitman and Emerson and William James and Louis Brandeis celebrated."[144]

◆▸◀◆

What Would Brandeis Do?

BRANDEIS REMAINED hungry for facts and optimistic about human perfectibility until the end. During his final years on the Supreme Court, after Chief Justice Hughes succeeded Chief Justice Taft, the views Brandeis had expressed in dissenting opinions began to be embraced by a majority of his colleagues. In cases ranging from the First Amendment—in which the Hughes Court struck down laws restricting free speech and free press—to economic liberty, in which the court overturned its previous opinions striking down minimum wage laws,[1] the prophet gained honor in his own house and across the land. But although his intellectual vigor was unimpaired, his physical vitality began to ebb around 1937. To protect his strength, Mrs. Brandeis insisted that he sit rather than stand to greet guests at his Sunday teas.[2] But a bad flu and then a mild heart attack caused him to miss most of the court's sittings in January 1939, and he wrote half the number of opinions that he had produced in his prime. Without warning, he retired from the court after a full day of work on February 13, 1939, sending a one-sentence note to President Roosevelt. He had recently turned eighty-three. The same day, he wrote to his sister-in-law Jennie Taussig Brandeis: "I want you to know promptly that I am not retiring from the Court because of ill health. Mine seems to be as good as heretofore. But years have limited the quantity and intensity of work possible, and I think the time has come when a younger man should assume the burden."[3]

During the two years that were left to him, Brandeis continued to be fully engaged with the Zionist cause. In May 1939, the British government declared that an independent Jewish state would not be created for ten years, that Jewish immigration would be severely restricted, and that after 1944, no Jews could immigrate to Palestine without the permission of the Arabs. Brandeis's response was poignant. "Where will a poor Jew go now?" he asked.[4] Although appalled, he was unbowed. He discussed the refugee situation with President Roosevelt and wrote to his son-in-law Jacob Gilbert: "I am deeply shocked, but not surprised, at British actions re Palestine. I am not, however, in any way discouraged. The great work in Palestine will go forward."[5]

Jacob Gilbert's son Frank recalls the final summers on Cape Cod, when his grandfather and grandmother were helped into a canoe and sat in the bottom, facing each other happily, as their daughter and her husband paddled them toward the center of town and back to the beach. Frank and his brother Louis produced a mimeographed newspaper called "The Chatham Chatter"—Brandeis suggested the slogan, "Quality Not Quantity"—and Frank's job was to read articles to his grandfather, whose hunger for facts was unabated. As the Nazis advanced, Brandeis preferred to avoid the distractions of a radio in his house and relied on his grandson to bring him news from the front—a duty he dubbed "the Gilbert News Service." Each day, Frank ran a quarter mile across the fields from his own house to his grandfather's with the latest bulletins.[6]

Although German victories in Greece threatened the possible fall of Palestine, Brandeis remained confident in an Allied victory and certain of the need for a Jewish state. He remained until the end, in the words of the economist Alvin Johnson, "a serenely implacable democrat."[7] In April 1941, he told a friend: "It has been established that the Jews require a state of their own for their continued existence. The Germans have established that fact. The Jews have established their capacity to build such a state. That is the essential groundwork for the future effort."[8] And in late September 1941, Brandeis wrote to his grandson that he was fortunate to have closed the Gilbert News Service before the Nazi advance on Russia. Nevertheless, he ended on a characteristic note of optimism. The Russians had kept the Nazis "quite fully occupied" for three months, he wrote. "[T]he Russians promise to continue their energetic fighting. If they keep this promise, the rains and the winter may help bring to Hitler deserved disaster." Although Pearl Harbor was two months away, Brandeis had faith in Franklin Roosevelt's ability to mobilize America in defense of liberty. "Surely," he concluded, "our President will do his part."[9]

A few days after writing these words, having returned from a drive with his wife through Rock Creek Park, Brandeis suffered a second heart attack. He fell into a coma on October 4 and died at 7:15 p.m. on Sunday, October 5. A year later, his ashes were placed at the entrance of the University of Louisville Law School. Four years later, Alice Brandeis's ashes joined those of her husband.[10] A mosaic near the entrance of the law school today, displayed a few feet from Brandeis's resting place, includes one of his axioms, which serves as an epitaph: "Knowledge is Essential to Understanding, and Understanding Should Precede Judging."[11]

The day after Brandeis died, members of the Supreme

Court and former clerks, such as Dean Acheson, then assistant secretary of state, gathered at the austere apartment on California Street for a memorial service. A string quartet played Beethoven. "During these years of retreat from reason, his faith in the human mind and in the will of people to understand and grasp the truth never wavered or tired," Acheson said, ascribing to Brandeis "the faith of the prophets and poets, of Socrates, of Lincoln."[12] (He might have added Jefferson.) A year later, this august group reconvened at the Supreme Court for more formal tributes. There were remarks by the attorney general, by judges including Learned Hand, and an insightful response by Chief Justice Harlan F. Stone, whose elevation Brandeis had applauded. Striking a nicely Jeffersonian note, the chief justice called Brandeis a great lawgiver and "a great American because of his abiding faith in the principles of liberty, justice, and equality of opportunity which were proclaimed by those characteristically American documents, the first Virginia Bill of Rights, the Declaration of Independence and the Constitution." Stone continued:

> For him those principles were not concerned alone with the tyrannies of eighteenth century government which gave them birth. They were equally to be taken as guaranties that the social and economic injustices which attend the development of a dynamic and increasingly complex society should not prevail. . . .
>
> By exhaustive research to discover the social and economic need and consequences of regulation of wages and hours of labor, of rate-making for public utilities, of the sources and evils of monopoly, and in many another field, he laid the firm foundation of those judicial decisions which for nearly a quarter of a century were to point the way for the development of law adapted to the industrial civilization of the twentieth century. . . .
>
> In cases involving the validity of legislation or the ap-

plication of statute or common law to new fact situations, his opinions, like his briefs at the Bar, give us the results of his extensive researches into the social and economic backgrounds of the questions presented, buttressed by expert opinion and accounts of the experiences in other states and countries. His statements of fact and law were simple, direct, orderly, powerful, proceeding to their conclusion with convincing logic. In their discussions of the principles of constitutional government and of civil liberty they rise to heights of dignity and power which place them among the great examples of legal literature.[13]

In the seventy-five years since Brandeis's death, on the hundredth anniversary of his confirmation hearings, his reputation among members of the Supreme Court remains high. Three justices—Ruth Bader Ginsburg, Stephen Breyer, and Elena Kagan—have explicitly invoked Brandeis as a model for their own jurisprudence.

Justice Ruth Bader Ginsburg has identified Brandeis as one of her models for his craftsmanship and his ability to combine a dedication to judicial restraint with a readiness to defend civil rights and liberties when our constitutional values required it. "Brandeis worked hard on his opinions as evidenced by the number of drafts he composed. He cared not only about reaching the right bottom line judgment; he cared as much about writing opinions that would enlighten other people," she told me.[14] "His opinions are inspirational for that reason." Ginsburg also admires Brandeis's collegiality and his determination to dissent only when he felt the public needed to hear his separate views. "One major way in which he influences me is demonstrated in Alex Bickel's book compiling his unpublished opinions,"[15] Ginsburg said. "Not many people would go through the labor of writing an opinion and then ask, 'Is this opinion really needed?' His dissents were all the more powerful because of his self-imposed restraint. He did not dissent, as some judges do, whenever he disagreed with the court's judgment."

In terms of legal philosophy, Ginsburg has modeled herself on Brandeis's progressive judicial restraint, generally deferring to legislatures unless the laws in question clash with essential civil rights and liberties. "I consider myself perhaps the most restrained justice on this court in respecting the legislative product and, in this regard, Brandeis was pathmarking for me," Ginsburg said. "When the court's majority gets it egregiously wrong, you must defend civil liberties." Ginsburg also admires Brandeis's philosophy of statutory as well as constitutional interpretation. "His—I won't call it pragmatism—his purposive interpretation placed him among jurists who interpret the Constitution and statutes sensibly," she said. "He certainly was not an admirer of what was once called legal classicism, which seems to me similar to today's originalism"—that is, the view that the Constitution should be interpreted in light of the original understanding of its framers and ratifiers. She added, "The health care case decided in June 2015[16] is illustrative. I cannot imagine Brandeis saying that because the law reads, 'exchange established by the state,' it must be interpreted in a way that would wreck the entire act. No responsible member of Congress would have wanted an outcome so bizarre. Salvage, not destruction, was the proper course."

As an advocate at the ACLU arguing for sex equality in the 1970s, Ginsburg was especially influenced by the Brandeis brief in the *Muller* case, despite the fact that it defended maximum hours laws for women on grounds that seem paternalistic today. Her brief in *Reed v. Reed* (1971), a case successfully challenging a state law preferring men to women as estate administrators, was self-consciously Brandeisian. "The *Reed* brief was intended to be kin to a Brandeis brief, replete with social and economic references," she told me. "He was the model for our presentation of information showing what conditions for women really were." Still, Ginsburg sought to overturn the paternalistic presumption implicit in *Muller v. Oregon*, namely, the notion that women workers needed special protection that men did not. "The Brandeis brief in *Muller* does speak of woman's physical weakness and the need to preserve her health because she's going to bear children. To win that case, he had to take the position he did, because the court had ruled in *Lochner*, just three years before *Muller*, that laws restricting the hours men could work were unconstitutional," Ginsburg recalled. Still, she considers Brandeis's influence to be critical both for cases in which she has been in the majority and those in which she wrote in dissent. "If you speak of Brandeis as a model for me," Justice Ginsburg concluded, "it would be first as an advocate inaugurating the Brandeis brief, and then as a judge, in his efforts to come to the right judgment and to explain that judgment in a way intelligent readers can comprehend."

Justice Stephen Breyer, too, embraces Brandeis as a model. His fact-heavy appendixes and opinions are also inspired by the Brandeis brief. In his rationalism, empiricism, deference to choices reached by democratic participation, and pragmatism, Breyer, a former Harvard Law School professor of antitrust, is in many respects Brandeis's heir. When I asked Breyer how Brandeis had influenced him, he gave a multifaceted answer. "He did strongly believe that he wanted to look into the facts and circumstance of a particular case in some depth, and he thought the values will grow out of an understanding of what's actually at stake," Breyer told me.[17] "And also, I think he felt this both about federal government and also about state governments. Of course state governments are important. We all know the phrase, 'the laboratories' and 'experiment'—very important." Breyer's book *The Court and the World* notes that Brandeis, in his *Whitney* concurrence, embraced a methodology of constitutional balancing—weighing the imminence of a threat against the seriousness of a harm—that European courts have embraced as well.[18] Breyer thinks that Brandeis would have endorsed his idea of looking to foreign laws and opinions by "nations trying to cooperate in dealing with problems that now are facing us." (Brandeis, after all, cited foreign statutes in his famous Brandeis brief.) "And he felt, I think, very much, as Holmes did, in respect to the Constitution, Congress has a great deal of leeway—but *should*, in a democracy, the legislature *should*. But, but, there comes a point, and not further than that. Now we can go through all kinds of reasoning to discover what that point is. But no, not that. And he explains it very eloquently, in respect to free speech, in respect to other important values. . . . I think Brandeis had a way of approaching that that I find absolutely admirable."

Justice Elena Kagan has adopted another powerful Brandeisian rhetorical device, posing questions about whether the legislature was unreasonable to reach the conclusion it did before including a blizzard of facts to establish that the legislature was entirely reasonable. Kagan views it as a great honor to sit in Brandeis's seat, held in the interim by William O. Douglas and John Paul Stevens. She expressed to me her deep admiration for the force and style of his opinions, commenting on their "coupling of eloquence and rhetorical suasion with superb analytics and lawyerly precision."[19] Her favorite Brandeis opinion is *Whitney*, which she thinks contains "the most powerful, and also the most beautiful, statement of First Amendment values ever written." In that opinion and others, Kagan thinks, Brandeis demonstrated a "real feel for American history," showing how "the founders' ideals expressed themselves both in their own moment and in the time since." "That understanding of the long sweep of American history," she said, "at times made him prescient about the future and imbued his opinions with a deep wisdom." And she admires how he rooted his legal arguments in facts. Even his most rhetorical passages, she notes, are never "abstract or high-blown," but instead gain their force from "his grounded understanding of the way the world works." She says she could not, and does not try to, emulate him: "Both our worlds and our talents are too different." But she finds it inspirational "to sit in his chair and have the chance to reflect on his constitutional vision."

All of the current Supreme Court justices invoke Brandeis in different ways. Chief Justice Roberts, for example, has endorsed Brandeis's principle of "constitutional avoidance"—the idea that the court will not ordinarily decide a constitutional question if there is another, narrower ground on which the case can be decided[20]—in cases ranging from voting rights to terrorism. And he has pledged to try to persuade his colleagues to converge around narrow, unanimous opinions—avoiding broad constitutional rulings and resisting the urge to file separate dissents and concurrences—in the interest of shoring up the nonpartisan legitimacy of the court.[21] Other justices—including Scalia and Clarence Thomas—also invoke Brandeis's principle of "constitutional avoidance." And Brandeis's dissent in *Olmstead*, the wiretapping case, has been invoked by justices of diverse perspectives who are united in their devotion to protecting privacy, from Samuel Alito[22] and Anthony Kennedy[23] to Ruth Bader Ginsburg.[24] Justice Sonia Sotomayor's pathbreaking concurring opinion in *U.S. v. Jones*, which called for a reexamination of the court's approach to electronic privacy cases, was entirely in the Brandeisian spirit. Indeed, in a sign of Brandeis's bipartisan appeal in other cases involving privacy, he appears in *Chandler v. Miller* both in Justice Ginsburg's majority opinion striking down mandatory drug tests for state judicial candidates and in Chief Justice William Rehnquist's dissenting opinion insisting that the court should have deferred to the state law as a sign of respect for a state laboratory of democracy.[25]

Given that Brandeis has been embraced by both liberal and conservative justices on the Supreme Court, it may seem surprising that he does not have more acolytes today among civil libertarian liberals and libertarian conservatives, who are his natural heirs. On the progressive left, some critics of corporate bigness are not equally suspicious of bigness in government, and they rush to embrace centralized regulations of the economy that Brandeis would have mistrusted. Some progressives also reject Brandeis's emphasis on economic opportunity rather than racial equality. As the scholars Joseph Fishkin and William E. Forbath have noted, there have been two movements for constitutional equality during the past two centuries that have interacted uneasily with each other—one focusing on the diffusion of wealth and the other on the inclusion of previously excluded groups such as minorities and women.[26] The first movement, of which Brandeis was the shining example, flourished in the nineteenth and early twentieth centuries, from the Jacksonian era through the New Deal. It insisted that constitutional democracy could not be preserved without constitutional restraints on what Jackson called the "moneyed interests," Brandeis called "our financial oligarchy," and Franklin Roosevelt called the "economic royalists."[27] But during the Great Society era, liberals began to focus less on a political economy that maintained a broad middle class and more on opening up already abundant economic opportunities to women, minorities, and other previously excluded groups.[28] This second movement had less interest in the southern economic populists such as Jefferson, Jackson, and Brandeis, whose passions were devoted to restraining oligarchy rather than a more inclusive conception of racial equality.

The progressive ambivalence about Brandeis today also may reflect his dedication to small government and deference to the states. Like most of his colleagues, he joined opinions upholding the mandatory sterilization of so-called defectives[29] and the exclusion of a Chinese American child from public school.[30] He also voted to limit congressional power—for example, joining

Chief Justice Taft's opinion striking down the 1919 child labor tax law.[31] Some modern progressives believe that Brandeis was too romantic, failing to embrace their conviction that we live in a Hamiltonian, not a Jeffersonian, world, and that on certain issues—from health care to the environment—only big government is strong enough to curb big business. Brandeis, for example, might have questioned the federally created insurance exchanges in the Affordable Care Act, preferring (as the act itself does) exchanges created by the states. As he wrote to his daughter Elizabeth proposing what he called "national-state provisions for 'unemployment insurance'": "The Federal Govt should leave the providing wholly to the States; but as a 'discourager of hesitancy' should lay an excise tax after a day fixed upon every employer who shall not have made provision thereupon under some adequate state law. The federal tax should go into the U.S. General revenue fund, i.e. not be specifically appropriated to unemployment compensation, lest by doing so we start national provision."[32]

As for the libertarian Right, it once lionized Brandeis, as Albert Jay Nock's biography of Jefferson demonstrates. Today, however, some libertarian critics of a centralized federal government lack a similar mistrust of centralized corporate power, and in their deregulatory zeal are indifferent to the ways that unchecked oligarchies in the private sector can also threaten liberty. Some libertarians have also been reluctant to embrace Brandeis in the post–New Deal era because of a general aversion to the big government that they attribute to the constitutional achievements of Progressivism, including the Sixteenth Amendment, authorizing a federal income tax, and the Seventeenth, authorizing the direct election of senators, both adopted in 1913. Randy Barnett, a leading libertarian intellectual of constitutional reform, has proposed to mitigate the effects of the Sixteenth and Seventeenth amendments with a "repeal amendment" that would give the states the power to repeal any federal regulation or law with a two-thirds majority.[33] And while libertarian defenders of judicial engagement may lament Brandeis's deference to progressive laws passed by state legislatures, liberal and conservative defenders of judicial restraint may find Brandeis's commitment to restraint inconsistent, given his tendency to uphold laws of which he approved on policy grounds and to strike down those he opposed.

Still, Brandeis's hour seems to be coming around at last. Both the libertarian Right and the civil libertarian Left have invoked his inspiring vision of intellectual privacy in their shared opposition to warrantless surveillance by the National Security Agency. The civil libertarian Alan Dershowitz has noted that Brandeis is the only person who would appear at or near the top of two separate lists of the most influential justices and the most influential lawyers in American history.[34] In a poll of leading libertarian and civil libertarian scholars and judges by *Reason* magazine, the libertarian journal of ideas, four out of the fourteen respondents identified Brandeis as their favorite Supreme Court justice, largely because of his dissenting opinion in *U.S. v. Olmstead*, the wiretapping case.[35] Moreover, libertarians are also rediscovering Brandeis's defense of transparency and his criticisms of the curse of bigness, which, at least indirectly, influenced the libertarian guru Frederick Hayek. In his 1945 article "The Use of Knowledge in Society," Hayek strikes a Brandeisian note by arguing that central planning boards are less efficient than open markets because any given central planner can know far less than the collective knowledge of large numbers of individuals living in society.[36] In 1938, Hayek participated with Walter Lippmann in a Paris symposium on Lippmann's book *The Good Society* (1936), which channels Brandeis's antistatism by rejecting centralized planning and the government regulation of monopoly.[37] Hayek praised the book as "a brilliant restatement of the fundamental ideals of classical liberalism."[38]

Brandeis's greatest legacy today is his insistence on lifelong self-education, inspiring citizens who are trying to make up their own minds about how to apply the Constitution in a changing world. His personal example encourages us to use our moments of leisure to develop our intellectual and ethical faculties as well as our capacity for empathy and reason. With Brandeis's daunting Athenian self-discipline in mind, we can attempt, within the limits of our all-too-human weaknesses and fallibilities, to eat and drink less and read and think more, exercising our minds and bodies to prepare ourselves for the privileges and duties of citizenship. Brandeis reminds us that the task of deciding what the Constitution means is a responsibility of all citizens, one that requires immersing ourselves in facts and considering the best arguments on all sides of contested questions, so that we can translate and preserve constitutional principles in light of changed circumstances. In confronting a challenging and novel constitutional question, therefore, it's often helpful to ask, WWBD: What would Brandeis do? Although the answers are never clear, the thought experiment is always illuminating.

How, for example, would Brandeis approach the transformation of privacy in the modern age by new technologies such as cloud computing? Now that our "papers and effects" are stored not in desk drawers, as at the time of the framing, but in the digital cloud—that is, distributed servers owned by Google or Yahoo that can be accessed virtually with web browsers—should the government be able to seize the data at will? The current Supreme Court has said yes in many circumstances, because of two implausible doctrines that have prevented the Fourth Amendment from keeping pace with changes of technology. First, the court has held that if you surrender data to a third party, even for a limited purpose, it generally loses all Fourth Amendment protections. This means that if you turn over your private papers to Google, Google can be compelled to turn them over to the government. Second, the court has held that the only expectations of privacy that are entitled to constitutional protections are those that society is prepared to accept as reasonable. The circularity of this reasoning is obvious: as people adapt to technologies that enable greater invasions of privacy, our constitutional protections are correspondingly diminished.

Brandeis would never have tolerated these arid abstractions, which have the effect of giving citizens less privacy in the age of cloud computing than they had during the founding era. In translating the Constitution into the challenges of our time, he might have looked to the states as laboratories of democracy: according to an ACLU study, eleven states have rejected the "third-party" doctrine, which says that surrender of data for one purpose eliminates constitutional protection for all purposes, and nine more states have indicated that they might reject it in the future.[39] As an alternative, Brandeis might hold, with some states, that government intrusions must be no greater than necessary, encouraging judges to balance the intrusiveness and effectiveness of the search against the seriousness of the crime. Or he might attempt to define how much privacy citizens in a free society should be entitled to, regardless of society's expectations. Or he might look to European democracies, some of which, as Justice Breyer notes, adopt a proportionality principle that balances the justification for the search against its impact on the affected party. What's clear is that Brandeis would have considered it a duty actively to engage in the project of constitutional translation in order to preserve the framers' values in a startlingly different technological world.

The Supreme Court has yet to resolve squarely whether ubiquitous surveillance that tracks our movements in public violates the Fourth Amendment if it doesn't involve physical trespass by government officials. Brandeis would have had no hesitation in saying yes. By menacing our ability to control the expression of our beliefs, thoughts, emotions, and sensations, ubiquitous surveillance poses a threat to cognitive liberty, intellectual privacy, and the anonymous dissent on which democratic self-government relies. Although five Supreme Court justices have suggested that ubiquitous surveillance that tracks someone's movements in public for a month requires a warrant, Brandeis might have gone further, holding that month-long tracking of an individual's movements in public is unreasonable and unconstitutional even with a warrant. By recognizing the connections between the First Amendment rights of political dissent and the Fourth Amendment rights of intellectual privacy, Brandeis would have insisted on at least as much protection against ubiquitous surveillance in the twenty-first century as "the makers of our Constitution" demanded in the eighteenth century.

And what of free speech? Brandeis's doctrinal conclusions about the First Amendment were eventually embraced by the modern Supreme Court, which has held since the 1960s that speech can be suppressed only if it is intended—and likely—to cause imminent lawless action. This principle, the crown jewel of the American free speech tradition, is Brandeis's most enduring constitutional achievement. At the same time, Brandeis's philosophical vision has met with more resistance. The court has repeatedly endorsed Holmes's metaphor of free trade in ideas, while rejecting Brandeis's competing notion that the First Amendment protects the positive liberty of citizens to engage in public deliberation as well as the negative liberty of citizens to be free from any governmental restrictions on speech. "The concept that government may restrict the speech of some elements of our society in order to enhance the relative voice of others is wholly foreign to the First Amendment,"[40] the court wrote with a Holmesian flourish in 1976.

Brandeis certainly would have deplored the court's decision in *Citizens United v. FEC* (2010), which struck down restrictions on corporate campaign spending. ("He obviously would not have been a fan of *Citizens United*, not at all," Justice Ginsburg told me.)[41] As Brandeis wrote in his *Liggett* dissent (which was cited by Justice Stevens and the other dissenters in *Citizens United*), legislatures throughout the nineteenth and early twentieth centuries imposed a host of regulations to ensure that the corporate form did not threaten the autonomy and deliberative powers of citizens. Campaign finance regulations on corporations implicate three of Brandeis's greatest concerns—the peril of corporate bigness, the importance of public deliberation, and the imperative of judicial restraint.

The Supreme Court in 2012 applied the *Citizens United* decision to strike down the century-old restrictions imposed by Montana's 1912 Corrupt Practices Act, which forbade Montana corporations from making campaign expenditures supporting or opposing a candidate or political party. In doing so, the justices overturned the findings of the Montana Supreme Court noting the long history of political corruption in the state, dating back to Progressive Era–scandals about corporate control of the state legislature and judiciary, that had provoked Montana citizens to pass the law in the first place. (More than half the states had similar laws on the books before *Citizens United* called them into question.) The Montana Supreme Court quoted a 1913 history of Montana emphasizing that industrial corporations—such as the quartz mining and railroad monopolies—controlled the state, "thus converting the state government into a political instrument for the furthering and accomplishment of legislation and the execution of laws favorable to the absentee stockholders of the large corporations and inimical to the economic interests of the wage earning and farming classes who constitute by far the larger percentage of the population in Montana."[42] The same year, Brandeis himself was making the same case against the oligarchic power of the railroad monopolies in *Other People's Money*.

What would Brandeis have made of the coming threats to

free speech and privacy in the Internet age? He would have recognized, surely, that the lawyers at Google and Facebook have more influence over who can speak and who can be heard and who can escape his or her past today than the justices of the Supreme Court, and he would have been concerned about the ways in which concentrated corporate power may threaten public deliberation rather than encourage it. He would have appreciated that the most important recent developments in free speech have involved not only the libertarian rulings of the Supreme Court but the Federal Communications Commission's endorsement of "net neutrality"—namely, the rule that Internet service providers must treat all content equally and cannot delay, block, or throttle any lawful content or applications. More generally, Brandeis would have encouraged the FCC and other regulatory bodies to explore the free speech implications of antitrust regulations as they approved the merger of media and broadband companies such as the one between Comcast and NBC or AOL and Time Warner. In controlling both the production and distribution of content, the merged media behemoths have the power to favor their own content over that of their competitors on a range of platforms.

One of the most dramatic clashes between privacy and free speech in the Internet age involves the 2014 decision by the Court of Justice of the European Union recognizing a "right to be forgotten." The decision forces us to balance European notions of dignity or honor against the American notion of complete freedom of public deliberation. Although Brandeis, in his early article on the right to privacy, had emphasized dignity over liberty, he came, by the time of his *Whitney* concurrence, to strike the opposite balance. For this reason, I imagine he would have criticized the right to be forgotten as a threat to freedom of thought and deliberation.

In *Google Spain v. AEPD*,[43] the European court held that Internet users in Europe have the right to demand that Google and other search engines remove truthful but embarrassing information about them that is "inadequate, irrelevant or no longer relevant, or excessive." The opinion delegated to Google's lawyers the responsibility for balancing the free speech interests of the public in receiving true information against the dignitary interests of individuals who felt that they were misrepresented online. If Google guesses wrong or refuses to remove the data, it faces fines of up to 1 percent of its annual income, which in 2014 was $66 billion. These fines concentrated Google's mind: since the decision, it has removed 42 percent of the more than three hundred thousand take-down requests it has received.[44] Google emphasizes that it has removed embarrassing data relating to private figures—such as a news story in the United Kingdom about a minor crime—while leaving up data relating to public figures—such as a news story in Hungary about the decade-old conviction of a high-ranking public official. But the BBC has published a list of the links on its website that Google has decided to remove from its search engine,[45] including those to stories about individuals who clearly would be considered public officials in the United States—for example, an article about the former chair of Merrill Lynch who left the firm in 2007 after colossal losses following the collapse of subprime loans to U.S. homeowners with poor credit histories.[46] Brandeis surely would have insisted on unfettered public access to stories about the personal misdeeds of our financial oligarchs. And he would have deplored the idea of allowing either judges or private corporations to decide what kind of truthful speech is relevant or irrelevant to public discourse. The mature Brandeis, I think, would have concluded that this decision was one that citizens have to make for themselves.

Still, the Internet vindicates Brandeis's warnings about the complexities of promoting deliberation by citizens in bounded small-scale communities. On the one hand, citizens are finding on social media such as Facebook and Twitter, in blogs, and in

comments sections across the Web some kind of digital fulfillment of the Periclean commonwealth that Brandeis viewed as
a model for the "political duty" of "public discussion." When
freed from the need to submit their speech to censors and
intermediaries—with troubling exceptions in China, Iran, and
other repressive states—citizens can deliberate, respond, and refine their views on matters of public interest in ways that approach Brandeis's ideal. On the other hand, the same Web
communities are full of the idle gossip that Brandeis lamented
in his famous article on the right to privacy—and on a scale that
makes Brandeis's concerns of the invasions of social privacy by
the Kodak camera and the instant press look quaint.

Facebook has more than 1.5 billion monthly users at the
moment, and its wall posts and news feeds are full not only
of deliberation about public issues but also of less elevating
content—photos, chat, self-exposure, and speculations about
the private lives of others. In his earlier work Brandeis worried
that this kind of gossip could crowd the public sphere and leave
less space and attention for matters of public concern. Brandeis
also would have worried about the polarization of speech on
the Internet into "communities of interest" that often amount
to electronic mobs, relentlessly insisting upon more and more
extreme versions of their positions, and more and more con-
formity to their extremism. At their worst, these echo chambers can represent the death of public reason. Noting that when
communities of like-minded people deliberate, they tend to
become more extreme, the scholar Cass Sunstein has suggested
that more speech on the Internet may lead to less exposure to
competing points of view, less reasoned deliberation, and more
group polarization.[47] If this hypothesis is true, it might call into
question Brandeis's faith in the value of counter-speech ("the
fitting remedy for evil counsels is good ones") and his faith
in "the power of reason as applied through public discussion,"
which was the basis for his rejection of "silence coerced by law."

The fact that Internet mobs can polarize so quickly, exaggerating the influence of extreme views, also challenges Brandeis's belief in the importance of time as a precondition for reasoned deliberation. His faith that reason could prevail only "[i]f there be time to expose through discussion the falsehood and fallacies" is hard to reconcile with the warp speed of the Twittersphere, where fallacies and extreme opinions can go viral in seconds.

Brandeis, however, would have insisted on empirical evidence for what has been called the "Filter Bubble"[48] effect—the claim that people are building online echo chambers that reinforce, rather than challenge, their existing points of view. And the empirical evidence is mixed. On the one hand, a 2011 study of Twitter found that individuals tended to retweet points of view that coincided with their own, leading to self-segregation by right- and left-leaning users.[49] On the other, a peer-reviewed study commissioned by Facebook found that although people's choice of friends as well as the stories they read on Facebook are skewed toward their existing ideological preferences, the effect is less extreme than had been feared. The study also found that individual choices about what stories to click on have a more significant influence than the Facebook algorithm about whether people encounter conflicting perspectives.[50] An independent study found that "ideological segregation on the Internet is low in absolute terms, higher than most offline media (excluding national newspapers), and significantly lower than segregation of face-to-face interactions in social networks," concluding that "Internet news consumers with homogeneous news diets are rare."[51]

Faced with this ambiguous evidence, I imagine that Brandeis would have been cautiously optimistic about the possibility of achieving reasoned deliberation in bounded communities online. (He was always optimistic, after all, about the potential of all individuals to develop their faculties of reason.) He would have insisted that individual citizens—not government or judges—bear the ultimate responsibility for using social networking technologies to fulfill their "political duty" of public deliberation, rather than to play video games, gossip, rant, or amuse themselves to death. Recall Brandeis's strenuous conception of the importance of leisure as a condition of personal and social fulfillment. He felt individual workers had to decide between idle amusements and meaningful self-improvement, between wasting our time as consumers and elevating ourselves into engaged citizens. He certainly would have been a fan of massive open online courses, or MOOCS, and if he were giving his MIT lectures on business today, he would have been delighted that they were available free and online.

Brandeis might have been concerned, however, by the Internet's tendency to increase the trends toward digital monopoly by eliminating physical barriers to consolidation, such as the cost of real estate. The result is vast network power by online megastores—from Amazon to iTunes—that can more easily crush their rivals than the chain stores of Brandeis's day. This fulfills Brandeis's worst fears about the transformation of citizens into consumers, the suppression within citizens of the consciousness of being also a producer, and the isolation of producers and consumers from each other.[52]

The decision to suspend traditional enforcement of the antitrust laws in the 1980s, as well as the globalizing power of the Internet, accelerated the power of the distributors, setting in motion a tremendous concentration of power in the hands of megastores such as Wal-Mart and Amazon that makes Brandeis's fears of the power of chain stores to crush independent business look understated. As Barry Lynn notes, between 1917 and 1979, administrations from both parties ensured that no chain store controlled more than a fraction of sales in any region in the United States, repeatedly threatening the Great Atlantic Pacific and Tea Company, or A&P, with violations of antitrust law. Once the government stopped enforcing that law in the 1980s, Wal-Mart became five times larger, relative to the size of the U.S. economy, than A&P was at its zenith. Indeed, Wal-Mart has become a de facto monopoly, selling more than half the groceries and detergents in many small and large markets.[53]

As a result, giant chain stores such as Wal-Mart and Amazon can sell products for less than they pay for them, in order to drive less well-capitalized retailers out of business. The megastores can also set different prices for the same product, pitting producer against producer, and bankrupting many of them in the process. The supply chain has become so consolidated that today two companies—Proctor and Gamble and Colgate-Palmolive—hold between them more than 80 percent of the U.S. toothpaste market.[54] This trend has also put pressure on independent producers, such as authors and publishers, who are no longer able to set the prices for their creative work in the face of the power of the giant distributors.

Brandeis might have supported efforts to check the power of Amazon and restore the power to set prices to producers, such as the "fixed book price agreements" that countries in the European Union have long adopted to allow bookstores to promote less popular but culturally significant books rather than concentrate only on best sellers. He also might have been sympathetic to the U.S. publishers who are trying to maintain the price of e-books against Amazon's decision to use its 90 percent market power to sell e-books for less than it paid for them. He might even have approved of the side deal between Apple and five of the biggest publishers that would have allowed the publishers to set e-book prices but guaranteed that books distributed in Apple's iBooks always had the lowest price. Antitrust regulators chose to shut the practice down, charging that it was a classic case of horizontal competitors colluding to force Amazon to change its business practices. European regulators, by contrast, have launched antitrust investigations into Amazon, Google, and Facebook that Brandeis would have supported. For Brandeis, book pricing should offer reasonable rewards for the individual creative author, not the giant distributor, and he might even have tolerated a looser definition of cartels as a way of maintaining a degree of competition in the publishing industry. Brandeis might have been surprised, however, by the fact that authors and freelance artists are now the most visible representatives of the producing classes, and that small tech start-ups can imagine no greater success than being acquired by tech giants like Google. Google's decision to improve its Wall Street balance sheets by disaggregating its various units into a decentralized holding company called Alphabet would have given him only wan satisfaction.

There remains a lively debate about whether national online and physical megastores such as Amazon, Wal-Mart and Target, by shutting down family-run businesses, have discouraged local democratic participation in the ways that Brandeis predicted. Critics worry that when Wal-Mart moves into a region, it often closes down entire main streets of family-owned shops, from hardware stores to local markets, in surrounding towns, harming workers in their capacity as citizens rather than consumers.[55] As Brandeis put it, "[T]he chain store, by furthering the concentration of wealth and of power and by promoting absentee ownership, is thwarting American ideals."[56] In Europe and Asia more than in America, there is a political consistency today for legal responses to the curse of bigness. If Brandeisian privacy laws forbidding the publication of true but embarrassing private facts are "alive and well and flourishing in Paris,"[57] as one scholar has noted, then Brandeisian anti–chain store laws, too, are alive, at least, in Japan and Germany. Japan has regulated large department stores since 1937, when the imperial government adopted a department store law to protect small business from competition from chain stores.[58] (The law has been relaxed recently in response to pressure from the United States.) Anti–chain store laws continue to be enforced in Germany. When Wal-Mart entered the German market in 1997, it struggled in the face of price regulations forbidding retailers from selling below costs and strict zoning regulations designed to protect small retailers.[59] Wal-Mart also struggled with German laws, of which Brandeis would have approved, protecting industrial democracy and giving workers' councils the ability to participate in decisions affecting working conditions.[60] Germany also has long used Sunday closing laws to protect local business against competition by megastores. After Germany transferred control over Sunday closing hours to the states rather than the federal government, some of the states relaxed the restrictions, leading, according to one study, to lower consumer prices.[61]

In other words, the economic evidence remains mixed today, as it was in Brandeis's day, about whether laws protecting small businesses by regulating megastores help or harm consumers, economic productivity, efficiency, and, ultimately, democracy. Brandeis believed that it was permissible to sacrifice efficiency and growth if this preserved self-governance and democratic participation. But now that the Internet has created other opportunities for democratic participation, the costs and benefits of the economic protectionism he believed necessary for democracy are certainly worth reexamining with an open mind. Brandeis himself would have expected no less.

In attempting to channel Brandeis's thoughts on contemporary constitutional debates, of course, all of us can plausibly reach different conclusions. But Brandeis's greatest legacy can be found not in his views on specific questions about liberty or political economy but in his inspiring example urging us to grapple with these questions on our own. He expressed his faith in the lifelong imperative of self-education in a beautiful letter to his daughter Susan on her birthday in 1919:

You have been happily born into an age ripe for change; and your own horror of injustice properly beckons you to take an active part in effecting it. In laying your plans, bear in mind that time, the indispensable, is a potent factor, and that your own effectiveness is to be measured in terms of a life-time; and that you should have before you half a century of persistent, well directed effort with ever growing power and influence. Be not impatient of time spent in educating yourself for the task, nor at the slowness of that education of others which must precede real progress. Patience is as necessary as persistence and the undeviating aim.

This sounds fearfully solemn and must not be permitted to mar the day which should be full of joy and sunshine; but I can never think of your future without this vision of a noble, useful and significant life.[62]

All this from a lawyer and a judge! But Louis Brandeis was more than a Supreme Court justice; he was a constitutional philosopher who assumed the mantle of Jefferson and a social philosopher who was one of the inventors of American modernity. Today, ideological extremists on the left and right grievously lack Brandeis's sense of balance and proportion, his acute awareness of human limitations, and his faith in the possibility of transcending them through self-education on a human scale. But as the richness of traditional cultures increasingly comes under attack by technology, and as the dark side of particularism increasingly needs to be disinfected by the sunlight of universal reason, Brandeis must again be heard. And as the centralizing tendencies of democracies, corporations, and technologies around the world continue to threaten human individuality and liberty, Brandeis's warnings about the dangers of size and the duties of public deliberation may help us to preserve the values of the American framers and make them truly our own. This will require work. As Brandeis put it, "If we would guide by the light of reason, we must let our minds be bold."[63]

Introduction

1. JORDAN A. SCHWARZ, THE NEW DEALERS: POWER POLITICS IN THE AGE OF ROOSEVELT 113 (1994).

2. *Id.*

3. MELVIN I. UROFSKY, LOUIS D. BRANDEIS: A LIFE 705 (2009).

4. SCHWARZ, *supra* note 1, at 113.

5. UROFSKY, *supra* note 3, at 705.

6. ALPHEUS THOMAS MASON, BRANDEIS: A FREE MAN'S LIFE 636 (1946).

7. *Isaiah* 28:17.

8. *Isaiah* 49:7.

9. ROBERT A. BURT, TWO JEWISH JUSTICES: OUTCASTS IN THE PROMISED LAND 19–20 (1988).

10. JACOB DE HAAS, LOUIS D. BRANDEIS: A BIOGRAPHICAL SKETCH 32 (1929).

11. *See* New State Ice Co. v. Liebmann, 285 U.S. 262, 311 (1932) (Brandeis, J., dissenting).

12. Albert W. Alschuler, Law Without Values: The Life, Work, and Legacy of Justice Holmes 58–59 (2002).

13. Nelson Lloyd Dawson, Louis D. Brandeis, Felix Frankfurter, and the New Deal 13 (1980).

14. Remarks of Paul A. Freund, *in* Proceedings of the Bar of the Supreme Court of the United States and Meeting of the Court In Memory of Associate Justice Louis D. Brandeis 29 (1942).

15. Alfred Lief, Brandeis: The Personal History of an American Ideal 478 (1936).

16. Philippa Strum, Louis D. Brandeis: Justice for the People 401 (1984).

17. Letter from Louis D. Brandeis to Susan Brandeis Gilbert (June 15, 1927), *in* The Family Letters of Louis D. Brandeis 453 (Melvin I. Urofsky & David W. Levy eds., 2002).

18. Strum, *supra* note 16, at 401.

19. *Id.*

20. *Id.*

21. *Id.* at 402.

22. Albert Jay Nock, Jefferson 334 (1926).

23. *Id.* at 125.

24. *Id.* at 293.

25. Letter from Louis D. Brandeis to Pauline Goldmark (Nov. 15, 1929), *in* The Family Letters of Louis D. Brandeis, *supra* note 17, at 487.

26. Nock, *supra* note 22, at 25.

27. *Id.* at 142–43.

28. Lewis J. Paper, Brandeis 42 (1983).

29. Nock, *supra* note 22, at 50–51.

30. *Id.* at 49.

31. *Id.* at 50.

32. *Id.* at 52.

33. *Id.* at 55 n.1.

34. Garry Wills, *The Aesthete*, NEW YORK REVIEW OF BOOKS (Aug. 12, 1993).

35. NOCK, *supra* note 22, at 328.

36. MASON, *supra* note 6, at 640.

37. *Id.*

38. NOCK, *supra* note 22, at 110–11.

39. *Id.* at 115.

40. MASON, *supra* note 6, at 605.

41. NOCK, *supra* note 22, at 200–201.

42. Steven G. Calabresi & Larissa Price, *Monopolies and the Constitution: A History of Crony Capitalism* 30 (Nw. Univ. Sch. of Law Faculty Working Paper No. 214, 2012), http://scholarlycommons .law.northwestern.edu/facultyworkingpapers/214.

43. *Id.* at 32.

44. *Id.* at 31.

45. *Id.* at 33.

46. *Id.* at 35.

47. NOCK, *supra* note 22, at 198.

48. DE HAAS, *supra* note 10, at 46.

49. LOUIS BRANDEIS, OTHER PEOPLE'S MONEY AND HOW THE BANKERS USE IT 138 (1933).

50. NOCK, *supra* note 22, at 269.

51. *Id.* at 272.

52. EDWARD A. PURCELL, JR., BRANDEIS AND THE PROGRESSIVE CONSTITUTION 12 (2000).

53. *Id.* at 13.

54. LIEF, *supra* note 15, at 205.

55. *Id.* at 478.

56. *To Thomas Jefferson from Benjamin Banneker, 19 August 1791,* FOUNDERS ONLINE, NATIONAL ARCHIVES (Aug. 19, 1791), *available at* http://founders.archives.gov/documents/Jefferson/01-22-02-0049.

57. *From Thomas Jefferson to Benjamin Banneker, 30 August 1791,* FOUNDERS ONLINE, NATIONAL ARCHIVES (Aug. 30, 1791), *available at* http://founders.archives.gov/documents/Jefferson/01 -22-02-0091.

58. Louis D. Brandeis, True Americanism: Speech Delivered at Faneuil Hall, Boston (July 4, 1915), *in* BRANDEIS ON ZIONISM: A COLLECTION OF ADDRESSES AND STATEMENTS BY LOUIS D. BRANDEIS 8 (Zionist Org. of Am. 1999).

59. Christopher A. Bracey, *Louis D. Brandeis and the Race Question*, 52. ALA. L. REV. 859, 880, 884 (2001).

60. *Id.* at 873, 876.

61. *Id.* at 878–79.

62. LIEF, *supra* note 15, at 256.

63. RICHARD KLUGER, SIMPLE JUSTICE: THE HISTORY OF *BROWN V. BOARD OF EDUCATION* AND BLACK AMERICA'S STRUGGLE FOR EQUALITY 125 (2011).

64. *From Thomas Jefferson to Benjamin Banneker, 30 August 1791, supra* note 57.

65. NOCK, *supra* note 22, at 312.

66. *Id.* at 313.

67. *Id.* at 42.

68. *Id.* at 313.

69. Whitney v. California, 274 U.S. 357, 375 (1927) (Brandeis, J., concurring).

70. STRUM, *supra* note 16, at 237.

71. ALFRED ZIMMERN, THE GREEK COMMONWEALTH: POLITICS AND ECONOMICS IN FIFTH-CENTURY ATHENS 51 (5th ed. 1931).

72. Letter from Louis D. Brandeis to Alice G. Brandeis (Mar. 28, 1914), *in* THE FAMILY LETTERS OF LOUIS D. BRANDEIS, *supra* note 17, at 246.

73. Brandeis, True Americanism: Speech Delivered at Faneuil Hall, Boston (July 4, 1915), *in* BRANDEIS ON ZIONISM, *supra* note 58, at 6.

74. *Id.* at 6–7.

75. Letter from Louis D. Brandeis to Alfred Brandeis (Feb. 18, 1925), *in* THE FAMILY LETTERS OF LOUIS D. BRANDEIS, *supra* note 17, at 402.

76. *Id.*

77. Letter from Louis D. Brandeis to Susan Brandeis (Feb. 17,

1925), *in* THE FAMILY LETTERS OF LOUIS D. BRANDEIS, *supra* note 17, at 401.

78. MASON, *supra* note 6, at 584.

79. *Id.* at 585.

80. NOCK, *supra* note 22, at 48.

Chapter 1: The Curse of Bigness

1. Letter from Louis D. Brandeis to Susan Brandeis (Apr. 15, 1917), *in* THE FAMILY LETTERS OF LOUIS D. BRANDEIS 303 (Melvin I. Urofsky & David W. Levy eds., 2002).

2. GERSHOM SCHOLEM, THE MESSIANIC IDEA IN JUDAISM AND OTHER ESSAYS ON JEWISH SPIRITUALITY 84 (1971).

3. Ernest Poole, *Introduction* to LOUIS D. BRANDEIS, BUSINESS—A PROFESSION xi (1914).

4. Christopher A. Bracey, *Louis Brandeis and the Race Question*, 52 ALA. L. REV. 859, 869–70 (2001).

5. ALPHEUS THOMAS MASON, BRANDEIS: A FREE MAN'S LIFE 27 (1946).

6. *Id.* at 28.

7. HOWARD MORLEY SACHAR, A HISTORY OF JEWS IN AMERICA 73 (1992).

8. LEWIS J. PAPER, BRANDEIS 27 (1983).

9. Letter from Louis D. Brandeis to Stella and Emily Dembitz (Apr. 22, 1926), *in* THE FAMILY LETTERS OF LOUIS D. BRANDEIS, *supra* note 1, at 423.

10. MASON, *supra* note 5, at 31.

11. PAPER, *supra* note 8, at 27.

12. Poole, *supra* note 3, at xi.

13. MASON, *supra* note 5, at 3.

14. *Id.* at 38–39.

15. Letter from Louis D. Brandeis to Amy B. Wehle (Dec. 2, 1877), *in* THE FAMILY LETTERS OF LOUIS D. BRANDEIS, *supra* note 1, at 10.

16. STEPHEN W. BASKERVILLE, OF LAWS AND LIMITATIONS: AN INTELLECTUAL PORTRAIT OF LOUIS D. BRANDEIS 72 (1994).

17. PAPER, *supra* note 8, at 16.

18. MASON, *supra* note 5, at 16.

19. Letter from Louis D. Brandeis to Frederika Dembitz Brandeis (July 20, 1879), *in* THE FAMILY LETTERS OF LOUIS D. BRANDEIS, *supra* note 1, at 20–21.

20. Letter from Louis D. Brandeis to Frederika Dembitz Brandeis (Nov. 12, 1888), *in id.* at 31–32.

21. Letter from Louis D. Brandeis to Alice Goldmark (Sept. 7, 1890), *in id.* at 36–37.

22. Letter from Louis D. Brandeis to Alice Goldmark (Sept. 13, 1890), *in id.* at 41.

23. Letter from Louis D. Brandeis to Alice Goldmark (Apr. 15, 1908), *in id.* at 118.

24. Letter from Louis D. Brandeis to Alice Goldmark (Jan. 5, 1911), *in id.* at 160.

25. Letter from David Riesman to the author (Sept. 28, 1987).

26. DAVID MCCULLOUGH, TRUMAN 273 (1992).

27. Letter from David Riesman to the author, *supra* note 25.

28. PHILIPPA STRUM, LOUIS D. BRANDEIS: JUSTICE FOR THE PEOPLE 298 (1984).

29. MASON, *supra* note 5, at 77.

30. THE FAMILY LETTERS OF LOUIS D. BRANDEIS, *supra* note 1, at 75–76 n.1.

31. *Id.* at 81 n.6.

32. MELVIN I. UROFSKY, LOUIS D. BRANDEIS: A LIFE 778 (2009).

33. ALFRED LIEF, BRANDEIS: THE PERSONAL HISTORY OF AN AMERICAN IDEAL 51 (1936).

34. NEIL RICHARDS, INTELLECTUAL PRIVACY: RETHINKING CIVIL LIBERTIES IN THE DIGITAL AGE 16 (2015).

35. Samuel D. Warren & Louis D. Brandeis, *The Right to Privacy*, 4 HARV. L. REV. 193, 195 (1890).

36. *Id.* at 196.

37. RICHARDS, *supra* note 34, at 18.

38. Letter from Louis D. Brandeis to Alice Goldmark (Nov.

29, 1890), *in* THE FAMILY LETTERS OF LOUIS D. BRANDEIS, *supra* note 1, at 55.

39. RICHARDS, *supra* note 34, at 4.

40. *Id.* at 5.

41. *Id.* at 31.

42. PAPER, *supra* note 8, at 39.

43. BASKERVILLE, *supra* note 16, at 107–12.

44. LIEF, *supra* note 33, at 38–39.

45. MASON, *supra* note 5, at 103.

46. UROFSKY, *supra* note 32, at 134.

47. *Id.* at 146.

48. *See* Clyde Spillenger, *Elusive Advocate: Reconsidering Brandeis as People's Lawyer,* 105 YALE L.J. 1445, 1502–11 (1996)

49. UROFSKY, *supra* note 32, at 63–5.

50. Letter from Louis D. Brandeis to Alfred Brandeis (July 28, 1904), *in* THE FAMILY LETTERS OF LOUIS D. BRANDEIS, *supra* note 1, at 90.

51. *Id.* at 91.

52. UROFSKY, *supra* note 32, at 153.

53. *Id.* at 154.

54. LIEF, *supra* note 33, at 200.

55. A.L. TODD, JUSTICE ON TRIAL: THE CASE OF LOUIS D. BRANDEIS 48–49 (1964).

56. LOUIS D. BRANDEIS, *How Boston Solved the Gas Problem, in* BUSINESS—A PROFESSION, *supra* note 3, at 93.

57. Letters from Louis D. Brandeis to Alfred Brandeis (May 20 and 27, 1906), *in* THE FAMILY LETTERS OF LOUIS D. BRANDEIS, *supra* note 1, at 102–03.

58. LOUIS D. BRANDEIS, *Industrial Co-operation, in* THE CURSE OF BIGNESS: MISCELLANEOUS PAPERS OF LOUIS D. BRANDEIS 35–36 (Osmond K. Fraenkel ed., 1934).

59. LOUIS D. BRANDEIS, *Efficiency and Social Ideals, in id.,* at 51.

60. Whitney v. California, 274 U.S. 357, 375 (1927) (Brandeis, J., concurring).

61. UROFSKY, *supra* note 32, at 253.

62. BRANDEIS, *Efficiency and Social Ideals, supra* note 59, at 51.

63. *Id.*

64. STRUM, *supra* note 28, at 160.

65. *See* Richard P. Adelstein, *"Islands of Conscious Power": Louis D. Brandeis and the Modern Corporation*, 63 BUS. HIST. REV. 651–52 (1989).

66. *Industrial Relations—Final Report and Testimony*, U.S. Comm. On Indus. Relations, 64th Cong. 991 (1916) (testimony of Louis D. Brandeis) [hereinafter *Brandeis Testimony*], *in* THE CURSE OF BIG-NESS, *supra* note 58, at 49.

67. *Id.*

68. LIEF, *supra* note 33, at 198.

69. *Brandeis Testimony, supra* note 66, at 72–3.

70. Louis D. BRANDEIS, *Efficiency by Consent, in* BUSINESS—A PROFESSION, LOUIS D. BRANDEIS SCHOOL OF LAW LIBRARY, http://louisville.edu/law/library/special-collections/the-louis-d.-brandeis -collection/business-a-profession-chapter-5.

71. STRUM, *supra* note 28, at 165.

72. *Id.*

73. *Brandeis Testimony, supra* note 66, at 73.

74. *Id.* at 79.

75. *Id.* at 80.

76. *Id.*

77. *Id.* at 83.

78. *Id.* at 76.

79. UROFSKY, *supra* note 32, at 165.

80. *Id.* at 167.

81. *Id.* at 179.

82. *Id.* at 180.

83. Letter from Louis D. Brandeis to Alfred Brandeis (June 19, 1907), *in* THE FAMILY LETTERS OF LOUIS D. BRANDEIS, *supra* note 1, at 111.

84. Louis D. BRANDEIS, *The New England Transportation Monopoly, in* BUSINESS—A PROFESSION, *supra* note 3, at 268–69.

85. *Id.* at 271.

86. Letter from Louis D. Brandeis to Alfred Brandeis (June

15, 1909), *in* THE FAMILY LETTERS OF LOUIS D. BRANDEIS, *supra* note 1, at 125.

87. *Id.* at 115 n.2.

88. 208 U.S. 412 (1908).

89. Lochner v. New York, 198 U.S. 45, 75 (1905) (Holmes, J., dissenting).

90. THE FAMILY LETTERS OF LOUIS D. BRANDEIS, *supra* note 1, at 116 n.5.

91. Muller v. Oregon, 208 U.S. 412, 421 (1908).

92. 347 U.S. 483 (1954).

93. Brief for the State of Oregon at 43, Muller v. Oregon, 208 U.S. 412 (1908), http://pds.lib.harvard.edu/pds/view/2574849?n= 52&s=4&printThumbnails=no.

94. 243 U.S. 629 (1917).

95. LOUIS D. BRANDEIS, *The Constitution and the Minimum Wage*, *in* THE CURSE OF BIGNESS, *supra* note 58, at 64.

96. *Id.* at 65.

97. *Id.*

98. *Id.* at 69.

99. *See* UROFSKY, *supra* note 32, at 479.

100. Pac. States Box & Basket Co. v. White, 296 U.S. 176 (1935).

101. Letter from David Riesman to the author (July 12, 1996).

102. Letter from Louis D. Brandeis to Alice G. Brandeis (Oct. 27, 1909), *in* THE FAMILY LETTERS OF LOUIS D. BRANDEIS, *supra* note 1, at 131.

103. *Id.* at 116.

104. *Id.* at 116–17.

105. *Id.* at 123.

106. JORDAN A. SCHWARZ, THE NEW DEALERS: POWER POLITICS IN THE AGE OF ROOSEVELT 117 (1994).

107. Theodore Roosevelt, The New Nationalism (Aug. 31, 1910), http://www.presidentialrhetoric.com/historicspeeches/roosevelt _theodore/newnationalism.html.

108. *See* JAMES L. PENICK, JR., PROGRESSIVE POLITICS AND CONSERVATION: THE BALLINGER-PINCHOT AFFAIR (1968).

109. MASON, *supra* note 5, at 256.

110. *Id.* at 257.

111. Letter from Louis D. Brandeis to Alice G. Brandeis (Apr. 23, 1910), *in* THE FAMILY LETTERS OF LOUIS D. BRANDEIS, *supra* note 1, at 147–48.

112. MASON, *supra* note 5, at 276.

113. Letter from Louis D. Brandeis to Alfred Brandeis (May 1, 1910), *in* THE FAMILY LETTERS OF LOUIS D. BRANDEIS, *supra* note 1, at 150.

114. LIEF, *supra* note 33, at 178.

115. JAMES CHACE, 1912: WILSON, ROOSEVELT, TAFT AND DEBS—THE ELECTION THAT CHANGED THE COUNTRY 18 (2005).

116. *Id.* at 17.

Chapter 2: Other People's Money

1. William Kolasky, *The Election of 1912: A Pivotal Moment in Antitrust History*, 25 ANTITRUST 82 (2011), http://www.wilmerhale.com/uploadedFiles/WilmerHale_Shared_Content/Files/Editorial/Publication/The%20Election%20of%201912%20-%20Kolasky.pdf.

2. LOUIS D. BRANDEIS, *The Regulation of Competition Against the Regulation of Monopoly, in* THE CURSE OF BIGNESS: MISCELLANEOUS PAPERS OF LOUIS D. BRANDEIS 109 (Osmond K. Fraenkel ed., 1934).

3. Letter from Louis D. Brandeis to Alice G. Brandeis (Nov. 15, 1911), *in* THE FAMILY LETTERS OF LOUIS D. BRANDEIS 175 (Melvin I. Urofsky & David W. Levy eds., 2002).

4. JAMES CHACE, 1912: WILSON, ROOSEVELT, TAFT AND DEBS—THE ELECTION THAT CHANGED THE COUNTRY 194 (2005).

5. Letter from Louis D. Brandeis to Alfred Brandeis (Aug. 29, 1912), *in* THE FAMILY LETTERS OF LOUIS D. BRANDEIS, *supra* note 3, at 194.

6. CHACE, *supra* note 4, at 195.

7. *Id.*

8. Woodrow Wilson, Campaign speech at Lincoln, Nebraska

(delivered on Oct. 5, 1912), *as reprinted in Woodrow Wilson: The Fear of Monopoly*, ENCYCLOPAEDIA BRITANNICA, http://kids.britannica.com/presidents/article-9116986 (last visited Apr. 30, 2015).

9. BRANDEIS, *Competition, supra* note 2, at 109.

10. BARRY C. LYNN, CORNERED: THE NEW MONOPOLY CAPITALISM AND THE ECONOMICS OF DESTRUCTION, 122 (2010).

11. *Id.*

12. LOUIS D. BRANDEIS, *The Solution of the Trust Problem, in* THE CURSE OF BIGNESS, *supra* note 2, at 134.

13. LOUIS D. BRANDEIS, *The Democracy of Business, in* THE CURSE OF BIGNESS, *supra* note 2, at 140.

14. *Id.*

15. *Id.* at 141.

16. Letter from Louis D. Brandeis to Alfred Brandeis (Mar. 2, 1913), *in* THE FAMILY LETTERS OF LOUIS D. BRANDEIS, *supra* note 3, at 209–10.

17. SIMON JOHNSON & JAMES KWAK, 13 BANKERS: THE WALL STREET TAKEOVER AND THE NEXT FINANCIAL MELTDOWN, 28 (2011).

18. LOUIS BRANDEIS, OTHER PEOPLE'S MONEY AND HOW THE BANKERS USE IT 141 (1933).

19. Donald L. Miller, *Program 17: Capital and Labor—John Pierpont Morgan and the American Corporation, in* A BIOGRAPHY OF AMERICA (Annenberg Media 2000), http://www.learner.org/biographyofamerica/prog17/transcript/page03.html.

20. BRANDEIS, OTHER PEOPLE'S MONEY, *supra* note 18, at 3.

21. *Id.* at 4–5.

22. *Id.* at 8.

23. *Id.* at 14.

24. *Id.* at 12–13.

25. *Id.* at 13.

26. *Id.*

27. *Id.* at 15.

28. *Id.*

29. *Id.* at 19.

30. *Id.* at 133.

31. *Id.* at 134.
32. *Id.* at 110.
33. *Id.* at 112–13.
34. *Id.* at 111.
35. *Id.* at 114.
36. *Id.* at 35.
37. *Id.* at 137.
38. *Id.* at 138.
39. *Id.* at 139.
40. *Id.* at 140.
41. *Id.*
42. *Id.* at 130.
43. *Id.* at 133.
44. *Id.* at 134.
45. *Id.* at 136.
46. *Id.* at 62.
47. *Id.* at 65.
48. *Id.* at 67.
49. *Id.* at 70.
50. *Id.* at 71.
51. *Id.* at 60.
52. *Id.* at 146–47.
53. *Id.* at 109.
54. *Id.* at 142.
55. *Id.* at 152.
56. *Id.*
57. MELVIN I. UROFSKY, LOUIS D. BRANDEIS: A LIFE 182 (2009).
58. THOMAS K. MCCRAW, PROPHETS OF REGULATION: CHARLES FRANCIS ADAMS; LOUIS D. BRANDEIS; JAMES M. LANDIS; ALFRED E. KAHN 101, 141 (1986).
59. UROFSKY, *supra* note 57, at 397.
60. Norman Hapgood, *Introduction* to BRANDEIS, OTHER PEOPLE'S MONEY, *supra* note 18, at xiv.
61. Myers v. United States, 272 U.S. 52 (1926) (Brandeis, J., dissenting).

62. Hapgood, *supra* note 60, at xxxvii.

63. ALPHEUS THOMAS MASON, BRANDEIS: A FREE MAN'S LIFE 598 (1946).

64. ARTHUR M. SCHLESINGER, JR., 3 THE POLITICS OF UPHEAVAL: 1935–1936, THE AGE OF ROOSEVELT vi (2003).

65. UROFSKY, *supra* note 57, at 694.

66. NELSON L. DAWSON, LOUIS D. BRANDEIS, FELIX FRANKFURTER, AND THE NEW DEAL 31 (1980).

67. *Id.* at 17.

68. UROFSKY, *supra* note 57, at 710.

69. LYNN, *supra* note 10, at 114–15.

70. *Id.* at 116.

71. *'Volcker Rule' Supporters Step Up Their Fight*, FOX BUSINESS (Aug. 1, 2011), http://www.foxbusiness.com/markets/2010/03/29/volcker-rule-supporters-step-fight/.

72. Michael Snyder, *Megabanks: The Banking Oligarchy That Controls Assets Equivalent to 60 Percent of America's GNP*, THE ECONOMIC COLLAPSE (Apr. 26, 2010), http://theeconomiccollapseblog.com/archives/megabanks-the-banking-oligarchy-that-controls-assets-equivalent-to-60-percent-of-americas-gnp.

73. BRANDEIS, *supra* note 18, at 30.

74. *Id.* at 139.

75. Ryan Grim & Shahien Nasiripour, *Senate Votes for Wall Street; Megabanks to Remain Behemoths*, THE HUFFINGTON POST (May 25, 2011, 4:25 PM), http://www.huffingtonpost.com/2010/05/06/senate-votes-for-wall-str_n_567063.html.

76. BRANDEIS, *supra* note 18, at 137.

77. LYNN, *supra* note 10, at xii.

78. *Id.* at 13.

79. 2 *Nomination of Louis D. Brandeis: Hearings Before Subcomm. of the S. Comm. on the Judiciary on the Nomination of Louis D. Brandeis to be an Associate Justice of the Supreme Court of the United States*, 64th Cong. 124 (1916) [hereinafter 2 *Brandeis Confirmation Hearings*].

80. LOUIS D. BRANDEIS, *On Maintaining Makers' Prices, in* THE CURSE OF BIGNESS, *supra* note 2, at 125.

81. Dr. Miles Med. Co. v. John D. Park & Sons Co., 220 U.S. 373 (1911).

82. David F. Shores, *Vertical Price-Fixing and the Contract Conundrum: Beyond Monsanto*, 54 FORDHAM L. REV. 377 (1985)

83. 2 *Brandeis Confirmation Hearings, supra* note 79, at 110.

84. *Id.* at 111.

85. VICKI HOWARD, FROM MAIN STREET TO MALL: THE RISE AND FALL OF THE AMERICAN DEPARTMENT STORE 43–44 (2015).

86. Leegin Creative Leather Prods. v. PSKS, Inc., 551 U.S. 877 (2007).

87. United States v. Colgate & Co., 250 U.S. 300 (1919).

88. LOUIS D. BRANDEIS, The Living Law: An address delivered before the Chicago Bar Association (Jan. 3, 1916), *in* BUSINESS —A PROFESSION (1914), LOUIS D. BRANDEIS SCHOOL OF LAW LIBRARY, http://louisville.edu/law/library/special-collections/the-louis -d.-brandeis-collection/business-a-profession-chapter-21.

89. Letter from Louis D. Brandeis to Alfred Brandeis (Jan. 28, 1916), *in* THE FAMILY LETTERS OF LOUIS D. BRANDEIS, *supra* note 3, at 282.

90. Letter from Louis D. Brandeis to Alfred Brandeis (Feb. 12, 1916), *in* THE FAMILY LETTERS OF LOUIS D. BRANDEIS, *supra* note 3, at 295.

91. A.L. TODD, JUSTICE ON TRIAL: THE CASE OF LOUIS D. BRANDEIS 95 (1964).

92. UROFSKY, *supra* note 57, at 454.

93. TODD, supra note 91, at 37.

94. UROFSKY, *supra* note 57, at 440–41.

95. *1912 Presidential Election*, 270 To WIN, http://www.270to win.com/1912_Election/ (last visited June 4, 2015).

96. TODD, supra note 91, at 71.

97. *Id.* at 70.

98. LIFE, Feb. 10, 1916, at 248–49.

99. *Id.*

100. EZEKIEL RABINOWITZ, JUSTICE LOUIS D. BRANDEIS: THE ZIONIST CHAPTER OF HIS LIFE 49–50 (1968).

101. UROFSKY, *supra* note 57, at 445.

102. Todd, *supra* note 91, at 85.

103. *Id.* at 87.

104. *Id.* at 152.

105. *Id.* at 87.

106. *Id.* at 92–93.

107. *Id.* at 29.

108. Urofsky, *supra* note 57, at 446.

109. William Howard Taft, Anti-Semitism in the United States 23 (1920).

110. Alpheus Thomas Mason, William Howard Taft: Chief Justice 199–200 (1965).

111. Remarks of Senator George W. Norris, *in* Proceedings of the Bar of the Supreme Court of the United States and Meeting of the Court In Memory of Associate Justice Louis D. Brandeis 34, 36 (1942).

112. *Id.* at 34.

113. 2 *Brandeis Confirmation Hearings, supra* note 79, at 234.

114. *Id. See also* 1 *Nomination of Louis D. Brandeis: Hearings Before Subcomm. of the S. Comm. on the Judiciary on the Nomination of Louis D. Brandeis to be an Associate Justice of the Supreme Court of the United States,* 64th Cong. 59 (1916) (statement of Thomas J. Walsh).

115. *To Confirm the Nomination of Louis D. Brandeis, to be an Associate Justice of the Supreme Court of the U.S., June 1, 1916,* GovTrack, https://www.govtrack.us/congress/votes/64-1/s147.

116. Rabinowitz, *supra* note 100, at 53.

Chapter 3: Laboratories of Democracy

1. Ashwander v. Tenn. Valley Auth., 297 U.S. 288 (1936).

2. *Id.* at 347 (Brandeis, J., concurring).

3. The Family Letters of Louis D. Brandeis 301 n.2 (Melvin I. Urofsky & David W. Levy eds., 2002).

4. Peter G. Renstrom, The Taft Court: Justices, Rulings, and Legacy 63 (2003).

5. Adams v. Tanner, 244 U.S. 590 (1917) (Brandeis, J., dissenting).

6. ALPHEUS THOMAS MASON, WILLIAM HOWARD TAFT: CHIEF JUSTICE 216–17 (1964).

7. *Adams*, 244 U.S. at 597.

8. *Id.* at 613.

9. *Id.* at 615 (citing Holden v. Hardy, 169 U.S. 366 (1898)).

10. Truax v. Corrigan, 257 U.S. 356 (1921).

11. *Id.* at 356–57 (Brandeis, J., dissenting).

12. Duplex Printing Press Co. v. Deering, 254 U.S. 443 (1921).

13. *Id.* at 482 (Brandeis, J., dissenting).

14. *Id.* at 481.

15. *Id.* at 484.

16. Fed. Trade Comm'n v. Gratz, 253 U.S. 421 (1920).

17. *Id.* at 428.

18. *Id.* at 433 (Brandeis, J., dissenting).

19. *Id.* at 435.

20. GERALD BERK, LOUIS D. BRANDEIS AND THE MAKING OF REGULATED COMPETITION, 1900–1932 231 (2012).

21. *Id.*

22. Am. Column & Lumber Co. v. United States, 257 U.S. 377 (1921).

23. *Id.* at 418 (Brandeis, J., dissenting).

24. *Id.*

25. *Id.* at 415.

26. *Id.* at 416.

27. *Id.*

28. Maple Flooring Mfrs.' Assn. v. United States, 268 U.S. 563 (1925). *See* BERK, *supra* note 20, at 236.

29. New State Ice Co. v. Liebmann, 285 U.S. 262, 311 (1932) (Brandeis, J., dissenting).

30. Louis K. Liggett Co. v. Lee, 288 U.S. 517 (1933).

31. *Id.* at 580 (Brandeis, J., dissenting).

32. *See id.* at 568.

33. *Id.*

34. DAVID M. DORSEN, HENRY FRIENDLY: GREATEST JUDGE OF HIS ERA 42 (2012).

35. ALEXANDER M. BICKEL, THE UNPUBLISHED OPINIONS OF MR. JUSTICE BRANDEIS 152 (1957).

36. *Id.* at 140–41.

37. *Id.* at 123.

38. Letter from Louis D. Brandeis to Susan Brandeis (May 18, 1922), *in* THE FAMILY LETTERS OF LOUIS D. BRANDEIS, *supra* note 3, at 380.

39. MELVIN I. UROFSKY, A MIND OF ONE PIECE: BRANDEIS AND AMERICAN REFORM 127–28 (1971).

40. BRUCE ALLEN MURPHY, THE BRANDEIS/FRANKFURTER CONNECTION: THE SECRET POLITICAL ACTIVITIES OF TWO SUPREME COURT JUSTICES 91 (1982).

41. Letter from Louis D. Brandeis to Louis Brandeis Wehle (Jan. 19, 1932), *in* THE FAMILY LETTERS OF LOUIS D. BRANDEIS, *supra* note 3, at 518.

42. *Id.* at 532.

43. MURPHY, *supra* note 40, at 103.

44. NELSON LLOYD DAWSON, LOUIS D. BRANDEIS, FELIX FRANKFURTER, AND THE NEW DEAL 30–31 (1980).

45. Letter from Louis D. Brandeis to Elizabeth B. Raushenbush (Nov. 19, 1933), *in* THE FAMILY LETTERS OF LOUIS D. BRANDEIS, *supra* note 3, at 533–34.

46. DAWSON, *supra* note 44, at 33–34.

47. ADOLF A. BERLE & GARDINER C. MEANS, THE MODERN CORPORATION AND PRIVATE PROPERTY xli (rev. ed. 1967).

48. Letter from Louis D. Brandeis to Elizabeth B. Raushenbush (Apr. 22, 1934), *in* THE FAMILY LETTERS OF LOUIS D. BRANDEIS, *supra* note 3, at 538.

49. JORDAN A. SCHWARZ, THE NEW DEALERS: POWER POLITICS IN THE AGE OF ROOSEVELT 113 (1994).

50. Panama Ref. Co. v. Ryan, 293 U.S. 388 (1935).

51. Louisville Joint Stock Land Bank v. Radford, 295 U.S. 555 (1935).

52. Humphrey's Ex'r v. United States, 295 U.S. 602 (1935).

53. JAMES BRIAN STAAB, THE POLITICAL THOUGHT OF JUSTICE

Antonin Scalia: A Hamiltonian on the Supreme Court 141 (2006).

54. Myers v. United States, 272 U.S. 52, 293 (1926) (Brandeis, J., dissenting).

55. *Id.*

56. *Id.* at 295.

57. *Id.* at 291.

58. A.L.A. Schechter Poultry Corp. v. United States, 295 U.S. 495 (1935).

59. *Id.*

60. Melvin I. Urofsky, Louis D. Brandeis: A Life 705 (2009).

61. *Myers*, 272 U.S. 293 (Brandeis, J., dissenting).

62. Dawson, *supra* note 44, at 20.

63. Erie Railroad Co. v. Tompkins, 304 U.S. 64 (1938).

64. Akhil Amar, *Law Story*, 102 Harv. L. Rev. 688, 695 (1989).

65. Louis D. Brandeis, The Living Law: An address delivered before the Chicago Bar Association (Jan. 3, 1916), Louis D. Brandeis School of Law Library, http://louisville.edu/law/library/special-collections/the-louis-d.-brandeis-collection/business-a-profession-chapter-21.

66. Whitney v. California, 274 U.S. 357 (1927) (Brandeis, J., concurring).

67. Schenck v. United States, 249 U.S. 47, 52 (1919).

68. Abrams v. United States, 250 U.S. 616 (1919).

69. *Id.* at 630 (Holmes, J., dissenting).

70. David M. Rabban, Free Speech in its Forgotten Years 3–4 (1997).

71. Vincent Blasi, *The First Amendment and the Idea of Civic Courage: The Brandeis Opinion in* Whitney v. California, 29 Wm. & Mary L. Rev. 653, 654 (1988).

72. Rabban, *supra* note 70, at 359.

73. *Id.* at 358.

74. Blasi, *supra* note 71, at 671 n.81 (citing Philippa Strum, Louis D. Brandeis: Justice for the People 3–4 (1984)).

75. Rabban, *supra* note 70, at 318.

76. Letter from Louis D. Brandeis to Susan Goldmark (Dec. 7, 1919), *in* THE FAMILY LETTERS OF LOUIS D. BRANDEIS, *supra* note 3, at 353.

77. Schaefer v. United States, 251 U.S. 466, 482 (1920) (Brandeis, J., dissenting).

78. *Id.* at 493.

79. *Id.* at 495.

80. Pierce v. United States, 252 U.S. 239 (1920) (Brandeis, J., dissenting).

81. *Id.* at 269.

82. *Id.* at 272.

83. *Id.* at 273.

84. RABBAN, *supra* note 70, at 362.

85. David Skover & Ronald Collins, *A Curious Concurrence: Justice Brandeis' Vote in* Whitney v. California, 2005 SUP. CT. REV. 333 (2005).

86. Blasi, *supra* note 71, at 656.

87. *Id.* at 657.

88. *See generally* Skover & Collins, *supra* note 85.

89. *Whitney*, 274 U.S. at 376.

90. *Id.*

91. Brandenburg v. Ohio, 395 U.S. 444 (1969).

92. *Whitney*, 274 U.S. at 375.

93. *Id.* at 375 n.2.

94. Thomas Jefferson, First Inaugural Address (Mar. 4, 1801), THE AVALON PROJECT AT YALE LAW SCHOOL, http://avalon.law.yale.edu/19th_century/jefinau1.asp.

95. *Whitney*, 274 U.S. at 375.

96. Johann N. Neem, *Developing Freedom: Thomas Jefferson, the State, and Human Capability*, HISTORY, Apr. 2013, at 37–38, Western CEDAR.

97. Jefferson, First Inaugural Address, *supra* note 94.

98. *Whitney*, 274 U.S. at 375.

99. Jefferson, First Inaugural Address, *supra* note 94.

100. *Whitney*, 274 U.S. at 375–76.

101. *Id.* at 377.

102. *Id.*

103. Blasi, *supra* note 71, at 672 n.81 (citing Robert Cover, *The Left, the Right, and the First Amendment: 1918–1928*, 40 MD. L. REV. 349, 385 (1981)).

104. *Whitney*, 274 U.S. at 375.

105. PHILIPPA STRUM, LOUIS D. BRANDEIS: JUSTICE FOR THE PEOPLE 237 (1984).

106. ALFRED ZIMMERN, THE GREEK COMMONWEALTH 209 (5th ed. 1956).

107. STRUM, *supra* note 105, at 238.

108. *Id.* at 62.

109. Blasi, *supra* note 71, at 697.

110. New York Times Co. v. Sullivan, 376 U.S. 254 (1964); Blasi, *supra* note 71, at 692.

111. NEIL RICHARDS, INTELLECTUAL PRIVACY: RETHINKING CIVIL LIBERTIES IN THE DIGITAL AGE 30–33 (2015).

112. Paul Raushenbush, *Why Don't You Just Convert?*, *in* MY NEIGHBOR'S FAITH: STORIES OF INTERRELIGIOUS ENCOUNTER, GROWTH, AND TRANSFORMATION 106 (Jennifer Howe Peace, Or N. Rose & Gregory Mobley eds., 2012).

113. Walter Brandeis Raushenbush, Brandeis as Jurist: Craftsmanship With Inspiration, Lecture at the University of School of Law 4–5 (Jan. 26, 1965).

114. RICHARDS, *supra* note 111, at 25.

115. Int'l News Serv. v. Assoc.'d Press, 248 U.S. 215 (1918).

116. *Id.*

117. *Id.* at 250 (Brandeis, J., dissenting).

118. ALBERT JAY NOCK, THOMAS JEFFERSON 70 (1926).

119. Letter from Thomas Jefferson to Isaac McPherson (Aug. 13, 1813), *in* THE WRITINGS OF THOMAS JEFFERSON (Andrew A. Lipscomb & Albert Ellery Bergh eds., 1905), 3 THE FOUNDERS' CONSTITUTION, art. 1, § 1, cl. 8, http://press-pubs.uchicago.edu/founders/documents/a1_8_8s12.html.

120. *Id.*

121. SIVA VAIDHYANATHAN, COPYRIGHTS AND COPYWRONGS:

The Rise of Intellectual Property and How it Threatens Creativity 23–24 (2003).

122. *Int'l News Serv.*, 248 U.S. at 250 (Brandeis, J., dissenting).

123. *Id.* at 262.

124. Richards, *supra* note 111, at 33.

125. Gilbert v. Minnesota, 254 U.S. 325 (1920).

126. *Id.* at 335–36 (Brandeis, J., dissenting).

127. *Id.* at 335.

128. *Id.* at 337–38.

129. *Id.* at 338.

130. Olmstead v. United States, 277 U.S. 438 (1928).

131. U.S. Const. amend. IV.

132. Carol S. Steiker, *Brandeis in* Olmstead: *"Our Government is the Potent, the Omnipresent Teacher,"* 79 Miss. L.J. 145, 148–49 (2009).

133. Urofsky, *supra* note 60, at 627.

134. Dorsen, *supra* note 34, at 30.

135. *Olmstead*, 277 U.S. at 474 (Brandeis, J., dissenting).

136. *Id.* at 473–74.

137. *Id.* at 474 (citing Boyd v. United States, 116 U.S. 616 (1886)).

138. Akhil Reed Amar, The Law of the Land: A Grand Tour of our Constitutional Republic 336 n.1 (2015).

139. *Olmstead*, 277 U.S. at 474–75.

140. *Id.* at 477–78.

141. Richards, *supra* note 111, at 5.

142. *Id.* at 3.

143. Steiker, *supra* note 132, at 156.

144. *Id.* at 161.

145. *Olmstead*, 277 U.S. at 472.

146. *Id.* at 479.

147. *Id.* at 485.

148. *See* Tracey L. Meares, *The Legitimacy of Police Among Young African-American Men* (Yale Law Sch. Faculty Scholarship Series Paper No. 528, 2009), http://digitalcommons.law.yale.edu/fss_papers/528.

Chapter 4: The Perfect Citizen in the Perfect State

1. Louis D. Brandeis, The Jewish People Should Be Preserved: Address Delivered Upon Brandeis's Acceptance of Position as Chairman of the Provisional Committee for General Zionist Affairs (Aug. 30, 1914), *in* BRANDEIS ON ZIONISM: A COLLECTION OF ADDRESSES AND STATEMENTS BY LOUIS D. BRANDEIS 44 (Zionist Org. of Am. 1999).

2. *Id.*

3. Louis D. Brandeis, What Loyalty Demands: Address at the New Century Club on the Occasion of the 250th Anniversary of the Settlement of the Jews in the United States (Nov. 28, 1905), http://louisville.edu/law/library/special-collections/the-louis-d.-brandeis-collection/what-loyalty-demands-by-louis-d.-brandeis.

4. EZEKIEL RABINOWITZ, JUSTICE LOUIS D. BRANDEIS: THE ZIONIST CHAPTER OF HIS LIFE 1 (1968).

5. JACOB DE HAAS, LOUIS D. BRANDEIS: A BIOGRAPHICAL SKETCH 51 (1929).

6. Louis D. Brandeis, Sympathy for the Zionist Movement (Dec. 1910), *in* BRANDEIS ON ZIONISM, *supra* note 1, at 36.

7. DE HAAS, *supra* note 5, at 51.

8. PHILIPPA STRUM, LOUIS D. BRANDEIS: JUSTICE FOR THE PEOPLE 180 (1984).

9. *Id.* at 233.

10. 3 LETTERS OF LOUIS D. BRANDEIS, 1913–1915 110 n.2 (Melvin I. Urofsky & David W. Levy eds., 1973).

11. DE HAAS, *supra* note 5 at 52.

12. STRUM, *supra* note 8, at 231.

13. DE HAAS, *supra* note 5 at 53.

14. STRUM, *supra* note 8, at 232.

15. Louis D. Brandeis, The Jewish Problem, How to Solve It: Address at the Conference of Eastern Council of Reform Rabbis (June 1915), *in* BRANDEIS ON ZIONISM, *supra* note 1, at 31 n.12.

16. Louis D. Brandeis, To Be a Jew: Address at the Young Men's Hebrew Association of Chelsea, Mass. (May 18, 1913), *in* BRANDEIS ON ZIONISM, *supra* note 1, at 39.

17. *Id.* at 40.

18. Letter from David Riesman to the author (July 12, 1996).

19. Brandeis, To Be a Jew, *supra* note 16, at 42.

20. Sarah Schmidt, *Horace M. Kallen and the "Americaniza-tion" of Zionism*, 28 Am. Jewish Archives 59, 61 (April 1976).

21. *Id.* at 62.

22. Melvin I. Urofsky, Louis D. Brandeis: A Life 410 (2009).

23. Sarah Schmidt, Horace Kallen: Prophet of American Zionism 59 (1995).

24. Horace M. Kallen, *Democracy Versus The Melting Pot: A Study of American Nationality*, The Nation (February 25, 1915) (quoted in Theories of Ethnicity: A Classical Reader 92 (Werner Sollors ed., 1996)).

25. *Id.* at 87.

26. Urofsky, *supra* note 22, at 410.

27. Strum, *supra* note 8, at 237–38.

28. *Id.* at 242.

29. *Id.* at 240.

30. Alfred Zimmern, The Greek Commonwealth: Politics and Economics in Fifth-Century Athens 49 (5th ed. 1931).

31. *Id.* at 158.

32. Louis Brandeis, Other People's Money and How The Bankers Use It 137 (1933).

33. Zimmern, *supra* note 30, at 201 n.1.

34. *Id.* at 204.

35. Louis D. Brandeis, True Americanism: Speech Delivered at Faneuil Hall, Boston (July 4, 1915), *in* Brandeis on Zionism, *supra* note 1, at 5.

36. Zimmern, *supra* note 30, at 271

37. Louis D. Brandeis, A Call to the Educated Jew: Address at a Conference of the Intercollegiate Menorah Association (Jan. 1915), *in* Brandeis on Zionism, *supra* note 1, at 67.

38. Zimmern, *supra* note 30, at 449.

39. *Id.* at 448.

40. Urofsky, *supra* note 22, at 405.

41. Rabinowitz, *supra* note 4, at 17–18.

42. *Id.* at 18.

43. Brandeis, The Jewish Problem, *supra* note 15, at 35.

44. De Haas, *supra* note 5, at 62–63.

45. *Id.* at 66.

46. Rabinowitz, *supra* note 4, at 31.

47. Lewis J. Paper, Brandeis 262 (1983).

48. Louis D. Brandeis, Members, Money, Discipline: Note to Morris Rothenberg, Chairman of the Zionist Council of Greater New York (Feb. 18, 1917), *in* Brandeis on Zionism, *supra* note 1, at 112.

49. John B. Judis, Genesis: Truman, American Jews, and the Origins of the Arab/Israeli Conflict 136–37 (2014).

50. De Haas, *supra* note 5, at 56.

51. *Id.* at 79.

52. Louis D. Brandeis, The Fruits of Zionism: Address Delivered During Brandeis's Time as Chairman of the Provisional Executive Committee for General Zionist Affairs (1914–1915), *in* Brandeis on Zionism, *supra* note 1, at 49.

53. *Id.* at 52.

54. *Id.* at 56.

55. Greetings from Louis D. Brandeis, 1 The Menorah J. 4 (Jan. 1915).

56. Brandeis, A Call to the Educated Jew, *supra* note 37, at 60–65.

57. Louis D. Brandeis, Group Liberty: Address at the Collegiate Zionist Society of Columbia University (May 2, 1915), *in* Brandeis on Zionism, *supra* note 1, at 70.

58. Brandeis, The Jewish Problem, *supra* note 15, at 13.

59. *Id.*

60. *Id.* at 22.

61. *Id.* at 19.

62. *Id.* at 21.

63. *Id.* at 20.

64. *Id.*

65. *Id.* at 24.

66. *Id.* at 20.

67. *Id.* at 24.

68. *Id.* at 25.

69. *Id.* at 28.

70. *Id.* at 29.

71. Louis D. Brandeis, The Common Cause of the Jewish People: Address at a Meeting of the Jewish Congress Organization Committee in Carnegie Hall (Jan. 24, 1916), *in* BRANDEIS ON ZIONISM, *supra* note 1, at 105.

72. *Id.* at 103–04.

73. DE HAAS, *supra* note 5, at 76.

74. *Id.* at 53.

75. Letter from Louis D. Brandeis to Alice G. Brandeis (July 16, 1916), *in* THE FAMILY LETTERS OF LOUIS D. BRANDEIS 296 (Melvin I. Urofsky & David W. Levy eds., 2002).

76. PAPER, *supra* note 47, at 260–61.

77. DE HAAS, *supra* note 5, at 77.

78. *Id.* at 90.

79. RABINOWITZ, *supra* note 4, at 59.

80. *Id.* at 63.

81. UROFSKY, *supra* note 22, at 519–20.

82. RABINOWITZ, *supra* note 4, at 72.

83. JUDIS, *supra* note 49, at 149.

84. ANITA SHAPIRA, BEN-GURION: FATHER OF MODERN ISRAEL 49 (2014).

85. Letter from Louis D. Brandeis to Regina Wehle Goldmark (Dec. 20, 1917), *in* THE FAMILY LETTERS OF LOUIS D. BRANDEIS, *supra* note 75, at 315.

86. UROFSKY, *supra* note 22, at 521.

87. DE HAAS, *supra* note 5, at 50.

88. Letter from Louis D. Brandeis to Alice G. Brandeis (Oct. 14, 1917), *in* THE FAMILY LETTERS OF LOUIS D. BRANDEIS, *supra* note 75, at 314.

89. DE HAAS, *supra* note 5, at 95.

90. *Id.* at 96.

91. PAPER, *supra* note 47, at 263–64.

92. Jonathan D. Sarna, *Louis D. Brandeis: Zionist Leader,* 11 BRANDEIS REV. 27 (Winter, 1992)

93. DE HAAS, *supra* note 5, at 96–97.

94. *Id.* at 97.

95. PAPER, *supra* note 47, at 267.

96. DE HAAS, *supra* note 5, at 101.

97. *Id.* at 113.

98. "HALF BROTHER, HALF SON": THE LETTERS OF LOUIS D. BRANDEIS TO FELIX FRANKFURTER 274 (Melvin I. Urofsky & David W. Levy eds., 1991).

99. Letter from Louis D. Brandeis to Alice G. Brandeis (June 22, 1919), *in* THE FAMILY LETTERS OF LOUIS D. BRANDEIS, *supra* note 75, at 335.

100. DE HAAS, *supra* note 5, at 109, 114 n.1.

101. *Id.* at 114.

102. Letter from Louis D. Brandeis to Alice G. Brandeis (July 1, 1919), *in* THE FAMILY LETTERS OF LOUIS D. BRANDEIS, *supra* note 75, at 340.

103. DE HAAS, *supra* note 5, at 116.

104. Letter from Louis D. Brandeis to Alice G. Brandeis (July 10, 1919), *in* THE FAMILY LETTERS OF LOUIS D. BRANDEIS, *supra* note 75, at 347.

105. *Id.*

106. DE HAAS, *supra* note 5, at 116.

107. Louis D. Brandeis, The Pilgrims Had Faith: Address at the Second Annual Conference of the Palestine Land Development Council (May 27–28, 1923), *in* BRANDEIS ON ZIONISM, *supra* note 1, at 127.

108. *Id.* at 132.

109. Louis D. Brandeis, Efficiency in Public Service: Address to the American Delegation at the London Conference (July 14, 1920), *in* BRANDEIS ON ZIONISM, *supra* note 1, at 121–22.

110. *Id.* at 123–24.

111. Rabinowitz, *supra* note 4, at 128–29.

112. Louis D. Brandeis, The Only Promising Road: Address at a Zionist and Non-Zionist Conference in New York City (Feb. 17, 1924), *in* Brandeis on Zionism, *supra* note 1, at 143.

113. "Half Brother, Half Son," *supra* note 98, at 385.

114. Judis, *supra* note 49, at 162.

115. *Id.*

116. Louis D. Brandeis, Jews and Arabs: Address at Second Session of an Emergency Palestine Economic Conference (Nov. 24, 1929), *in* Brandeis on Zionism, *supra* note 1, at 151.

117. *Id.* at 152.

118. *Id.*

119. Judis, *supra* note 49, at 155.

120. Brandeis, The Only Promising Road, *supra* note 112, at 148.

121. Brandeis, Jews and Arabs, *supra* note 116, at 152.

122. *Id.* at 151–52.

123. "Half Brother, Half Son," *supra* note 98, at 420 n.4.

124. *Id.* at 435 n.1.

125. *Id.* at 438–39.

126. *Id.* at 440.

127. Urofsky, *supra* note 22, at 735.

128. *Id.* at 736.

129. Steven Lehrer, The Reich Chancellery and Fuhrer-bunker Complex: An Illustrated History of the Seat of the Nazi Regime 111 (2006).

130. Letter from David Riesman to the author (Sept. 28, 1987).

131. Urofsky, *supra* note 22, at 739.

132. Paper, *supra* note 47, at 387.

133. *Id.* at 388.

134. Judis, *supra* note 49, at 156.

135. "Half Brother, Half Son," *supra* note 98, at 620.

136. Judis, *supra* note 49, at 156.

137. Dan Senior & Saul Singer, Start-Up Nation: The Story of Israel's Economic Miracle xii (2009).

138. Letter from Louis D. Brandeis to Jacob H. Gilbert (Jan. 2,

1931), *in* The Family Letters of Louis D. Brandeis, *supra* note 75, at 510.

139. *Zionism and its Impact: Impact of Jewish Settlement on Arab Palestinian Economy and Society*, Zionism & Israel Information Center (July 15, 2005), http://www.zionism-israel.com/impact_of_zionism.htm.

140. Brandeis, True Americanism, *supra* note 35, at 5.

141. Brandeis, The Fruits of Zionism, *supra* note 52, at 50.

142. Brandeis, True Americanism, *supra* note 35, at 9–11.

143. Horace Kallen, Cultural Pluralism and the American Idea 25 (1956).

144. The Legacy of Horace M. Kallen 33 (Milton Ridvas Konvitz ed., 1987).

Epilogue

1. Alpheus Thomas Mason, Brandeis: A Free Man's Life 632–33 (1946).

2. *Id.* at 633.

3. Letter from Louis D. Brandeis to Jennie Taussig Brandeis, (Feb. 13, 1939), *in* The Family Letters of Louis D. Brandeis 552 (Melvin I. Urofsky & David W. Levy eds., 2002).

4. Melvin I. Urofsky, Louis D. Brandeis: A Life 740 (2009).

5. Letter from Louis D. Brandeis to Jacob H. Gilbert (May 29, 1939), *in* The Family Letters of Louis D. Brandeis, *supra* note 3, at 554.

6. Frank Gilbert, Unpublished Talk, Indianapolis (Oct. 2010).

7. Alexander M. Bickel, The Unpublished Opinions of Mr. Justice Brandeis 163 (1957).

8. Mason, *supra* note 1, at 636.

9. Gilbert, *supra* note 6.

10. The Family Letters of Louis D. Brandeis, *supra* note 3 at 566 n.3.

11. Laura Rothstein, *New biography pictures Brandeis as teacher*, Louisville Courier (Nov. 7, 2009), http://archive.courier-journal

.com/article/20091108/FEATURES06/911080327/New-biography
-pictures-Brandeis-teacher.

12. MASON, *supra* note 1, at 638.

13. Response of the Honorable Harlan F. Stone, Chief Justice
of the United States, PROCEEDINGS OF THE BAR OF THE SUPREME
COURT OF THE UNITED STATES AND MEETING OF THE COURT IN
MEMORY OF ASSOCIATE JUSTICE LOUIS D. BRANDEIS 48–55 (1942).

14. Telephone Interview with Justice Ruth Bader Ginsburg,
Associate Justice, The Supreme Court of the United States (Aug.
25, 2015).

15. *See* BICKEL, THE UNPUBLISHED OPINIONS OF MR. JUSTICE
BRANDEIS, *supra* note 7.

16. King v. Burwell, No. 14-114 (U.S. June 25, 2015).

17. Quotations in the paragraph from interview with Justice
Stephen Breyer, Associate Justice, The Supreme Court of the
United States, in Phila., Pa. (Sept. 17, 2015), http://library.fora.tv/
2015/09/17/Justice_Stephen_Breyer_The_Court_and_the_World.

18. Stephen Breyer, THE COURT AND THE WORLD: AMERICAN
LAW AND THE NEW GLOBAL REALITIES 261 (2015).

19. Telephone Interview with Justice Elena Kagan, Associate
Justice, The Supreme Court of the United States (Oct. 2, 2015).

20. *See, e.g.,* Bond v. United States, No. 12-158, slip op. at 9
(U.S. June 2, 2014) (citing Ashwander v. Tenn. Valley Auth., 297
U.S. 288, 347 (1936) (Brandeis, J., concurring)).

21. Jeffrey Rosen, *Robert's Rules,* THE ATLANTIC (Jan./Feb.
2007), http://www.theatlantic.com/magazine/archive/2007/01/rob
ertss-rules/305559/.

22. *See* United States v. Jones, 132 S. Ct. 945, 959 (2012)
(Alito, J., concurring).

23. City of Ontario v. Quon, 560 U.S. 746, 758 (2010).

24. Chandler v. Miller, 520 U.S. 305, 322 (1997).

25. *Id.* at 324 (Rehnquist, C.J., dissenting).

26. Joseph Fishkin & William E. Forbath, *Wealth, Common-*
wealth, & the Constitution of Opportunity: A Story of Two Traditions
(Univ. of Tex., Pub. Law Research Paper No. UTPUB632, 2015),
http://ssrn.com/abstract=2620920.

27. Joseph Fishkin & William E. Forbath, *The Anti-Oligarchy Constitution*, 94 B.U. L. Rev. 669, 671 (2014).

28. Fishkin & Forbath, *supra* note 26.

29. *See* Buck v. Bell, 274 U.S. 200 (1927).

30. *See* Gong Lum v. Rice, 275 U.S. 78 (1927).

31. *See* Baily v. Drexel Furniture, 259 U.S. 20 (1922).

32. Letter from Louis D. Brandeis to Elizabeth Brandeis Raushenbush (Sept. 16, 1933), *in* The Family Letters of Louis D. Brandeis, *supra* note 3, at 531–32.

33. Randy E. Barnett, *The Case for a Repeal Amendment*, 78 Tenn. L. Rev. 813–822 (2011).

34. Alan M. Dershowitz, *The Practice*, N.Y. Times, Sept. 27, 2009, at BR13.

35. *Who Should Reign Supreme?*, Reason (July 2005), https://reason.com/archives/2005/07/01/who-should-reign-supreme/1.

36. F.A. Hayek, *The Use of Knowledge in Society*, 35 Am. Econ. Rev. 519 (1945).

37. James R. Hurtgen, The Divided Mind of American Liberalism 50 n.17 (2002).

38. F.A. Hayek, *The Transmission of the Ideals of Economic Freedom*, 9 Econ. J. Watch 163, 167 n.4 (2012).

39. Jay Stanley, *The Crisis in Fourth Amendment Jurisprudence*, Am. Const. Soc'y for Law & Pol'y (May 2010).

40. Buckley v. Valeo, 424 U.S. 1, 48–49 (1976).

41. Telephone Interview with Justice Ruth Bader Ginsburg, *supra* note 14.

42. W. Tradition P'ship, Inc. v. Attorney Gen. of State, 2011 MT 328, ¶ 27, 363 Mont. 220, 232, 271 P.3d 1, 9 *cert. granted, judgment rev'd sub nom.* Am. Tradition P'ship, Inc. v. Bullock, 132 S. Ct. 2490 (2012), (quoting Helen F. Sanders, 1 History of Montana, 429–30 (1913)).

43. *See* C-131/12, Google Spain v. Agencia Española de Protección de Datos, Mario Costeja González, ECLI:EU:C:2014:317, http://curia.europa.eu/juris/document/document.jsf?text=&docid=152065&pageIndex=0&doclang=EN&mode=req&dir=&occ=first&part=1&cid=305802.

44. *Transparency Report*, Google (Jan. 7, 2016), http://www
.google.com/transparencyreport/removals/europeprivacy/?hl=en.

45. Neil McIntosh, *List of BBC web pages which have been re-moved from Google's search results*, BBC Internet Blog, http://www
.bbc.co.uk/blogs/internet (last visited Jan. 11, 2016).

46. Robert Preston, *Merrill's Mess*, BBC News: Preston's Picks (Oct. 29, 2007), http://www.bbc.co.uk/blogs/thereporters/
robertpeston/2007/10/merrills_mess.html.

47. Cass R. Sunstein, Going to Extremes: How Like Minds Unite and Divide 81 (2009).

48. Eli Pariser, The Filter Bubble: How the New Personalized Web is Changing What We Read and How We Think (2012).

49. M.D. Conover et al., *Political Polarization on Twitter*, Proceedings of the Fifth International AAAI Conference on Weblogs and Social Media (July 2011), https://www.aaai.org/
ocs/index.php/ICWSM/ICWSM11/paper/viewFile/2847/3275.

50. Farhad Manjoo, *Facebook Use Polarizing? The Site Begs to Differ*, N.Y. Times (May 7, 2015), http://www.nytimes.com/2015/
05/08/technology/facebook-study-disputes-theory-of-political
-polarization-among-users.html?_r=1.

51. Matthew Gentzkow & Jesse M. Shapiro, *Ideological Segregation Online and Offline*, 126 Quart. J. of Econ. 1799, 1831 (2011).

52. Barry C. Lynn, Cornered: The New Monopoly Capitalism and the Economics of Destruction 55 (2010).

53. *Id.* at 6.

54. *Id.* at 5.

55. Hedrick Smith & Rick Young, *Is Wal-Mart Good for America?* Pbs Frontline (Nov. 16, 2004), http://www.pbs.org/wgbh/
pages/frontline/shows/walmart/transform/isgood.html.

56. Louis K. Liggett Co. v. Lee, 288 U.S. 517, 548–52 (Brandeis, J., dissenting).

57. Jeanne M. Hauch, *Protecting Private Facts in France: The Warren & Brandeis Tort is Alive and Well and Flourishing in Paris*, 68 Tulane L. Rev. 1219, 1238 (1994).

58. Jean Heilman Grier, *Japan's Regulation of Large Retail Stores: Political Demands Versus Economic Interests*, 22 U. Pa. J. Int'l Econ. L. 5–6 (2001).

59. Phoebe Jui, *Walmart's Downfall in Germany: A Case Study*, J. of Int'l Mgmt. (May 16, 2011), https://journalofinternational management.wordpress.com/2011/05/16/walmarts-downfall-in-germany-a-case-study/.

60. Jack Ewing, *Wal-Mart: Struggling In Germany*, Bloomberg Business (Apr. 10, 2005), http://www.bloomberg.com/bw/stories/2005-04-10/wal-mart-struggling-in-germany.

61. Karthik Reddy, *Regulating shop opening hours harms both consumers and workers*, Institute of Economic Affairs (Aug. 16, 2011), http://www.iea.org.uk/blog/regulating-shop-opening-hours-harms-both-consumers-and-workers.

62. Letter from Louis D. Brandeis to Susan Brandeis (Feb. 24, 1919), *in* The Family Letters of Louis D. Brandeis, *supra* note 3, at 328.

63. New State Ice Co. v. Liebmann, 285 U.S. 262, 311 (1932) (Brandeis, J., dissenting).

ACKNOWLEDGMENTS

Janet Malcolm suggested to Ileene Smith, the editor of the Yale Jewish Lives series, that I write about Brandeis, and I'm grateful to both of them for a superb assignment. Leon Wieseltier encouraged me to begin with a review essay for the *New Republic* of Melvin Urofsky's 2009 biography of Brandeis that became the building block for this book. I finally buckled down to write after joining the National Constitution Center, when Ileene Smith gave me a tight deadline followed by a swift and deft edit. At the Constitution Center, Paul Finkelman, scholar in residence, wrote helpful background memos on Brandeis's early years, confirmation hearings, and views on Zionism that prompted me to read the primary sources, and Danieli Evans, senior fellow for constitutional studies, offered suggestions for the introduction and epilogue. Legal fellows Laura Beltz and Lana Ulrich carefully checked the text and endnotes. Akhil Amar, the great teacher who first kindled my passion for the Constitution, closely read the manuscript for Yale University Press and offered a competing view of Brandeis that provided necessary balance. Series editors Anita Shapira and Steven J. Zipperstein offered useful perspective on Brandeis's role in twentieth-century Jewish history. Melvin Urofsky and Philippa Strum, Brandeis's greatest living biographers, generously read the manuscript and corrected errors of fact and judgment. Thanks to other friends and colleagues who read and improved the manuscript, including Albert Foer, Frank Foer, Frank Gilbert, Judith Goldstein, Barry Lynn, Hank Meijer, William Nitze, and Laura Rothstein. Justices Stephen Breyer, Ruth Bader Ginsburg, and Elena Kagan generously read the manuscript and offered insights about their predecessor's influence. My colleagues and students at the George Washington University Law School helped me test ideas about Brandeis as we learned about him together. The late David Riesman first shared his recollections of clerking for Brandeis during our independent study in college, and the late Alan Westin gave me his treasured bust of Brandeis before he died in 2013. Thanks to Leon Black for supporting the Yale Jewish Lives Series to increase public understanding of Jewish identity. Thanks finally to Doug DeVos and the Board of Trustees of the National Constitution Center, and to all of my wonderful NCC colleagues, for working with me on behalf of our inspiring mission of promoting nonpartisan constitutional education and debate. I wish LDB could have seen the NCC—we call it constitutional heaven, which is surely where he is now.

FORTHCOMING TITLES INCLUDE: